Pauline Jewett

Pauline Jewett

A Passion for Canada

Judith McKenzie

McGill-Queen's University Press
Montreal & Kingston · London · Ithaca

© McGill-Queen's University Press 1999
ISBN 0-7735-1822-3

Legal deposit first quarter 1999
Bibliothèque nationale du Québec

Printed in Canada on acid-free paper

McGill-Queen's University Press acknowledges the
financial support of the Government of Canada
through the Book Publishing Industry Development
Program for its activities. It also acknowledges the
support of the Canada Council for the Arts for its
publishing program.

Canadian Cataloguing in Publication Data

McKenzie, Judith, 1951–
Pauline Jewett: a passion for Canada
Includes bibliographical references and index.
ISBN 0-7735-1822-3
1. Jewett, Pauline, 1922–1992. 2. Canada. Parliament.
House of Commons – Biography. 3. Simon Fraser
University – Presidents – Biography. 4. Legislators –
Canada – Biography. 5. Educators – Canada –
Biography. I. Title.
FC631.J48M34 1999   328.71'92   C98-901153-4
F1034.3.J48M34 1999

Typeset in Palatino 10/12
by Caractéra inc., Quebec City

To the McKenzie clan:
Susan, David, Mary, Tory, and the late John Galbraith McKenzie

Contents

Preface

It is my hope that the life history that unfolds in the forthcoming pages will be seen by the family, friends, and academic and political colleagues of Pauline Jewett as an accurate, balanced, and thoughtful account of her life and legacy. The life of Pauline Jewett is an enriching story of the accomplishments that are possible when a woman has the will, self-confidence, and courage to follow her dreams. As will become evident, Pauline experienced a number of disappointments in both her personal and her public life. However, she had the drive and perseverance to continue her quest to make a difference through public service.

As a public figure, Pauline was often sought out by journalists for political responses to international incidents, particularly when she served as external affairs critic for the New Democratic Party from 1979 to 1987. On at least eight occasions she was part of an expert panel on *The Journal* and *The National*, Canada's most watched news programs. Her opinion was solicited on such diverse issues as Canada's involvement in NATO, the U.S. invasion of Grenada, Star Wars, apartheid, and the testing of the cruise missile in Canada. Her official political career had begun some fifteen years earlier when she served as a Liberal member of Parliament from 1963 to 1965. During her years as a Liberal Party supporter and sitting member, she developed strong beliefs about Canadian nationalism and sovereignty. Over time, her passionate nationalism established the philosophical framework for her other political beliefs.

Pauline's main policy interests were international relations and peace and disarmament, but she also had a great affection for young people and was committed to removing obstacles that stood in the way of their intellectual and social development. She believed strongly in accessibility to education, particularly in postsecondary institutions. During her tenure as president of Simon Fraser University, she was adamant in her views on what a university should be. Often, these views were not in the mainstream of popular opinion. Although a pivotal amount of Pauline's career as an academic and politician coincided with the early stages of the second wave of the Canadian women's movement, she faced a significant number of social and gender barriers. Yet she achieved considerable success in both her public careers. Despite the lack of a favourable climate for women in her chosen occupations, she did not shy away from controversy or underestimate her abilities. While much of this book will be focused on Pauline's public life, some discussion and interpretation of her private life is necessary in order to gain a richer understanding of her story.

Unlike some individuals who have been the subject of biographies, Pauline was very private about her personal life. Her friends and family were the guardians of numerous boxes of her personal effects, yet she kept very little that has been of assistance in chronicling her life. She was not a prolific letter writer or diary keeper, and her preferred mode of communication was the telephone. Therefore, many of the interpretations of her life contained in this biography have been premised on the reminiscences of her family, friends, and acquaintances.

While Pauline never married or had children of her own, she was a devoted daughter, sister, and aunt, and she placed a high value on shared history. She also treasured the importance of friendship. Her friends and family loved the informal side of Pauline – the Quebec Nordiques hockey fan, Toronto Blue Jays supporter, classical music and art aficionado, cowboy song chanteuse, and car enthusiast. Although she loved the excitement of parliamentary life, her happiest hours were spent in the quiet solitude of her summer retreat on Constant Lake. She had a serious side, to be sure, as an ardent nationalist, feminist, and socialist who had a vision of what Canada should be. Over her long and distinguished career, she never stopped pursuing this vision. However, she also loved having fun. It is my hope that this book finds the balance that Pauline herself was so committed to in her own life.

I would like to express my appreciation to Pauline's sister Catharine Kushneriuk and brother Fred Jewett for their assistance in providing me with background information and family stories. Their feedback and constructive commentary on earlier drafts were most appreciated. I would also like to thank Pauline's friends who graciously agreed to be interviewed for this book. My special thanks go to Doris Anderson, Pauline's close friend, who met with me on several occasions and kindly reviewed an earlier draft. Despite her busy schedule, Doris provided me with some twenty-two pages of her memories of Pauline, which gave me more insight into the essence of this important woman. This practice of sisterhood was most appreciated. Jill Vickers, Pauline's friend and colleague from Carleton University, provided me with introductions to several of Pauline's friends and family members. Without this early encouragement, *A Passion for Canada* would never have been begun. I am also grateful to Lyn Grey, Margaret Mitchell, and Dawn Black, who spent many hours with me during a research trip to British Columbia in August 1997. Thanks also to Pat Armstrong, Marion Dewar, Audrey McLaughlin, Bunny Pound, and Norm Fenn for sharing their Pauline stories with me.

I would like to acknowledge the assistance of Geoffrey Hopkinson of the Canadian Broadcasting Corporation for giving me access to a wide assortment of archival video material. Sylvia Bashevkin of the University of Toronto and David Docherty of Wilfrid Laurier University enthusiastically embraced my idea of this biography, and their encouragement to pursue this research project inspired me. The technical and administrative assistance of Sherry Howse of the Department of Political Science at Wilfrid Laurier University was invaluable in moving the project towards completion. Another thank-you is reserved for my friend and syntax coach Eleanor Ball, who volunteered to edit this manuscript and spent many hours encouraging me to capture the passion of Pauline Jewett. If I have been able to do this successfully, the credit is largely due to Eleanor's efforts. I would also like to acknowledge the financial assistance provided by the Office of Research at Wilfrid Laurier University and the WLU Academic Development Fund in supporting this biographical project. A final thank-you must go to the editors at McGill-Queen's University Press. Philip Cercone, Joan Harcourt, and Joan McGilvray were enthusiastic and committed to this project, and their encouragement and professionalism were much appreciated. The thorough and sympathetic editing by Carlotta Lemieux resulted in a much-improved manuscript.

There are two names in this biography that might cause confusion: Doris Andersen and Doris Anderson. The former, a West Coast journalist, wrote a short biography of Pauline in 1987 entitled *To Change the World*. The latter, the close friend of Pauline, is the former editor of *Chatelaine*, former president of the Advisory Council on the Status of Women, and author of several books, including an autobiography, *Rebel Daughter*. I have taken references from books by both these writers. A second source of confusion surrounds the spelling of Constant Lake, which some sources spell "Constan." I have followed the spelling used in *The Gazetteer of Canada* and referred to the lake as Constant Lake but have retained the name Constan Associates for the property owners.

Pauline Jewett had many possible titles. She could have been called Dr or Professor Jewett, although she had an aversion to this kind of formality. She might have been called Aunt Pauline by five young people, but she bristled at this address as well. On occasion, she was called Ms Jewett, though this did not really suit her either. When interviewing her, journalists typically resorted to Miss Jewett. Her good-humoured colleague from the New Democratic Party, Jim Fulton, called her PJ when she joined the caucus in 1979, and I am told that she quite liked this nickname. However, by all accounts, her preferred form of address and the one she usually insisted on was simply Pauline. For this reason, I have taken the liberty of using her first name in a rather liberal way throughout this book.

To conclude, a research project such as this often becomes an obsession and is always a preoccupation. During the past two years, my sons David and Bryan have shown great patience and understanding and have been my biggest boosters. I thank them both for their love and support.

Introduction

We must remember that our primary obligation is always to the people we study, not to our project or to a larger discipline. The lives and stories that we hear and study are given to us under a promise, that promise being that we protect those who have shared with us. And, in return, this sharing will allow us to write life documents that speak to the human dignity, the suffering, the hopes, the dreams, the lives gained, and the lives lost by the people we study. These documents will become testimonies to the ability of the human being to endure, to prevail, and to triumph over the structural forces that threaten at any moment to annihilate all of us.

Norman K. Denzin, *Interpretive Biography*, 1988

There are many challenges in documenting the life of a woman. Biographers of men are inclined to emphasize the public accomplishments of their subject and focus almost exclusively on the man himself. Biographers of women tend to avoid this spotlight approach because it prevents them from examining interconnections between particular groups of women and denies the importance of group experience. It has been well documented that the lives of women are different from those of men. Differences in socialization, values, methods of communication, and opportunity structures invariably influence the lifestyles and belief systems of women. These differences ultimately lead to varying interpretations of the meanings of power, equality, and justice, to name just a few.

Given Pauline Jewett's stature as a public figure, it is possible to identify a number of important markers that reflect critical points in her public life. These critical events are called "epiphanies" by literary theorists and have been defined as "interactional moments and experiences which leave marks on people's lives."[1] Unquestionably, there were several of these in Pauline's public life. Less evident are the private events that left an indelible imprint on her life. In giving meaning to these, I have relied on the stories told me by her friends, acquaintances, and family. As is the case with all stories, they tend to be ambiguous and are subject to multiple interpretations.[2] In the final analysis, this has required intervention and intuition in creating a story out of the clues presented.

The traditional chronological (cradle to grave) structure of biography does not tend to work well in recording the lives of women. It has been claimed that the linear model has a male bias and that male stories have a tendency to be obsessed with order, linearity, conflict, and a struggle with separation from authority figures, often the mother or father.[3] Elspeth Cameron and Janice Dickin claim that the lives of women are best described as "episodic, fragmented, dispersed and distinguished by marginality, discontinuity and improvisation."[4] Although some men in Canadian politics have experienced similar discontinuity and fragmentation in their lives, it is particularly true for women both inside and out of politics. Fragmentation, marginality, and discontinuity were all evident in Pauline Jewett's life. She did not have a smooth entry into academic life. Moreover, after losing her seat in the federal election in 1965, she did not pursue electoral politics again for seven years. By the early 1970s, she had reached some important conclusions about herself and her politics, and ultimately switched her loyalties from the Liberal Party to the New Democratic Party. Although Pauline did not marry or have children – two events that traditionally introduce major interruptions into the lives of women – her life can best be seen as a web of events and relationships that did not necessarily coincide with linear time.

Pauline held the inveterate belief that the Parliament of Canada was important and did indeed matter. As a political scientist, she was acutely aware of the criticism of Parliament advanced by fellow academics. These critiques claimed that Canada's Parliament had become moribund and served little useful purpose. Real politics were practised elsewhere, they argued. Mounting evidence of growing cynicism, bolstered by public opinion polls, supported the claim that Canadians were becoming increasingly negative about the value of Canada's legislative institutions and the parliamentarians who served in them. In spite of these allegations, Pauline remained resolute in her conviction that Parliament was the cradle of democracy in Canada and that visionary politicians could make a difference.

In legislative terms, Pauline was not a prime minister, premier, party leader, or cabinet minister – the usual benchmarks of a successful career in Canadian politics. But her failure to reach any of these pinnacles does not mean that her life in politics was unimportant. She was the external affairs critic for the New Democratic Party during the tumultuous Reagan years in Washington and represented an important voice imploring the Canadian government not to become implicated in the escalation of the Cold War. She was also an important member of the joint Senate and House of Commons committees examining the Meech Lake Accord and Canada's external affairs. Although a minority party member on both these committees, she made important contributions to their deliberations and final reports.

As an academic, Pauline never developed "a grand theory" or wrote a classic book or essay. However, as the first woman president of a co-educational public university in Canada, she broke an important barrier and blazed a trail for women in academic administration. Despite a concerted effort by several groups to undermine her administration at Simon Fraser University, Pauline did not retreat from the principles she had established when she assumed the presidency, many of which mirrored her strong belief in Canadian nationalism and sovereignty.

Over the past two years, I have grown to know and admire Pauline Jewett. At times, it has been difficult not to fall into the classic trap of biographer – of being taken over by one's subject or falling in love with the person. The ultimate failure of a biographer is to create a hagiography. According to Leon Edel, "the secret of this struggle is to learn to be a participant-observer."[5] Although I never had the pleasure of meeting Pauline, I have attempted to present her life in an objective, truthful, and balanced manner, blending a chronological approach with one that highlights the self-discoveries she made over her lifetime. It is my hope that this life history of Pauline Jewett will be seen as an important addition to the biographical literature on great Canadian women who have made a contribution to public life in this country.

The "stylish" Mae Simpson Jewett and her children in the backyard of their St Catharines home. Pauline (left), Catharine (right), and Frederick Chandler (standing), c. 1930. Courtesy of Catharine Kushneriuk

Mae Simpson Jewett and her children in the living room of their St Catharines home. Catharine (left), Pauline (right), and Frederick Chandler (standing), c. 1940. Courtesy of Robert S. Jewett

Pauline's father, Coburn Jewett, whom Pauline described as "an egalitarian to beat all egalitarians" and whom the British press called "the quiet Canadian," c. 1945. In 1946 he was made a Commander of the British Empire (CBE) by the British government for his contribution to the construction of the Gander air base. Courtesy of Catharine Kushneriuk

Pauline's graduation picture from Queen's University, 1944.
She earned an honours bachelor of arts degree in political
science and philosophy, and was awarded a gold medal
as the top-ranking student in politics.
Courtesy of Catharine Kushneriuk

Pauline standing in the courtyard of Harvard University in
Cambridge, Massachusetts, c. 1949. Pauline began her
studies in government in 1945 and completed her PH D in
1950. Courtesy of Catharine Kushneriuk

Pauline and her leader, Lester B. Pearson, taking a tour of the Warkworth Penitentiary in her riding of Northumberland, c. 1965. Unfortunately for Pauline, she was to lose the election later that year after serving for just two years as a Liberal member of Parliament. Courtesy of Robert S. Jewett

Pauline congratulating high school students at a graduation ceremony in Deep River, Ontario, 21 December 1966. Pauline always had a great affection for young people and was particularly pleased to see them excel in school.
Courtesy of Catharine Kushneriuk

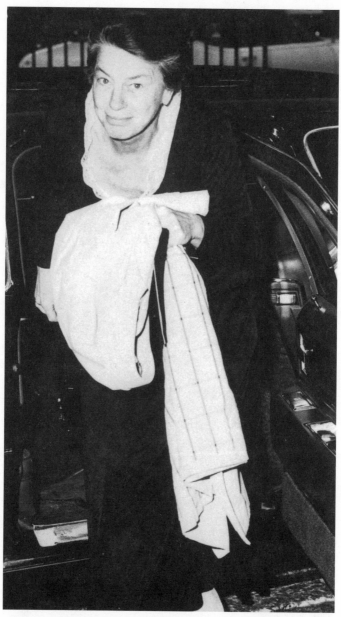

Pauline stepping out of a limousine on the way to her installation as president of Simon Fraser University in Vancouver, British Columbia, 1974. Pauline was the first woman to be named president of a public, co-educational university in Canada. Courtesy of Lyn Grey

Madame President, c. 1977. Pauline is looking thoughtful in this formal photograph taken during her presidency of Simon Fraser University. She had much to be thoughtful about, given the difficult problems she assumed as president. Courtesy of Doris Anderson

Four "sisters" of the New Democratic Party, c. 1987: Marion Dewar (left), Audrey
McLaughlin (second from left), Margaret Mitchell (second from right), and Pauline.
Pauline, Margaret Mitchell, and Marion Dewar were instrumental in supporting
Audrey McLaughlin's candidacy as party leader. Courtesy of Margaret Mitchell

Pauline and her Constan Associate friend, Norm Fenn, on the occasion of her sixty-fifth birthday, December 1987. Always a car enthusiast, Pauline celebrated this birthday by purchasing a Jaguar automobile and was thereafter fondly referred to by her NDP friends as the Jaguar socialist. Courtesy of Doris Anderson

Pauline with the future leader of the New Democratic Party, Audrey McLaughlin (second from right), c. 1988. Standing with them are Anita Hagan (left), the MLA from British Columbia who served as Pauline's campaign manager, and Dawn Black (right), Pauline's constituency assistant from New Westminster–Coquitlam. Dawn succeeded Pauline as the MP for New Westminster–Coquitlam in 1988. Courtesy of Catharine Kushneriuk

Madam Chancellor. Pauline looks a little mischievous in this picture as chancellor attending a graduation at Carleton University, c. 1990.
Courtesy of Carleton University, Mike Pinder Photography

Pauline with actor Peter Ustinov (left) at the graduation ceremony at Carleton University, 1990. Ustinov was awarded an honourary doctor of laws at this convocation. Courtesy of Carleton University, Mike Pinder Photography

Pauline Jewett, Order of Canada. Pauline was thrilled to receive this honour
from Governor General Ray Hnatyshyn in April 1992. Less than three months
later, she succumbed to cancer at the age of sixty-nine.
Courtesy of Catharine Kushneriuk

Pauline with her close friend Doris Anderson, c. 1990, taken at a spa.
Courtesy of Doris Anderson

Pauline Jewett

I know there is only so much each of us can do in the great
struggle to overcome the injustices and inequalities in the
world today and the awesome disparities between rich and
poor, North and South. And there is only so much each of
us can do to end the arms race and bring about disarmament and peace. But if each of us does our bit working with
others doing their bits, the ensuing avalanche of public
awareness and concern in this and in other countries can
surely secure the survival of our planet. That is the challenge before us – peace, justice, equality. Let us, the graduating class of this university, make Carleton as proud of us
as we are proud of Carleton, our alma mater. Your alma
mater and now mine, too.

> Pauline Jewett's address to the graduating class at
> Carleton University on being awarded an honourary
> doctor of laws degree, 12 June 1987

· 1 ·

The Early Years

Political thought embraces the credo that early influences in the formative years immutably shape an individual's political attitudes, mores, and value systems. Family, school, religion, and one's peers are agents of political socialization, and in Pauline Jewett's case they left an indelible imprint. The historical context in which one lives also influences one's ideals and beliefs. There is little question that the era in which Pauline's life unfolded, against the backdrop of the Great Depression, the Second World War, and the second wave of the Canadian women's movement,[1] were critical factors influencing the choices she made in both her public and her private life. There is also compelling evidence that birth order and dynamics within the family can play a significant role in determining the course one steers in life.

There was nothing extraordinary about the Jewett family. It was not a family of considerable wealth or exalted social position. Nor was it a poor one, made poorer by depression or wartime tragedy. It was not ravaged by scandal, illness, or family secrets. Indeed, Pauline grew up in a family that was characterized by its stability and civility. The only unusual thing about the Jewett family was its long-time presence in North America. The Jewetts were one of the oldest families on the continent, their arrival having been documented in the year 1638. In that year some twenty ships, holding at least three thousand persons, including the brothers Maximilian and Joseph Jewett, left Hull, England, landing in Charlestown (Boston) around the beginning of December. Although they were not Puritans like so many others in this group, Maximilian and Joseph Jewett also were seeking a resting place from religious oppression. They came from Bradford in the West Riding of Yorkshire, about two hundred miles north of London.

The Jewetts originally settled in the Rowley, Massachusetts, area and were attracted to the Maritimes sometime after the expulsion of the Acadians (1755). They travelled north to land along the St John River in what is now New Brunswick, and with a land grant in hand for title to property abandoned by the Acadians, they settled there at or around 1764. Family historians point out that the Jewetts were "planters," farmers who predated the arrival of the United Empire Loyalists.[2] Historically, most planters were the second or third sons of landowners in the American colonies who were denied a land legacy because of the prominence of primogeniture in New England. According to family lore, the Jewetts were eager to leave both the revolutionaries and the Loyalists behind. Whatever their reasons for leaving New England, it is known that they were highly successful farmers who flourished during the Civil War as major suppliers of foodstuffs to the Union army. This alliance suggests that the Jewetts were opportunists. Bartering and trading with the Americans were common characteristics of the Maritime economy at that time, and those who engaged in it were paid in American gold coin. The fact that the Jewetts were able to prosper is important, because many who made the exodus northward simply could not cope with the rigours of homesteading and eventually returned to New England.

Pauline's grandparents had a successful farm in Sunbury County, New Brunswick, near the parish of Sheffield, some seventeen miles below Fredericton on the St John River. Her grandmother, Harriet Elizabeth Yerxa, was a widow who brought with her a son, Elijah Yerxa, when she married Frederick Benjamin Jewett. Their marriage produced three more sons – John, Coburn, and George. According to family stories, this union was an interesting one for several reasons. Every year, Mrs Jewett travelled to Boston to visit relatives and go shopping, leaving her husband and sons behind. This was quite an extravagance for the period, since "time outs" for busy mothers and wives were not commonplace. Mrs Jewett had her own horse and carriage, a luxury few contemporaries enjoyed. This gave her considerable independence and may account for her rather autonomous nature. Elijah Yerxa eventually came to operate his own highly successful grocery store in the Fredericton area, and John Jewett inherited the family farm and the responsibility of caring for his aging parents. The youngest son, George, left the farm to join the Canadian war effort during the First World War. He settled in Montreal after the war and became a contractor. His firm, Jewett and

French, was involved in the construction of the Sun Life Building in Montreal.

The middle son, Coburn – Pauline's father – taught in local schools for several years until he had saved enough money to pay for his university tuition. At this time, it was unusual for the sons of farmers to attend university. Helped by a small loan from his father, Coburn entered McGill University in Montreal, where he studied civil engineering. On graduating in 1904, he started work with the contracting firm of Smith, Carey, and Chase in Campbellford, Ontario, as a junior engineer on the Seymour Power Development project, an independent power producer.

In 1909 Coburn met Mae Simpson, and after a brief courtship they were married that December. As the story goes, Coburn first spoke to Mae at a dance, though he had been watching her for some time from the porch of the local hotel, where the young bachelors lived. The Jewett men were all quiet and serious, with little inclination for womanizing, but Coburn was attracted almost instantly to young Miss Simpson, finding her very pretty and stylish. Mae Simpson had an eye for fashion, a passion that continued for her entire life. She was the daughter of a local entrepreneur, Nathan Alonzo Simpson, who operated a livery stable in Campbellford. A devoted father to his two children, he had done his utmost to provide them with all the advantages he could afford, including a formal education. Mae was sent to the Ontario Ladies' College[3] in Whitby, which was considered the most prestigious finishing school for young women in eastern Ontario. Her brother Morley, who was fourteen years younger, attended St Andrew's College in Aurora for a year.

Mae had had several suitors, all of whom could have offered her a good life, but she was attracted to the quiet Maritimer. Coburn had an impressive physical presence – some two hundred and fifty pounds on a six-foot frame. (His daughter Catharine's "larger than life" image of him evoked the Friendly Giant or Diamond Jim Brady.) Coburn was a well-educated and ambitious professional man with a good future, and although he seemed rather introverted, Mae was convinced she could draw him out and mould him into being more sociable. In many respects, Mae and Coburn were complete opposites. She was sociable, outgoing, and witty. He was quiet, intellectual, and steady. Having been socialized in a family with a strong matriarch, he was attracted to Mae's strength of character. She insisted that the word "obey" be struck from her wedding vows and that "cherish" replace it. This did not reflect a suffragette or feminist philosophy. Mae simply believed that no one should have to obey another in a marriage. Coburn willingly agreed to the change, and family members indicate that this was one of the first marriages in Canada where the word "obey" was not used. It proved to be a very happy marriage. Pauline once told a friend that whenever her mother was away, her father said it was as though all the clocks had stopped. None of the children can remember their parents ever having a harsh argument. The only problem was their mother's health.

Mae had been hampered by chronic mastoiditis since her teenage years and had been under the care of ear specialists at St Michael's Hospital in Toronto; she had frequent ear infections in the mastoid region of both inner ears. In those days, long before the discovery of penicillin, infections of this nature could fester and in some cases prove fatal. During the Jewetts' honeymoon to Quebec, Mae caught a cold and developed serious ear problems. By the time the honeymoon was over, the only possible treatment was surgery. The procedure was a radical one and called for the removal of a large portion of the mastoid bone in her inner ear. This reduced Mae's discomfort, but she was left totally deaf in one ear and with about fifty per cent hearing in the other. From then on, her balance and general health were fragile. She developed tinnitus, a continual ringing in her ears, and was particularly bothered by noise and vibrations. Some fifteen years later, she suffered another ear inflammation which further reduced her hearing, and in the following years her hearing continued to deteriorate. Many of Pauline's friends recalled her mother's deafness and observed that it affected Mae's ability to take part in conversations. To compensate, she always entered a room talking.

Pauline's father did not serve in the First World War, because men involved in industry were considered essential back home. Coburn was recruited to oversee a munitions plant in Campbellford that made shell casings. During this time the couple's first child, Frederick Chandler,[4] was born. Young Fred was a frail baby who failed to thrive; by the age of a year and a half, he was virtually back to his birth weight. His father took him to Toronto to consult with paediatric specialists at the Hospital for Sick Children, which at the time was housed in an ivy-covered house in downtown Toronto. There they met with the renowned paediatrician Dr Alan Brown, who confirmed that Fred was critically ill with celiac disease – a disease caused by an inability to digest gluten. This disorder is now managed through dietary restrictions, but in those days it almost always proved fatal. Fred was hospitalized under the watchful supervision of doctors and nurses for several months and had intermittent stays in the hospital for several years.

When the time came for Fred to be discharged, Dr Brown insisted that a trained nurse accompany them back to Campbellford. She remained with the family for more than three years. Dr Brown claimed that young Fred was the first known baby to be cured of celiac disease, and it is likely that the nursing care and diligence of Miss Johnston and the Jewett parents were largely responsible for his recovery. According to family members, Coburn was very "hands on" in helping his wife care for Fred. Over time, the child's condition improved and he was eventually able to attend regular school, but he required an inordinate amount of attention from both his parents, who also shouldered the great financial cost of treating his condition. It is likely that Fred's illness was the main reason why there was a five-year gap between their first and second children.

After the war, Coburn Jewett accepted a position as an engineer on the Welland Canal expansion project in the Niagara region of southwestern Ontario. For four years, the family lived in a large house in Port Weller which was quite close to the barracks in which the canal labourers lived. Apparently Mae Jewett was nervous around a number of these labourers, many of whom were of European origin and spoke little English, and she did not enjoy her four lonely years there with a sick baby boy. During their time in Port Weller, the Jewetts' second child, Catharine, was born. Not long afterwards they moved to a new residential development in the St Catharines area, where they stayed until the Second World War. At the time of the move, Fred was on the road to recovery and ready to start school. The Jewetts' desire to enrol him into a good school system was the motivation behind their relocation. For a number of years, Fred was a day student at Ridley College, the prestigious boys' school in St Catharines.[5] A year after their move, on 11 December 1922, Pauline was born.

The Jewetts' house in St Catharines was a substantial three-storey brick structure in an upscale new residential development known as Glenridge. While it is likely that Coburn Jewett could have afforded a grander house, he was not the type of man who felt the need to impress people with material possessions. By choosing a home that was within his means, he could spend his money on other things that gave him pleasure, such as a car. According to his son, Coburn had a car from 1910 onwards. His passion for cars appears to have been one of his few extravagances and one of the few departures from a rather conservative lifestyle. Although Coburn was a member of the St Catharines Club, he never had the desire for a network of male friends.

The transformation of Coburn Jewett which the young Mae Simpson had envisaged did not take place. He remained the solid, steady, and introverted man she had married, preferring a life of relative simplicity. The one social activity that he and Mae enjoyed together was auction bridge, but that ended with the deterioration of Mae's hearing after her second mastoid surgery. There is no question that the lack of a rich social life was a major disappointment to her, but she recognized that her husband had many good attributes, and over the years she gathered a wide circle of women friends with whom she enjoyed spending time, usually over afternoon tea.

A common pattern for many political women is the development of a strong attachment to the father and a relatively weak one to the mother. In an analysis conducted on eleven Canadian women legislators who have written their autobiographies or been the subject of a biography,[6] it was determined that six of them were strongly influenced by the political beliefs and partisanship of their fathers. For the most part, the mothers of these women were shadowy figures who seem to have had little influence on the political beliefs of their daughters. This may be because these mothers deferred to the political beliefs and partisanship of their husbands and were the "mindless matrons" which early voting research proclaimed them to be;[7] or perhaps they simply shared the same ideas as their husbands. The remaining five women had important adult political socialization experiences which had the effect of altering their political views.

There is considerable evidence that Pauline's relationship with her father was important. Close friends have suggested that he was the most significant influence in moulding her personality. He enjoyed her intellect, her athleticism, and her ambition. There appears to be little question that she adored him and admired his philosophy of life. She described him as "an egalitarian to beat all egalitarians" and often recounted the story of his support of Mae's request to have the word "obey" struck from their wedding vows. Although his position as a public servant prevented Coburn Jewett from publicly supporting one political party over another, it is clear that he had a deep admiration for Mackenzie King and the Liberal Party.

Long after her father's death in 1951, Pauline often brought him up in conversations. As one friend recounted, Pauline would be driving her car and chatting away – and then, on encountering a certain situation, she would recall the advice her father had given her to handle that very problem. Pauline was convinced that her father had been a major influence in her life. She described him as a gentle man with a strong social conscience:

During her childhood, Pauline witnessed a scene involving her father and a neighbour. The neighbour came to their home with a petition requesting that a Jewish family be refused permission to buy land and build a house on property adjoining the Jewetts' home in the somewhat superior suburb of Glenridge in St Catharines. Not only did her father refuse to sign, but with an anger she had never before seen him exhibit, he declared that if the petition were circulated he would organize another one demanding that the newcomers be allowed to buy. Buy and build they did, and they became friendly neighbours for many years.[8]

Another story concerns a report card that Pauline brought home early in her high school years. Her father looked at the results and in a calm voice said, "Pauline, you can do better than this." Nothing more was said. As far as Pauline was concerned, nothing more needed to be said. From that time forward, there was a noticeable change in her work ethic at school. As her brother has pointed out, their father never patronized Pauline; he always treated her as an equal.

Another well-known family story relates to a race that Pauline won at a school track meet. Apparently, she was terribly deflated when, next day, the winners' names were published in the *St Catharines Standard* and hers was not among them. Her father promptly contacted the editor, and in the next edition there was a special mention of Pauline's victory. This was not an ego-inflating exercise; her father's intervention had had only one objective – to ensure fairness of treatment. Throughout Pauline's young life, her father gave her similar nudges and words of encouragement which fostered her drive to achieve, while his egalitarianism led her to believe that the world could be hers if she was prepared to work hard.

In the late 1930s, Pauline's father was engaged by the British government as chief engineer on the Gander Air Base project. The establishment of the airport at Gander was a keystone of Britain's aviation strategy.[9] The British believed that it was important to hire Canadian engineers who were acquainted with local geological and climactic conditions, and F.C. Jewett's name had been put forward. On completion of the project, he was described by British newspapers as "the quiet Canadian."[10] Meanwhile, with the onset of war, he went to Ottawa with the Transport Department in a special unit. He was appointed chief of wartime construction of the British Commonwealth Air Training Scheme, in charge of the development and construction of more than a hundred airfields in Canada, which were to be used for training air force personnel. When Coburn accepted this position, he and his wife made the decision to sell the house in St Catharines and relocate to Ottawa. Fred had gone overseas, Catharine was launched on her nursing training, and Pauline had just started university in Kingston. Mae had grown tired of her husband's lengthy absences, and now that "the nest was empty," the time seemed right to move to Ottawa.

What was life like for Pauline growing up in St Catharines as a young girl and teenager? One of the early "truths" she learned was that life was not always fair if you were born a girl. If you were good at games such as "run sheep run" and baseball, people called you a tomboy, which to this day continues to have a rather derogatory meaning. A story about Pauline's desire to have a paper route illustrates her stubborn streak and her strong will to challenge this social norm of male dominance. At the age of ten, she decided that she wanted a paper route and she approached her father for help. According to Pauline, her father telephoned the *St Catharines Standard* to inquire how one went about getting a paper route. "He was told that the paper's policy precluded little girls having paper routes. And so there was this boy who had the paper route in the area, who, when I told him my problem, subcontracted part of his paper route to me. I think I was getting about twenty-five cents a week, but for me it was the height of achieving an ambition to have done this."[11] This was one of Pauline's first experiences with gender discrimination. In an interview with her niece, she recalled thinking that boys seemed to be unlimited in terms of the things that they could do: "Consciously, I was very aware that it was the boys [who] had the paper routes, the boys who had the key positions on the baseball teams, and it was the boys [who] set up the 'run sheep run' games, and the boys had the teddy bears instead of the dolls. And I know that I said to Mom and Dad, 'Oh, why wasn't I a little boy?' And it was then they began saying things like, 'Little girls can do those things, too.' They didn't really discourage me from those tomboyish things."[12]

Pauline's father had emphasized since early childhood that her gender should not discourage her from having lofty ambitions even if they were not traditional ones. He also instilled in Pauline the belief that there were lessons to be learned from setbacks and failures; throughout her life she had the ability to reflect on disappointments and contextualize them. While Pauline idolized her father, she could not have been totally objective about him, of course; it is likely that his introverted personality presented problems. Those who knew him have described him as dependable and "moderately sociable within the family," whereas his wife was a warm and sociable person who had a strong desire for companionship. Despite their differences, one senses that both were content working together as a team, providing a stable home for their three children.

According to Fred Jewett, his parents were a unit bound together by their children.[13] Achievement in school and a desire for excellence were important considerations to the father, while social graces and the development of good conversational skills were important to the mother. Because of their mother's condition, the Jewett home was serene rather than raucous. Loud voices, temper tantrums, and, above all, door slamming were strongly discouraged. One of the family rules, strictly enforced, was harmony at mealtime; any of the children who had arguments were asked to leave the table. While all this may seem like quite a regimented household, there were many smiles and plenty of laughter during these years.

One story that Pauline recounted to her friend Doris Anderson concerned her habit of occasionally sitting at the table with radio earphones on during dinner. In spite of her parents' objections, she continued to listen to her favourite program. Her father, who happened to know the radio announcer, arranged to have him announce on air that children who ate at the table with earphones were in danger of being skipped over when Santa Claus made his rounds that Christmas. Pauline apparently snatched the earphones off her head immediately, to the amusement of her father and mother.

As far as female role models were concerned, Mae Simpson Jewett was far from typical of her times. Although she was not involved in the suffrage movement or active in social service clubs, she was a practical, discerning, independent, intelligent woman. In certain respects, Alonzo Simpson had been inclined to overindulge his only daughter, and Mae's fragile physical condition led to further nurturing and pampering by her husband. Rather than being resentful about his wife's special needs, Coburn Jewett respected her intelligence and by all accounts was happy to be an active partner in the parenting of their three children. Furthermore, he always made sure that his wife had cleaning help, help with the children, and conveniences such as a laundry service.

Despite her fragility, Mae was a dominant force in the family. She was satisfied with her traditional lifestyle, though she realized that much had changed with the depression and the war. Women were entering the workplace in increasing numbers, and the opportunities now available to them had expanded well beyond the traditional roles. Mae's awareness that times had changed helps explain her very strong views about the type of life she wanted for her daughters. As Pauline observed, "She did not encourage any of us to follow traditional paths. She did not present marriage to us as the inevitable route to go as did the mothers of a great many of our friends."[14]

When Pauline was growing up, she often bristled against social snobbery and social do's and don'ts, rebelling against her mother's insistence that she follow certain practices. This indifference to social niceties stayed with Pauline most of her life and became part of her political style. Her ability to relate to people from all walks of life, not just from her own social strata, was an approach she employed throughout her political career. While on the campaign trail in an Ottawa riding for the NDP in 1972, Marion Dewar noted this characteristic: "I remember her sitting on a carton, surrounded by all sorts of people, chain-smoking and talking away to them, and it was as if she lived next door."[15] Similarly, Doris Anderson observed, "She knew all sorts of people, from janitors to Prime Ministers, and she valued all of them. I was amazed at the numbers of people who kept calling or coming to see her when she was ill."[16]

It appears that Pauline learned this important skill from her father. His unassuming nature and lack of social pretension likely dated back to his religious Maritime upbringing and his work. On the Welland Canal project and in his airport work it was necessary to relate both to assistant engineers and to unskilled labourers, many of whom had a limited command of the English language. Pauline also inherited her father's frugality. Aside from an occasional "exotic" taste in cars – also acquired from her father – Pauline was very careful with her money and rarely splurged on travel or extravagances. In fact, during the 1980s while serving as an MP, she lived in a nonprofit housing project in Centre Town, a moderate-income residential area in downtown Ottawa. Although she was a full-paying tenant, she had no desire to live in a more upscale residential neighbourhood.

Despite Pauline's obvious emulation of some of her father's traits and her open admiration of him, there is nothing to indicate that she and her mother had a troubled or strained relationship. Pauline often told the story about the day she skipped school to go to a movie with her first beau, a boy named Bev. A neighbour saw them coming out of the theatre and immediately telephoned Pauline's mother – who promptly said that Pauline had discussed her plans to attend the show that afternoon and had received permission to do so. Mae Jewett had strong ideas about people minding their own business. In the early 1960s, she and Pauline lived in the same apartment building, frequently spending their evenings together. By this time, Pauline was almost forty years old. Apparently, her mother once disapprovingly remarked that she had seen a certain man Pauline was dating leaving the building very early one morning. According to the story, Pauline paused and said, "So?" That was the last time her mother ever raised the subject of Pauline's comings and goings.

Yet there is considerable evidence that Pauline was devoted to her mother. It was typical of their relationship that after the death of her father, when her mother was quite lonely, Pauline recruited a group of her friends to have "tea and sympathy" with her on a weekly basis. Mae Jewett always brought out her best china and silver tea service during these visits, fostering the impression among Pauline's friends that her mother was from a much more privileged background than was the case. Certainly, her home in the Roxborough Apartments was impressive. This apartment hotel was considered one of Ottawa's smartest addresses when it opened in 1910. Backing onto the Rideau Canal, it had elevators, concierges, maid service, and an elegant communal dining room. As Mae often informed her visitors, it had been home to some of Ottawa's finest "gentlemen," including Louis St Laurent, Mackenzie King, and Paul Martin.

To put Pauline's early life into historical context, one might note that she was born two years after most Canadian women had won the franchise[17] and during a period when social activism entered a stage of relative dormancy. Although women had been active participants in the wartime economy during the First World War, this important role had largely been forgotten by the time Pauline was a teenager. Even the Persons Case[18] and the controversy it generated had taken place when Pauline was still a small child. Moreover, there is no evidence to suggest that Pauline's mother was a social or maternal feminist, in spite of her insistence that the "obey" clause be removed from her wedding vows. Pauline's formative youth was spent in an atmosphere of traditional values and family stability – and also in financial comfort, despite the hard times of the depression. But although the Jewetts were spared the financial hardships that many others endured, it is likely that the depression did leave some lasting impressions on Pauline and was a significant event that shaped her social and political consciousness.

BIRTH ORDER

There have been a number of compelling studies concluding that birth order has a profound influence on personality development.[19]

In the case of the Jewett family, it is likely that birth order did play a prominent role in shaping Pauline's personality. One of the perplexing questions in the area of personality psychology relates to why siblings are so different. It has been suggested by Frank J. Sulloway that siblings are different "because they exemplify Darwin's 'principle of divergence.'"[20] Having been observed in all species, diversity is a behavioural strategy used by siblings to compete for scarce resources, namely, parental attention. As children within a family grow up, claims Sulloway, they "undergo adaptive radiation in their efforts to establish their own individual niches within the family. By pursuing disparate interests and abilities, siblings minimize direct competition."[21] In the case of Pauline's father, it is evident that he attempted to minimize competition among his children by not comparing their achievements. One of his favourite expressions was "Comparisons are odious." Over the years, he was attentive to all his children and spent long periods, one-on-one, with each of his daughters and his son. However, despite the best intentions of any parents, it is virtually impossible to eliminate sibling rivalry within families.

Because Fred was a boy and was five years older than Catharine and seven years older than Pauline, it is more instructive to consider the Jewett sisters as a two-sibling family, or a "sister dyad." Catharine was a beautiful child and constantly had this attribute emphasized by her mother. During their elementary school years, Catharine, by her own admission, was bossy and dominated her little sister. In part, this occurred because she knew that it was her responsibility as the older sister to care for Pauline. Catharine's idea of fun was running a summer school for her sister and other children in the neighbourhood. The summer school was convened in the playroom of the Jewett home, where there were tables and chairs and a "real" blackboard. Catharine took this role very seriously and taught Pauline and the others everything she had learned the preceding year. Although the Jewett girls thought this was great fun, other neighbourhood children thought it too much work and dropped out of the school.

As the older daughter in the family, Catharine found her niche as the nurturing, pretty, and feminine child. She tended to pursue much more traditional interests than Pauline, both at an early age and later, graduating from nurses' training at the Royal Victoria Hospital in Montreal and later obtaining a diploma in public health nursing from McGill University. While working as a public health nurse in Deep River, Ontario, she met and married a young physicist, Steven Kushneriuk, with whom she raised three children. Pauline, on the other hand, was convinced that she was not pretty, and this became a lasting insecurity that had a profound effect on her self-image and her relationships with men. Throughout her life, she sought reassurance that she was attractive, sometimes seeking it in the wrong places with the wrong people.

I never had the feeling that I was particularly pretty and I do remember at a very early age thinking that I was not very attractive to boys. Catharine was the pretty one of the family. Even though our parents weren't pushing us into dates and early marriage, society around you made the assumption that's what you would do. I deliberately compensated for this by trying to make my conversation interesting and my ideas interesting. I remember constantly doing that to overcome what I felt to be my limits on attractiveness.[22]

At a young age, Pauline was motivated to find an unoccupied niche within the family to attract the attention of her parents – what Sulloway terms "parental investment."[23] As a result, both her interests and her personality were decidedly different from those of her older sister. Pauline was more sociable, happiest when surrounded by other people. She preferred playing games and participating in sports to reading and sedentary hobbies. Although she was not as well read in the classics as Catharine, she was an excellent student and an accomplished athlete. It was in these areas, scholarship and athleticism, that Pauline found her niche within the Jewett family.

It has also been claimed that birth order has an influence on political and social thought. Sulloway's study concluded that firstborns are inclined to respect the status quo, while the second of two children is distinctly radical.[24] It is evident that Pauline saw herself as the family radical, and she continued to play this role throughout her life. At the age of fourteen, she announced that she intended to become a criminal lawyer so that the wrongly accused and underprivileged would have a fair trial. Her father supported this ambition and never tried to dissuade her by promoting careers that were more traditional. He told her, "Most goals can be reached if you're prepared to struggle for them. Just say to yourself, 'I can lick my weight in wildcats!'" Pauline liked the sound of that, and it became a favourite family phrase whenever a challenging problem arose.[25] Shortly before her death, she repeated the phrase in her last interview with Charlotte Gobeil and laughed as she explained the history of the expression.

Sulloway's study of birth order also gives us some clues about political styles in attempting to understand the difference between the Jewett sisters. Using the work of British psychologist Hans Eysenck,[26] he presents a model with four styles of political thought: tough-minded support for the status quo, tender-minded support for the status quo, tender-minded support for liberal social change, and tough-minded support for radical change. The style most descriptive of the one Pauline emulated is tender-minded support for liberal social change. As a general rule, liberal reform movements such as antislavery, freethinking, socialism, and utopianism have been backed by laterborns and opposed by firstborns.[27] In examining liberal reformism among women, Sulloway found a correlation with birth order, noting that Mary Wollstonecraft, George Eliot, Florence Nightingale, Susan B. Anthony, Elizabeth Cady Stanton, Margaret Sanger, and Virginia Woolf were all laterborns.[28]

Despite the personality and philosophical differences between the Jewett sisters, there was genuine affection between them, though there was also tension; but rather than engaging with each other in areas where they did not agree, they usually made a concerted effort to downplay their differences of opinion in order to avoid dissension. Over the years, they called each other regularly, and after Pauline purchased her cottage on Constant Lake, the Kushneriuks spent a week there every summer. Although Pauline was very busy with her career, she came to Catharine's rescue in the summer of 1967 when Catharine was in an Ottawa hospital, recuperating from back surgery. Her husband and his sisters had been taking turns caring for the three Kushneriuk children, who ranged from eight to twelve years of age; but at the last moment, Steven Kushneriuk was called to go to Ann Arbor, Michigan, for a conference and arrangements for the children could not be made. Aunt Pauline (though she did not like being called that) stepped into the breach and volunteered to baby-sit for the week. She took the children to her cottage, and by all accounts everyone had a grand time. Pauline, the three children, and their Pekinese dog Ching went for long canoe trips on the lake, and Pauline prepared their favourite dishes for dinner. She was a notorious nighthawk but changed this behaviour when she realized that the children were early risers.

Although Pauline loved her niece and nephews and had a tremendous fondness for young people, she never felt totally comfortable in some of the traditional feminine roles. She was always indifferent to fashion, and when she first went to university she kept wearing the same outfit, though her mother had supplied her with a full complement of clothes. After two weeks, a senior student who had been assigned to keep a watchful eye on her marched into her room and, throwing several pieces of clothing on the bed, said, "Wear them!" Throughout her life, Pauline detested shopping for clothes. She would binge shop, buying four or five dresses at a time. She never trusted her own taste in fashion and usually persuaded her sister or a friend to accompany her on shopping jaunts. In her academic career, she did not have to bother much about her clothes, for the university environment did not necessitate much attention to wardrobe. As a parliamentarian, however, she became more clothes conscious, especially after being described as "frumpy" in a women's magazine. According to Pauline's friends, her choice of casual clothes usually accentuated her "great" legs. In the summer, she enjoyed wearing short-shorts and pumps à la Betty Grable in the 1950s.

It was much the same story with decorating her various apartments. When Pauline was president of Simon Fraser University, she invited Catharine to Vancouver to help her decorate the president's residence. As for her cooking – well, it wasn't legendary! Not that she was a bad cook, but her repertoire was rather limited and would not be described as gourmet. Nevertheless, she took pleasure in good food and was a most appreciative dinner guest, making contented sounds throughout the meal and offering flattering comments to the cook.

While Pauline had little interest in these traditionally femine occupations, she did have a number of outside interests that captured her passion. According to her friend Norm Fenn (the former director of athletics at Carleton University), PJ was a "jock." She loved sports, especially hockey and baseball, and had been a member of the Queen's tennis team and women's hockey team. Pauline was an avid fan of the National Hockey League. While at Simon Fraser University, she followed the fortunes of the Vancouver Canucks, and in her later Ottawa days, she became a passionate fan of the Quebec Nordiques and Toronto Blue Jays. She reportedly supported the Nordiques because "they were such a courageous little lot."[29] More than one of her friends have commented that Pauline would have been ecstatic when the Colorado Avalanche (the former Nordiques) won the Stanley Cup in the spring of 1996. She also had a passion for sports cars. Pauline owned a 1968 Shelby Cobra GT500 KR the year that she was running for the NDP in Ottawa West (1972). She and her friend Marion Dewar used to drive to coffee parties in Pauline's car – and, in Marion's words, they usually flew to these meetings! On her sixty-fifth birthday, Pauline treated herself to a slightly used, silver and green Jaguar XJS V12 which greatly amused her friends. Apparently, she had long harboured the desire to own a Jag.

Over the years, Pauline developed a keen interest in art. In the early fifties, she purchased several prints of José Orozco, the great Mexican painter. (These prints ended up at the cottage as her taste in art changed.) Later, she purchased several canvases by avant-garde French-Canadian painters, and she also owned a David Milne watercolour. Apparently, she was a great movie buff too and went to many foreign films in the 1950s and 1960s with her friend Lyn Grey. Reading was another passion. While Pauline certainly devoured volumes of scholarly books and journals, her pet passion was a good mystery or detective novel. She had a particular liking for the stories of Agatha Christie.

Pauline was different from many other young women of her time in her affinity for politics and her interest in current events. These two intellectual passions led to an early development of social consciousness, which began in adolescence. In a television interview in 1992, Pauline admitted to having had parliamentary ambitions when she was at high school and was voted the person in the graduating class most likely to become the first woman prime minister – a thoroughly unusual prediction in 1939–40.[30] She had already decided that she wanted to attend university and study law. Whether this was because she had a passion for the law or because law was the traditional "pathway" to Parliament is not clear. Whatever insecurities she had about her physical appearance were more than compensated for by a strong belief in herself and her abilities. This self-confidence sustained Pauline throughout her life.

In her final year at St Catharines Collegiate, Pauline applied herself well enough to win an entrance scholarship to Queen's University. She financed the lion's share of her university education through scholarships and academic awards, but she was always aware that her parents, especially her father, were behind her in her endeavours. This support was pivotal, since most young women of that era were encouraged to attend normal school,[31] nurses' training, or secretarial college, rather than university. From this point on, it was clear that Pauline was embarking on a mission that would lead her to pursue a different course. In the fall of 1940, in her eighteenth year, she set off to Queen's University in Kingston, Ontario, and began the second chapter of her life, one that would be extremely important in her decision to pursue a public career.

Off to Queen's and Harvard

Pauline began her university years at an opportune time. Although it was still not commonplace for young women to attend university, the Depression and wartime had the effect of increasing their attendance. This continued a trend that educational historians had observed since the 1920s, when there was a presence of women on university campuses.[1] In the case of Queen's University, Nicole Neatby reports that female students comprised about 40 per cent of the arts students during the 1920s and that the proportion of graduate students nationwide who were women peaked in 1929–30 when they comprised 28 per cent of graduate enrolment in Canada.[2] Nicole Neatby and Gladys Hitchman attribute this peak to the emancipation of women resulting from their participation during the First World War.[3]

Unlike the Ivy League image of Queen's today, it was known as a poor man's college in the 1920s.[4] However, Neatby suggests that the truth was somewhere in between its present image and its past one. An estimated 39 per cent of the freshman class in 1928–29 were said to be the sons and daughters of professionals.[5] Not only were more women entering university as undergraduates, but graduate school enrolments among women were up as well. The percentages of graduate students who were women, therefore, was quite impressive, and it is likely that their presence served as an inspiration to younger women undergraduates.

At the end of the 1930s as the Second World War loomed, universities began to encourage the enrolment of women to fill the places of young men who joined the forces. During the war, women formed a larger proportion of the student body than ever before. As Alison

Prentice and others have observed, female students constituted a "reserve army" much as they did in the labour force. And as with the labour force, it was assumed that these student spaces "would be occupied by men once the war was over."[6] However, women did not stop going to university after the war. In fact, more women than ever (some fourteen thousand) entered universities in September 1945.

When Pauline was ready for university in the fall of 1940, she was one of an estimated eight thousand Canadian women enrolled as undergraduate students. At that time, women accounted for 23 per cent of all university students.[7] The forties were a difficult time for Canada's universities, and Queen's was no exception. According to Herb Hamilton, the faculty and staff at Queen's had been decimated by enlistment or secondment to Ottawa, and intercollegiate athletics had been cancelled.[8] All able-bodied students were expected to train in some war-related capacity. In the case of women, they were required to register for work in one of a number of special activities for at least two hours each week.[9]

Pauline had not really considered going to any other university, and her selection was strongly endorsed by her father. It may well be that Coburn Jewett was familiar with the high profile that Queen's graduates had in the federal civil service and the excellent reputation for high academic standards which the university itself enjoyed. Unlike the University of Toronto and McGill University, Queen's did not allow fraternities and sororities. It was clearly spelled out in Queen's academic calendar that "by resolution of [the] Senate no student registered with the University may form or become a member of any chapter of any externally-affiliated fraternity or sorority at or near Kingston." In Coburn's opinion, these organizations were bastions of elitism and did not provide an environment supporting egalitarianism and equality.[10] It is also likely that he preferred the smaller size of Queen's, which was said to have a student body of seventeen hundred in 1940,[11] and the more conservative nature of Kingston compared with Toronto.

Although it was probably not a deciding factor in Pauline's choice of Queen's, there had been a long history of involvement by the women of the Queen's University Alumnae Association to "smooth the way for succeeding generations of women students."[12] In the early 1920s, a small group of former students and a faculty member, Dr Elizabeth Shortt, had committed themselves to developing residence space for women. At first, they leased and furnished an older house in Kingston called the Hen Coop. Led by Aletta Marty,[13] the group began a major fundraising drive, and by 1923 the Board of

Governors had authorized construction of a women's residence.[14] The university administration grudgingly supplied some funding for this project, though it assumed that the residence would be a white elephant and a major cash drain. To counter these criticisms, the alumnae insisted that they manage the residence themselves. And so the Ban Righ Board was established, which ran the women's residences effectively and with a profit for more than thirty years. By 1974, the construction of new residences ceased and the money that had accrued was put into a foundation – the Ban Righ Foundation – which was established to encourage continuing education for women. There is a certain irony that Pauline selected a university with this rich history of sisterhood, though Queen's was not in actuality a mecca of enlightened thinking; it was much like other universities in Canada in its treatment of women students.

There were special admonitions to women students in the Queen's calendar for the 1940–41 session. For example, "All first year women under twenty-five and not resident in the City of Kingston" were required to live in Ban Righ Hall or in one of its annexes.[15] Women students living in boarding houses also were subject to certain rules and regulations. The calendar stated, "Women students are under no circumstances permitted to lodge in houses in which any man other than the husband or son of the lodging-house keeper is living or lodging."[16] Male students, on the other hand, faced no restrictions relating to their living arrangements. While these regulations may not have drawn criticism back in 1940, their intent and message was clear. Women were to be sequestered and to be protected from men. The mores of the time were still rather Victorian and were decades away from advances in birth control. The universities took it upon themselves to do what they could to ensure that students would not "get in trouble." It is small wonder that co-educational residences were considered such a radical idea in the 1970s and 1980s, given the archaic treatment of women undergraduates just three decades earlier.

When Pauline enrolled at Queen's, her intention was to study law, specifically criminal law. However, her academic focus soon shifted, no doubt influenced by the changing world order during the war years. The political intrigue and stratagems embracing the war and Canada's involvement in it fascinated Pauline. It soon became apparent that her intellectual interests were increasingly in politics and international affairs. The Department of Political and Economic Science at Queen's was small, with just nine faculty. In 1940, the chair was W.A. Mackintosh, who later would become principal of Queen's.

Other faculty were C.E. Walker (professor), R.G.H. Smails (professor), C.A. Curtis (professor), F.A. Knox (professor), J.L. McDougall (assistant professor), J.A. Corry (the Hardy assistant professor of political and economic science), J.C. Cameron (head of the industrial relations section), and L.G. Macpherson (instructor).

The introductory course in political science was called Politics 2 and was taught by Professor Corry, a person with whom Pauline would have a bittersweet relationship. Politics 30, also taught by Corry, dealt with Canadian government and constitutional law. Politics 32 (recent political thought), Politics 33 (English constitutional history and law), Politics 34 (international politics), and Politics 35 (European governments) were the other political science courses offered, and **all** of them were taught by Corry. The courses were given on Mondays, Wednesdays, and Fridays at 9 and 11 AM and on Tuesdays, Thursdays, and Saturdays at 11 AM. For all intents and purposes, J.A. Corry was the only faculty member in the department who taught political science. During Pauline's undergraduate years, two other political scientists came to Queen's – J.E. Hodgetts and K.G. Crawford, director of the Institute of Local Government – but it is clear that if you were a student of political science at Queen's, you received a large dose of Corry and could not help but fall under his influence.

Professor Corry was a lawyer by training. Born in Perth, Ontario, he had gone west to study law and was awarded a Rhodes Scholarship in 1924. He spent the following year at Oxford University but did not embrace the socialist ideas that dominated the campus at that time. Moreover, Corry had been a committed disciple of the Harvard case method, also known as the Socratic method of instruction, and he found this approach to be sadly lacking at Oxford.[17] On returning to Canada, he had the good fortune to be offered a teaching position at the University of Saskatchewan Law School. After several years there, he applied for and received a graduate fellowship at Columbia Law School in New York City (1934–35), and in 1936 he was approached by Queen's to teach political science.

Despite his interest in politics and constitutional law, Corry was not at all confident that he was the right person for the job. Political science was still not recognized as an independent field of study. As Corry observed, "The subject was regarded as an adjunct of 'related' disciplines, and the meagre instruction in it was usually given by economists or historians, and sometimes by lawyers or philosophers."[18] But Queen's was looking for someone with a legal background and an interest in public administration, and Corry fitted the bill.[19] From then on, he *was* political science at Queen's. His ideological persuasion was never in doubt. He was born into a family of Clear Grits, and for most of his life he espoused classical liberalism and supported the Liberal Party.

Although Corry never saw himself as a political scientist, he anchored the department in this subject and had to learn the discipline at the same time as his students. He found teaching to be both demanding and challenging: "My teaching in Politics over twenty-five years was almost entirely given to undergraduates. We had, during that time, only occasional graduate students. For me, this was gratifying. I had not – and did not covet – the depth of knowledge in detail in particular areas that graduate students have a right to expect. My interests, my knowledge, and methods of teaching were well suited for arousing interest in undergraduates and encouraging them to think for themselves."[20]

In the spring of 1944, Pauline graduated with first-class honours in political science and philosophy and was awarded the gold medal as the top-ranking student in politics.[21] In examining her Queen's scrapbook, I noted that she achieved this honour largely as a result of strong grades in the third and fourth years of her undergraduate program. In her first year, she received a steady dose of BS and CS in her courses, which included philosophy, politics, and economics. These marks suggest that Pauline's interests may have lain elsewhere during her first couple of years at Queen's. She later commented, in an interview with Charlotte Gobeil, that it took until the age of twenty-one before her "framework for learning" was firmly establishe.[22] The scrapbook of her Queen's years contains pasted advertisements relating to a number of dances held at the university. Pauline told another interviewer that she "loved partying and dancing" and that "university was fun in that sense." She had a particular affinity for the sounds of the big bands and loved such songs as "In the Mood," "Night and Day," and her all-time favourite, Hoagy Carmichael's "Stardust." "You couldn't help but be a romantic with that kind of music," she said.[23] She was also active on the women's athletic teams and excelled at hockey and tennis.

Pauline's scrapbook contains a number of notices for meetings of the Students' Christian Movement. Apparently, she had signed up with the group on a whim. A young theology student, Glyn Firth, called her one day to find out why she had not been more active in the club. They went on to become lifelong friends. Pauline's parents thought Glyn was a serious beau, but in fact he was gay. This may have been Pauline's first friendship with a gay person, and it likely opened her eyes to the discrimination that people with this orientation endured. Glyn eventually became a United Church minister and spent most of his career working in underprivileged urban areas. He and Pauline maintained a relationship, mostly over the telephone, until his death in the late 1960s.

Like many other women students at Queen's, PJ joined the university's Army Reserve Unit in 1942. In total, some sixty young women travelled to Barriefield, a military base just outside Kingston, where they were trained in motor mechanics and army vehicle driving. This was a perfect assignment for Pauline because she had long had a fascination with cars and driving. She toyed with the idea of joining the RCAF, but she was advised to finish her studies, since many teachers would be required when the veterans returned after the war.[24] Encouraged by Jean Royce, the registrar, Pauline decided to pursue a master's degree at Queen's. She later credited Jean Royce with encouraging young women to maximize their potential and challenge the traditional norms set for them by society. Miss Royce thought that Pauline was an excellent candidate for graduate school and told her in her third year, "I am convinced that you can have a really outstanding career if you want it."[25]

A number of former Queen's women have reflected on the role that Jean Royce played in their lives. She was more than an administrator. Men and women alike firmly believed that she "ran" the university. As registrar of Queen's (1933–68), and as convenor of the Canadian Federation of University Women and convenor of the Standards Committee of the International Federation of University Women, Jean Royce had first-hand knowledge of who the promising women scholars were across the country. One former Queen's graduate wrote to her saying, "I shall never forget that day in your office at Queen's when, in a meeting with you, you suddenly leaned across your desk and said, 'Esther, what do you *really* want to do?' And, in your manner of asking, conveyed to me that I could be whatever I wanted to be and do whatever I wanted to do. And, for the first time in my life, I felt that the whole world was in my hands."[26] Another Queen's graduate, Kathleen Butcher Whitehead, had a similar story:

Then I got a call to go and see Miss Royce. As a freshman, I had received a real dressing down from her for failing the Christmas exam in English. She asked if I were interested in going to graduate school. The idea had simply never occurred to me. Going on in mathematics was not the normal thing it became later. She said that the Mathematics Department thought I should consider the possibility. I was completely taken aback, said that I was definitely not interested, and went off. However, she had planted the thought in my mind. That conversation probably represented the first real turning point in my life. Now I had to find out how to go on.[27]

Life at Queen's provided Pauline with many insights about the difficulties women faced in pursuing nontraditional occupations. One of her friends there, Lyn Grey, commented that women were not taken seriously academically, particularly "if you were attractive." She joked that if you were in science, "you had to wear your hair in a bun and wear lisle stockings." Lyn recalled applying for a student position at the marine field station in Nanaimo, British Columbia, and not being accepted because she "might disrupt the concentration of the male students." Another peer of Pauline's remembers a male professor boasting that he had never given a woman student a first-class standing in all his years of teaching. In short, it was not easy for bright young women to be taken seriously by certain male professors. An entrenched, accepted prejudice that women were somehow second-class students persisted.

This prejudice was not confined to women students; women faculty also had a very difficult time. Pauline later described the problems endured by Alice Vibert Douglas, the dean of women at Queen's for some twenty years. Dr Douglas had been selected to replace Winnifred Kydd as dean of women in 1939. At the time, she was an astrophysicist in the McGill Department of Physics, and she had previously been a doctoral research student with Rutherford and Eddington at Cambridge.[28] In addition to her role as dean of women, Dr Douglas later became a full professor in the physics department at Queen's. Over and above counselling women students, the dean of women was responsible for a plethora of menial tasks such as keeping tabs on the laundry and presiding over the dining hall. Pauline noticed that many of her peers demeaned Dr Douglas, and she wondered whether a male professor would be subject to that kind of abuse. The students seemed oblivious to the fact that Professor Douglas was an accomplished scientist who travelled widely. She was a pure scholar, yet she had to worry that not too many bed sheets went missing! These experiences must have alerted Pauline to the idea that life as a woman in the academy was not easy. Yet witnessing this discrimination first-hand did not dissuade her. If anything, it inspired her.

Three major stimuli explain Pauline's desire to pursue her academic career at the graduate level. First, she was urged by Jean Royce to continue her studies. Pauline was a driven young woman who, from time to time, needed to be prodded and praised. As a girl, this encouragement had come from her father. As a college student, the cheerleading role was assumed by Jean Royce and Professor Corry. Second, she possessed a fine intellect and had an excellent record of achievement at Queen's. She had been the top-ranking student in politics and had been awarded several scholarships to pursue her master's degree. However, perhaps the greatest single factor was her attendance at a summer conference on international relations. Pauline participated in a two-month students' conference on international affairs held in Twin Lakes, Connecticut, the summer after she graduated from Queen's.[29] Many of those attending were European students who had been unable to return to their native lands because of the war. Points of view from competing ideological perspectives were presented at this conference, and many diverse explanations for the causes of the war were debated. More importantly, a number of seminars were devoted to the issue of how peace could be maintained in the changing world order.[30] Pauline's lifetime preoccupation with world peace was undoubtably rooted in this period. As an intellectual environment for eager inquiring young minds, the conference was enriching and exhilarating. For Pauline, it was a paramount formative experience in terms of her intellectual evolution, fixing the framework on which she built her political ideas and ideals, and defining the direction her life would follow.

Pauline completed her MA at Queen's in June 1945, convocating in October of that year, and was accepted into the PH D program in government, at Harvard University in Cambridge, Massachusetts. There had been a rich history of Queen's women graduates attending Harvard. Four of the first ten Marty Scholarship recipients (1937–47)[31] attended Radcliffe, the women's college affiliated with Harvard, and many of the Queen's faculty held postgraduate degrees from Harvard. In other words, a well-established Harvard-Queen's pipeline existed for both graduate students and faculty. Harvard and Radcliffe were familiar with and obviously impressed by the level of scholarship of Queen's graduates. Pauline's father, however, regretted that she had abandoned her plans to study law; he was concerned about the career prospects for someone with a PH D. This ambivalence did not last long. Pauline was awarded the Henry Clay Jackson Fellowship in government to study at Harvard, and both her parents became enthusiastic about her plans to pursue a doctorate.

In the early 1940s, women admitted to Harvard had been taught mirror courses separately at Radcliffe College, but by the time Pauline arrived, this system had been changed and her courses were all taken with men. However, there continued to be an entrenched prejudice against women students. Pauline and the other woman in her class were told to use the back door and enter at the upper level of the classroom. They were also advised not to speak during class. This was hardly an environment conducive to learning. On more than one occasion, Pauline stated that Queen's had prepared her well for her studies at Harvard. Another Queen's graduate who went on to Radcliffe held a similar view: "In the first year, I was required to carry a full course load with term papers but no major thesis. I seem to remember getting AS across the board which brought a Master's degree almost automatically. Queen's had been much more demanding!"[32]

When Pauline began her PH D at Harvard, there were fourteen women enrolled in various doctoral programs, including one who, like herself, was studying political science. All fourteen lived in a women's residence on campus. They were a diverse group. Many were not from North America, so this was an enriching experience for Pauline, whose life had been centred in small-town southwestern and eastern Ontario.[33] At this time, the Harvard doctoral program involved a two-year residency requirement, during which compulsory courses and comprehensive examinations had to be successfully completed. In her second year at Harvard, PJ taught a fourth-year political science course to women students at Wellesley College, a private college for women nearby. This assignment formed the basis of an evaluation by the chairman of the Department of Government at Harvard. At twenty-four years of age, Pauline was more a peer to her twenty-five young women students than an authority figure:

One day in the midst of her lecture, she glanced up to see the department head slipping into a seat at the back of the classroom. Pauline stopped abruptly in the middle of a sentence, unable to collect her thoughts. The professor smiled and nodded for her to continue. As she resumed her stride she noticed the girls stealthily passing a note from one to another. Pauline watched despondently as it travelled up and down the aisles, certain that the professor could see the performance with equal ease from the rear of the classroom. She had never frowned upon the occasional passing of note, but she thought, "Why today of all days?" Unable to concentrate, she wound up her lecture and shot a series of questions at the students. To her great relief, the girls answered intelligently … At last, the bell rang and the professor rose and departed. The girls, usually quick to leave when the bell released them, stood in groups, whispering and glancing over at her. Finally, several of them went up and handed her the note they had been passing. It read, "The prof has just entered the class at the back. Let's rally around P."[34]

In fact, a good deal was at stake, including a letter of reference which could make or break Pauline's future career in the academy. In an interview with her niece, Pauline stated, "We worked terribly hard. Both in the first year in courses at Harvard, where the classes were 99 per cent men, and in the second year, teaching for the first time. We had to go out of that one year teaching with the kind of recommendation that would enable us to enter a world that was totally dominated by men and was expected to continue to be a world in which men would predominate. We knew that if we didn't work, work, and work, we wouldn't get jobs."[35]

During her time at Harvard, Pauline cultivated a friendship with an Afro-American student named Trish. Well in advance of the black civil rights movement, this friendship fostered a sensitivity in Pauline for human rights abuses in North America. Although Pauline had been exposed to instances of inequality from the time she was young, her friendship with Trish greatly increased her empathy for civil rights and humanitarian causes. Moreover, this bright and energetic black woman was not able to escape the fate that many women found themselves caught in – marriage. As Pauline later observed, "Your consciousness and awareness is not something that happens overnight. It builds up in little bits and pieces. It builds up when you visit somebody you went to Harvard with, who was a brilliant student there and that's not been where she's been able to develop. She's in Harlem and looking after a lot of small kids and her husband is THE powerhouse, he's THE person."[36]

Pauline's interest in international relations also continued to evolve during her years at Harvard:

All of us in the postwar years studying for our PH DS at Harvard really wanted to see one world. We were very pro-U.N. ... We were all sympathetic to Henry Wallace and the Progressive Party of the United States – the first major third party in my lifetime, anyway – and we wanted to see the end of the bomb. When Eisenhower came out with his open skies policy, we were all in favour of that. Mind you, in the period I'm talking about – graduate school in the postwar years – it was the first democratization of the university because of the DVA program and the GI bill in the States. Therefore, you met and mingled with a broad range of people from different income levels. You did not live totally in a social elite by any means ... Another thing was that people were coming to Harvard from all over the world. That gave me a broadening of horizons that Queen's had not done during wartime ... Intellectually, it was an extremely stimulating environment, but there was a high degree of awareness both through the friends you made and the work you studied of what the real world was like for a lot of people.[37]

During the second year of her two-year residency, Pauline fell in love for the first time. This love affair with Pete, an instructor at Wellesley, lasted for most of the year, but it ended badly with Pauline feeling that the young man had been less than honourable. All that is known about Pete is that he was a veteran of the United States Navy and that he helped Pauline "survive" the stress of her comprehensive exams in her second year.

Pauline fell into a common PH D dilemma over the next five years. The drop-out rate from doctoral programs is high for both men and women. After completing her two-year residency, she began work on her thesis, but in the spring of 1947 she received an offer to teach part- time at Queen's. She had mixed feelings. On the one hand, she was thrilled at the prospect of returning to her alma mater and was anxious to gain some additional teaching experience; there was the possibility of a permanent position at Queen's if she completed her degree and did a credible job at teaching. On the other hand, teaching would take valuable time away from completing her dissertation. This dilemma continues to plague people who are ABD (all but dissertation), and although many become highly competent teachers, they do so at the cost of never completing their theses. Ultimately, this may lead to termination or being denied tenure. Evidently, Pauline believed that she would be able to combine the two, and she accepted the teaching position.

In 1946–47 the Department of Political and Economic Science at Queen's had grown to twelve members with the arrival of M.C. Urquhart as an assistant professor in the economics section. The following year J.E. Hodgetts, who had been teaching Politics 30 (elements of political science), Politics 36 (politics of democracy), and Politics 37 (public administration), was promoted to assistant professor, having completed his PH D. Pauline and another lecturer, David Slater, were added to the department, bringing the faculty number to fifteen. Pauline taught several sections of Politics 36 and likely was involved in the supervision of students who were doing reading courses. In 1948, when V.W. Malach replaced David Slater as economics lecturer, Pauline again taught Politics 36.

Even though Pauline did not have a heavy teaching load and was considered a part-time member of the department, the fact remains that the early years of teaching can be both intellectually and physically draining. After the war, the student body was different from that which Pauline had been used to. Most of her students were men, and many of them were older than she was. As well, they were fresh from a war environment from which women had largely been absent. Pauline often told the story of the time she finished her lecture with the customary "Are there any questions?" and a male student rose and said, "Yeah – whatcha doin' tonight, babe?" Undoubtably, many of them had "rusty" social skills around women, particularly women in positions of authority. Some of them delighted in behaving like bad children – dropping marbles down the steps in the amphitheatre where she taught. She had lots of attention from them – whistles and catcalls – but not the kind of attention she wanted. It was all very frustrating; it was simply more difficult for a woman to gain the respect of the male students. Pauline once told a radio interviewer:

You won't believe this story, but it is absolutely true. I did have some trouble in the first couple of weeks in one of these large classes. There was a tendency for them to shoot craps at the back of the class and push each other around and laugh and go to sleep and what not. One day, when I was beginning to think that this class would never be disciplined, I got quite annoyed because this chap in the sixth row had gone to sleep and was snoring loudly and his mouth was wide open. And I reached behind me to the ledge of the blackboard and picked up a piece of chalk – and, by the way, at one time I had been centre-forward on the basketball team – and threw it, and it went right into his mouth. And he gagged and woke up and everyone looked at me with some admiration, I must say, and they behaved better after that chalk episode.[38]

The hours spent in lecture preparation, the grading of tests and assignments, and simply learning the ropes and assimilating different pedagogical methods of teaching were exhausting. Pauline had been given no instruction on how to teach. The only direction she had been given was, "Whatever you do, keep them amused." Added to the pressures associated with teaching was the ominous spectre of continuing work on her unfinished thesis. There was little opportunity to relax. Pauline found those two teaching years at Queen's "academically demanding and personally lonely times."[39]

One positive experience was making the acquaintance of Roslyn (Lyn) Grey in the spring of 1947, with whom she forged a lifelong friendship. Lyn was just embarking on her master of science degree in microbiology and had been working for the Defence Research Board. She was married to a mining-engineering student who had gone off to a job, and in his absence she became friendly with the assorted group of people (one of whom was Pauline) who lived at the student co-op just up the street from her apartment. The co-op had a number of rooms with a shared kitchen and shared bathroom, and during the school year it was home to full-time students. In summer a strange assortment of new tenants moved in, including military people, sessional instructors at Queen's, and graduate students.

A married couple in the co-op, Bud and Jeannie Cohen, had a large room where people tended to congregate during the evenings. Two of the more contentious topics of conversation involved Canada's military role in the postwar era and the atomic bomb. PJ and Lyn were pacifists who had strong opinions about peace. Bud Cohen, an army officer, and several others had equally strong views about Canada supporting the American and British position of maintaining a military presence. Lyn recalls that Pauline always "had the floor" during these evenings. Somehow, she managed to control the flow of the discussion at hand – a talent she had for her entire life. Other friends have described this talent as her ability to "hold court." Pauline would talk and others would listen. Even at this time, she had a presence that was admired by some and was intimidating to others.

In the summer of 1947, Pauline moved into Lyn's flat, having grown tired of the shared facilities at the co-op. Lyn remembers that summer as the one in which she and Pauline "met" D.H. Lawrence. The two of them devoured a number of his novels; they admired his writing because he "told it all." Lyn and Pauline also spent hours discussing such serious matters as the German concentration camps and the horrors of war – but, at the same time, many of their conversations revolved around men. Although Pauline was confident that people found her intelligent and entertaining, it was very important to her that men found her attractive.

Lyn had transferred to Queen's from Dalhousie University because there were no fraternities or sororities at Queen's. As a young Jewish girl growing up in Rothesay, New Brunswick, she had become all too familiar with anti-Semitism. Not only was she excluded from the sorority rush at Dalhousie, but her own parents were apologists for being Jewish. By the time she came to Queen's, her sense of identity had been shattered. Her parents often told unpleasant stories about Jewish people which left her questioning her roots. She encountered further anti-Semitism at Queen's, where the "only" men on campus during the war were described by some of the women as being Jewish cowards and pacifists. Lyn responded by joining the RCAF in 1943 and served until 1945.

Lyn credits Pauline with helping her redirect her personal anger from herself to more positive areas, including working towards making the system more fair.[40] "My parents, who came to visit me that summer [1947], considered Pauline to be a bad influence on me," she stated. "They were extremely conservative, a philosophy I did not share, so I welcomed Pauline's humanitarianism. Before she died, I told her that she had been the greatest positive influence in my life. She was surprised and touched by my revelation."[41] Lyn was an early supporter of the Co-operative Commonwealth Federation (CCF) and voted for Henry Cartwright, a Kingston lawyer, who was a candidate for the party. She had become aware of him through Pauline, who had spent a summer at his office searching titles when she was an undergraduate. Throughout most of her adult life, Lyn has remained a supporter of the New Democratic Party and has often worked on party campaigns. Much to her surprise, Pauline never asked her to work on one of her own campaigns as a New Democrat.

In September 1948 Pauline shared a flat with two friends from the co-op, Moira Howson and Marian Cowie. The following year, she moved again, this time into a spacious older house with two new "mates" – Jean Royce, the registrar at Queen's, and Kate Macdonnell. "Miss M.," as Pauline called her, had a brother who was active in the Conservative Party and later served as a minister in the Diefenbaker cabinet. As the story goes, one day Miss M. invited Pauline to join them for dinner: "Pauline, politics and conservatism created an explosive combination. She was soon arguing hotly. [He] became deeply offended, and Miss M. retired to her room in tears. Pauline followed her, bewildered by the reaction. 'But shouldn't I say something when I know it's right?' she asked. She learned then that viewpoints differ widely about what is right."[42]

After teaching at Queen's for two years, Pauline was shocked to learn in the spring of 1949 that her position there was being terminated. She later intimated that Queen's would have given her one more year as a part-time contract teacher; but whatever the conditions were, they were unacceptable to Pauline. The reasons for her dismissal were never explained to her, though Pauline suspected that the all-male selection panel had decided it would be better to have a man in that position. But she was never quite sure: "I thought, 'Is it because I'm not good enough?' That's what plagues a woman always … Even though I finally mastered this rambunctious class, am I not good enough? Am I not a good enough scholar? And then I thought, 'I bet it's because I'm a woman, but even then I couldn't believe it. I blamed myself. I thought it was because I hadn't taught well enough or wasn't sufficiently scholarly or whatever."[43]

It was not a question of Pauline's position suddenly disappearing. She was replaced by a young man named John Meisel, who also was a PH D candidate. Meisel went on to have a brilliant academic career, and it is likely that the men in the department recognized the potential of this young scholar, but all Pauline could see was the discrimination inherent in an old boy's network. A remote explanation is that it was Corry who made the decision, believing she would never complete her PH D as long as she was doing sessional teaching. However, this explanation has little credibility, given Pauline's reaction. Moreover, even though one in five women undergraduates in the arts program were women, women were largely absent from faculty positions. Even though Pauline had been Corry's star student and medal winner, her name is conspicuously absent from the discussion, in his memoirs, of the personnel in the Department of Political and Economic Science during the 1940s and 1950s:

As the end of the war came in sight, it was clear that the federal government would give generous financial support to veterans who wanted a university education. The universities would have to face, temporarily at least, a greatly increased enrollment, and severe problems in preparing for the bulge. Apart from the need for more adequate financing, the worst problem would be to find additional staff of sufficient competence to carry effectively the greatly increased teaching load ... We very quickly found two young men who had just finished graduate work in Political Science, both excellent teachers and now distinguished scholars. J.E. Hodgetts, who made his reputation in his fifteen years on the Queen's staff ... and went to posts of preeminence in the University of Toronto. John Meisel, who remained at Queen's for more than thirty years and became an internationally recognized authority on voting and elections left the university in 1980 to become Chairman of the CRTC. I could not have wanted two more congenial colleagues.[44]

Doris Anderson was amazed that Corry left Pauline out of his memoirs: "I can't imagine even a charter member of the Old Boys' Club like Corry leaving P. out after she had become a member of parliament and president of a major university."[45]

Later, when Pauline reflected on her teaching experience at Queen's, she could not deny being bitter about her treatment by the faculty, particularly by Professor Corry. As an undergraduate and a master's student, she had studied under him on many occasions. She had admired and trusted him. Although she had done her doctorate elsewhere, she considered him a mentor. Her dismissal epitomized the "ultimate betrayal" by Corry, for he had not recommended her as highly as he might have to keep her at Queen's. In fact, his mediocre recommendation was not simply a disappointment; it was a humiliation. Pauline used this term on numerous occasions to capture her sense of rejection over this event. It was the first major failure she experienced as an adult.

Until this time, Pauline had felt an intense loyalty to her alma mater and a deep trust and respect for the faculty there. This "betrayal" not only weakened her loyalty to Queen's, but it raised her awareness of the micropolitics practised in the academic environment. It would be years before she was able to put this incident into the context of the war years and the extraordinary measures the government took to make postsecondary institutions comfortable places for returning veterans. This experience was Pauline's first adult encounter with gender discrimination, and it significantly influenced her thinking, both in her future as a professor at Carleton University and later as a university president. There seems little doubt that this was indeed gender discrimination. Jill Vickers and June Adam later chronicled in their book *But Can You Type?* the fact that discrimination against women academics was rampant on Canadian university campuses.

It is evident to female academics that neither their male colleagues nor "the powers that be" in most Canadian universities are prepared to admit that these differences are the result of sex discrimination. There is something offensive for academics whose lives are supposedly dedicated to impartiality and objectivity to have to confess to such a crime. Hence women have been told that the differences have other causes. Women, we are told, are less well qualified than their male counterparts.[46]

Also noted by Vickers and Adam was the difficulty that academic women had – and continue to have – in complaining about this discrimination.

It is not, however, realistic for women in the academic profession to expect others to argue their cause. In many instances, it is difficult for academic women to pursue their own cause aggressively because they are without the security of rank and tenure or even without a full-time job. Perhaps the most important task is to convince academics that they should be concerned with the question of the status of women both within the universities and within society in the context of the university's role of shaping that society.[47]

Pauline's disappointment with Queen's haunted her for many years. While some academics, such as George Grant, were critical of J.A. Corry for other reasons,[48] Pauline took the experience personally and internalized the humiliation. In a twist of irony, she was offered the position of dean of women at Queen's after the retirement of Alice Douglas in 1958. By this time, Pauline had an institutional loyalty to Carleton University, had developed a comfort level with her colleagues there, and had no desire to return to the place where she had been so badly treated. She may also have recalled some of the other requirements of the position, such as laundry and dining-room supervision, tasks she found less than appealing. Still, Pauline considered the offer seriously and sought out Dr Douglas to ask her advice. According to Pauline, Douglas told her, "You went to Carleton as a lecturer in '55 and became an assistant professor in '56. Why go through the back door to come to Queen's when you have gone through the front door at Carleton?" Pauline turned down the job.

At this time in Canada there were a number of postwar policies that served to disadvantage women. "Veterans' preference" policies heavily influenced hiring decisions in the public service and universities by giving priority to veterans. Since only seven thousand women had served overseas, the large proportion of people taking advantage of this policy were men. According to Prentice and her associates, "The prime minister went so far as to request his cabinet ministers not to employ female secretaries ... Within the public service, the married women who had been persuaded to help run the burgeoning wartime bureaucracy were summarily discharged. Married women continued to be barred from the federal civil service until 1955."[49]

In hindsight, one can see that Pauline's termination from Queen's may have given her the impetus to complete her dissertation. Fuelled with determination, and with few alternatives, she returned to Ottawa at the end of May 1949 and worked nonstop on her doctoral thesis, "The Wartime Prices and Trade Board," for the next five months. In September 1949 she successfully defended the thesis, at last fulfilling all the requirements of her Doctor of Philosophy degree.

After being awarded the Marty Scholarship as well as an IODE fellowship, Pauline spent the next eight months in England, doing postdoctoral research at the London School of Economics and Oxford University. Her research involved a comparative analysis of the Canadian and British cabinets, but she never published a paper on the subject. It is likely that a good deal of the year was spent recovering from the rigours of her PH D, the heavy teaching load, and the stress and disappointment of losing her position at Queen's. She spent a good part of the time bicycling, generally enjoying herself, and touring around Europe. Nevertheless, this eight-month hiatus was useful in that it gave her time to reflect on her experiences as a graduate student and to develop a plan of attack for obtaining a teaching position at a Canadian university. She returned to Ottawa at the end of 1950 rejuvenated and refreshed and ready to assume a new challenge.

· 3 ·

Life in the Ivory Tower

Successful PH D candidates are strongly encouraged by their supervisors to make every effort to convert their doctoral dissertations into books. A strong publication on record lends credence to an application for teaching positions in the academy. Pauline recognized that this was an important strategy, but despite her best intentions and hours of effort, she was unable to complete the project. She believed that her inability to do this "haunted her career." In those days (and to large degree today) a "serious" academic had to have a book to his or her credit. Although academic journal publications and conference papers have, of course, been considered worthy scholarship, they are no substitute for a book. Pauline's failure to convert her thesis was a major setback in her academic career and planted a seed of doubt in her mind that she would ever be considered a strong research academic. Perhaps it was this failure that led to an erosion of her confidence in her writing and researching abilities. While her difficulty in securing a teaching position may partly be explained by gender and the veterans' preference, it is likely that her rather thin record in academic scholarship may have been an important factor. The fact remains, however, that she did have a PH D from Harvard and several years' teaching experience at Queen's University – credentials that made her an impressive candidate for an entry-level faculty position.

Although the early 1950s were difficult times for many new scholars, a number of men who were far less qualified than Pauline did gain permanent positions. However, Pauline entered the academic marketplace at a time when Canada's university system had not yet undergone an expansion to accommodate the baby boomers. The creation of new universities and the massive expansion of existing institutions did not take place until the mid-sixties. In this sense, it was not an opportune time, and faculty positions for new scholars were limited. Moreover, a system of intellectual snobbery had developed on Canadian campuses which had the effect of giving preference to those who had been born and educated in the United States or Britain. Many highly accomplished Canadian scholars had a series of contract positions and found permanent positions to be elusive. The end result was that there were few academic jobs available in Canada for a freshly minted PH D who happened to be a Canadian woman without academic publications.

Although Pauline's first preference was a job in academia, she applied for and was offered a position with the Canadian Nurses' Association (CNA) to direct a study of its organization. Pauline was hired in January 1951 and her report, *A Structure Study of the Canadian Nurses' Association*, was published in January 1952. This study made proposals to alter the association's by-laws and streamline its committee system, with the overarching objective of making the CNA a more effective voice for the nursing profession in Canada.

The job had many positive results for Pauline, including extensive travel across Canada. More important, it awakened a feminist consciousness in her, changing the way she perceived the world: "I suddenly met an enormous number of women who were powerhouses; who had in many cases gotten into their profession as an alternative avenue to what they thought they wanted to do, like being a doctor, and had subsequently used their work in the association to improve their profession. I heard a lot of talk about what made them believe there was only one profession for them and that was nursing. It made me angry on many occasions. It made me much more aware of the unfairness of things."[1]

Marion Dewar, who was then a public health nurse, was aware of Pauline's study long before the two of them met. As she recalled, Pauline's report on the CNA was a stinging assessment of the nursing profession in Canada; although the nurses were an intelligent group of women, they had been unable to organize themselves and were reluctant to take on this responsibility. Marion recalled thinking that "PJ's report was 'right on' and she was saying things about nursing in the 1950s that people are saying now about nursing."[2]

Pauline experienced difficulties writing the final draft, and its completion was largely due to the support and encouragement of her supervisor, Dr Muriel Uprichard. As the project coordinator of the nursing research project, Muriel proved to be very influential as both a role model and a mentor. Muriel was in her early forties, and she saw much of herself in Pauline. Obviously bright and articulate, Pauline simply lacked confidence in her own abilities. Muriel had selected her for the research position, and she prodded her to complete the report by the target deadline. This weakness that Pauline had in finishing her research expeditiously was to rear its head frequently throughout her varied careers. Meanwhile, Muriel and Pauline had a one-year relationship that proved very important to both of them. Muriel reappeared in Pauline's life during her Simon Fraser years in the mid-1970s, albeit with a decided reversal in roles.

Muriel Uprichard was born on the prairies to staunch Presbyterian parents who had traditional views about the role of women. Highly intelligent and ambitious, she was presented with limited occupational choices after completing high school, and she chose to attend normal school. Just nineteen years of age, she took less than a year to conclude that she was not well suited to the teaching profession. With all the courage and resolve she could gather, and with little encouragement from her parents, Muriel entered Queen's University with the help of an entrance scholarship. She never looked back, graduating with an honours BA in psychology. She went on to do graduate work at Smith College in the United States and was eventually awarded her PH D in psychology from the University of London. Her doctoral research investigated the effects of displacement on inner-city English children who had been evacuated during the Second World War. Like Pauline, her strong ambition was to teach at the university level in Canada, but there were no jobs to be had. She managed to find some part-time teaching positions, but it was difficult to support herself on academic stipend pay. Eventually, Muriel was hired to supervise the "state of the profession" report of the Canadian Nurses' Association. Her appointment had been contentious, since many within the organization believed that the project coordinator should come from the nursing profession. However, others believed that a non-health-care professional would be more objective. Clearly, Muriel accepted the position amidst controversy.

In June of that year (1951), Pauline decided to combine a research trip to Cape Breton with a visit to her relatives who lived in Sheffield, New Brunswick. Pauline, her sister Catharine, and a friend set out in Pauline's car, and several days later they arrived at the Keltic Lodge in Cape Breton. The next morning Pauline and Catharine received word that their father had died during the night. Catharine immediately took the train to Montreal and flew to Ottawa. Despite flooding in Nova Scotia, Pauline drove through the night and arrived the following evening. Coburn Jewett had not been well for some time and had suffered a number of small strokes. A more serious stroke had left him incapacitated, and he had entered a nursing home in Ottawa some six months earlier. Pauline was beside herself with grief, although it is likely that her grieving had begun earlier when his health had started to deteriorate.

After completing the report for the CNA, Pauline spent the next three years applying for university positions. During 1953 and 1954, she applied to eighteen Canadian universities and did not receive a single offer. Increasingly despondent over her job prospects, she hit one of the worst periods of despair in her life. Having her mother living in the same apartment building in Ottawa helped her survive this dark chapter: "I had Mother and what a lucky break that was. She was so tough, and so resilient and so mad and so good and so understanding. She was great during that very depressed period and tried to help me in getting my thesis shaped into a book. But there were hours and hours when I would come downstairs and play double solitaire. I didn't want to see people. I didn't want to go out."[3]

Not only were the opportunities in academia limited, but Pauline had a serious illness in the fall of 1953, and she spent several months in a nursing home near her mother's apartment on Elgin Street in Ottawa. The diagnosis then was glandular fever, but today the illness would probably be identified as mononucleosis. This virus attacks the white blood cells and causes fatigue and swollen glands. Because it is a virus, the only treatment is bed rest. The illness was no doubt a setback in Pauline's job search. Despite being frustrated by the lack of teaching prospects, she was only thirty years old and was not prepared to give up her ambition of becoming a university professor.

As an alternative to an academic position, Pauline began to consider a career in the public service; but although she knew a number of high-ranking men in the federal bureaucracy from her days at Queen's, she was unable to secure employment. George Grant, the famous Canadian political philosopher, talked about this connection between Queen's and Ottawa's civil service; and William Christian, in his biography of Grant, noted that O.D. Skelton, an occasional professor at Queen's, was the main architect of Canada's Department of External Affairs.[4] Pauline recalled being one of six candidates short-listed for a new category of public servant – the Privy Council officer. However, the all-male board came to the decision not to hire her in spite of her stellar performance in the interview and in spite of her substantial knowledge of federal-provincial relations. Once again, Pauline was convinced that gender was the issue: "At one point they said they couldn't have a woman in the Privy Council Office because there was no woman's bathroom. You know, you've heard stories like that, but that was actually said."[5]

By 1954, Pauline had blanketed the Canadian university market. She had also – for the first and possibly last time – seriously contemplated marriage. She had fallen head over heels in love, almost "beyond control," with a man named Ian[6] who worked in the public service. However, he decided to break off the relationship, a crushing blow to Pauline: "The chap decided after all that he didn't want to get married. He phoned at seven a.m. and he just said, 'I can't cope. I can't cope with you, your strength, your dominance, your millions of other things. Sorry.'"[7] Not long afterwards, Ian married someone else, which devastated Pauline.

Pauline finally got the break she needed when she was hired by Carleton College in 1955. Carleton had begun as the vision of a small group of academics and public servants who believed that there was a desperate need for facilities of higher education in the nation's capital. (The University of Ottawa partially fulfilled this need, but it was primarily a French-language institution.) Although officially named the Ottawa Association for the Advancement of Learning, the group of organizers became known as the Carleton Mafia or the First Avenue crowd. The group later included Russell (Rusty) A. Wendt, who became the dean of social science at Carleton, Paul Fox, Wilfrid Eggleston, James Gibson, John Porter, Allan Munn, Herbert Nesbitt, James Holmes, and Munro Beattie. The association began to meet informally in 1938. After war broke out in 1939, meetings were suspended until 1941. The group incorporated in 1943, and Carleton College offered its first courses in September of that year. In its first year of operation, 550 students registered for the academic year, a number far exceeding the expectations of the organizers of the college.[8] Initially, classes at Carleton College were held in the High School of Commerce and in Glebe Collegiate.

By 1944–45, enrolment had increased to 938 students, and it was clear that new arrangements would have to be made to accommodate returning veterans. A series of buildings were rented to cope with the expansion in enrolment, which swelled to more than 2,200 students by March 1945.[9] In September 1946 the college for the first time had its own building – a four-storey structure on the southwest corner of First Avenue and Lyon Street, formerly the home of the Ottawa Ladies' College.[10] Then, in April 1947, the Board of Governors announced that a gift of approximately forty acres had been made by private donors. This site, within a short distance of the city limits in the Dow's Lake area, became the future site of the college. In the spring of 1949 the first degrees from Carleton were awarded.[11]

In 1955, when Pauline was hired as a lecturer at Carleton, a full five years had passed since she had obtained her PH D. As she observed in a conversation with Peter Gzowski, "When I first started, our entire teaching staff was smaller than the economics department at Yale, but we were full of ideas and enthusiasm and all the different disciplines rubbed against each other."[12] As was the case with many universities at the time, there were few women on the faculty; in fact, there was only one other woman, and she too had the position of lecturer. Pauline discovered that a new colleague in the Department of Political Science, Ken McRae, who had been hired at the same time with the same qualifications, was being paid a thousand dollars a year more than she was. He was earning $5,400 at the rank of assistant professor, while Pauline was earning $4,400 with the rank of lecturer. In both absolute and proportional terms, a thousand dollars was not a paltry sum – it was a significant differential – but Pauline decided not to complain: "Like a lot of women, I was grateful; we spend so much of our time being grateful. And this was one occasion when I really was grateful to have a job and to be in an academic faculty and to be teaching, which was what I wanted to do."[13] Having experienced wage discrimination herself, this was an issue that raised its head time and time again in her working life. She strongly believed that wage gaps between men and women were unacceptable.

After a year, Pauline was promoted to assistant professor, and her salary rose accordingly. Meanwhile, she had been settling in at Carleton. Members of the First Avenue crowd soon became more than colleagues; they became friends. In September 1955, when Pauline attended her first general faculty meeting, the staff was so small that everyone could fit around one table. Pauline was running a little late, and by the time she arrived only one seat remained. Sitting across from her was a tall, tanned, handsome man with a captivating smile – Norm Fenn, the athletics director at Carleton. He immediately found her "interesting and attractive," and they gradually became friends. Occasionally they ran into each other on campus, especially in the house that had been converted into the School of Public Administration with a main floor seminar room. As director of athletics, Norm had taken over the basement as his equipment and training room, and Pauline often quizzed him about the "goings-on in the basement," saying they were distracting her students. This became a source of banter between the two and helped break the ice.[14]

During her first year at Carleton, Pauline and a number of her teaching colleagues as well as old friends from her Queen's days met regularly for social get-togethers. Included in this group were Bill Lawson and his future wife, Kate Macdonnell (Miss M.'s niece), Gordon Robertson, later clerk of the Privy Council, Lyn Grey, Tom Daly, a producer at the National Film Board, Dvora and Muni Frumhartz, and John and Marion Porter. One of the group had managed to obtain the LP record, *The Investigator*. This recording had been pirated from the CBC *Stage* satire on the U.S. Senate hearings on un-American activities. John Drainie played the part of the investigator, whose role was clearly modelled on Joseph McCarthy. Listening to this play became a regular activity at parties during the year. Given the left-wing ideology of some members of the group, it is likely that the issues of censorship and freedom of speech were prominent topics of conversation at these gatherings.

In the summer of 1956, Pauline was asked by John Porter, a colleague in the Sociology Department at Carleton, if she would be interested in renting a cottage for the summer at Constant Lake, some eighty miles northwest of Ottawa. She was told that it was a quiet and peaceful place and that it offered some spirited intellectual discussions in the evenings as Munro Beattie, another faculty member from Carleton, and his family also had a cottage there. Pauline went to see the property and thought she would give cottage life a try. What she did not know was that Norm Fenn had been approached by Munro and May Beattie about renting another cottage on the lake. Both Pauline and Norm had gone at different times to see the property but had no idea that each of them was being lobbied to rent cottages there.

As it turned out, Norm's and Pauline's cottages were side by side, though some distance apart. That winter, the owner of this group of cottages, Clifford Cole, decided to sell. The regular Constant Lake crowd, along with Norm and Pauline, talked about purchasing the property, but none of them individually could afford to buy it as a single block (the asking price was $26,000). The Wendts, also a Carleton connection, had visited Norm on several occasions the previous summer, and they too had fallen in love with Constant Lake. The cottage group decided to purchase the property collectively, which they did in 1957, and Constan[15] Associates was born. As initially conceived, the Constan Associates consisted of seven principals – the Porters, the Beatties, the Wades, the Frumhartzes, the Wendts, Norm Fenn, and Pauline. The Menchetti family became associates the following year. Having been employed for only a short time, Pauline had no savings, but her mother lent her the necessary down payment, even though she was less than impressed with the cottage property – as Doris Anderson related:

P brought Mae up for a weekend to see what she was investing in. For Mrs Jewett, who had always detested picnics, was nervous in cars and generally uncomfortable outdoors, the weekend was a disaster. As they strolled along the path that edged the shore in front of P's cottage, a snake ran across Mrs Jewett's shoe which sent her screaming back to the cottage. There was a terrifying thunderstorm in the middle of the night, during which she demanded to be taken back to the city immediately. Then, to complete the debacle, on the Sunday one of the cottages at the far end of the property near the Beattie's burned to the ground ... Nevertheless, Mrs Jewett came up with the money.[16]

The decision to participate in the purchase of the property was a watershed for Pauline. From St Catharines to Kingston, from Kingston to Cambridge/Boston, back to Kingston again, and finally to Ottawa, she had been without roots for years. At long last she had planted herself, and she called Constant Lake home, at least during the summer months, until her death some thirty-six years later. Another factor driving her decision to purchase the cottage was that as the self-appointed clan organizer, she wanted a venue for Jewett family gatherings. Neither Catharine nor Fred had the financial means, at that time, to purchase a recreation property, and both were busy with young families. Fred was with the Bank of Nova Scotia and had been transferred frequently in southwestern Ontario. Catharine lived in Deep River, where there were two magnificent beaches, so she and her husband saw no need to buy a cottage. Fred believes that Pauline's desire to have her family around her was one of the main reasons why she purchased the property.[17] The cottage was Pauline's "resting place" for the remainder of her life, and it became her real home as well as the site of family reunions. It was the place where she came to relax, where her closest friends were, and where she did most of her casual entertaining. Pauline's first weekend as a cottage owner made for many laughs over the years. It was the first time she had ever owned property and she was very excited. Exuberant when she awoke that first morning, she ran outside naked to perform a little dance to the sun. Startled to see Clifford Cole coming up the path from the lake, she darted behind her car, where she stayed until he had passed.

The property was about two hundred and seventy-eight acres in area and had ten cottages on it. They were seasonal, rather modest structures, accessed by a long gravel road. Pauline's cottage had a screened-in porch and weathered pine siding. At first, it had no indoor bathroom. There was one bedroom with a double bed, but there was also a partitioned room that Pauline used as a guest bedroom on occasion. If she invited friends who had children (or if she was busy working), she accommodated her visitors in a small guest cottage on her property. Inside the main living room was a pot-bellied stove, which Pauline lit in late August when the mornings and evenings turned cool. Like the other cottages, Pauline's was heavily screened by coniferous trees; the water's edge was some seventy-five feet away from her front porch. Robert S. Jewett, the nephew to whom she bequeathed the Constant Lake property, removed the guest cottage in 1994, and in the summer of 1996 he sold his share of the property to a member of the Menchetti family.

Constant Lake provided an anchor in Pauline's life. Wherever her careers might take her, the lake was always there, as were the people with whom she shared much of her life. The chemistry generated at Constant Lake was special. All the associates except Pauline and Norm had families, but rather than feeling isolated by this, Pauline enjoyed having the children around. She was, however, quite authoritarian when it came to establishing noise rules. There was a curfew of sorts about horseplay on the lake after ten o'clock at night. (When Pauline was not at the cottage, it was a cause for celebration by teenagers at the lake.)

The early years were spent renovating, and Pauline did most of the repairs herself. Stubborn and often frustrated when she was unable to do some odd job, she rarely asked for help. Many of the associates have since died, so it is difficult to recreate the vitality that this group of people embodied.[18] Pauline enjoyed a particularly close relationship with John Porter, and they often stayed up late debating the issues of the day long after everyone else had retired. On more than one occasion, Marion Porter became irritated by the amount of attention her husband paid to Pauline and she to him. It was difficult for the wives of the associates to relate to Pauline. She was an academic colleague of their husbands, and her interests were not wrapped up in raising children. On occasion, she was dismissive of the women, preferring the company and conversation of their husbands, and this caused some hurt feelings.

As for her relationship with Norm Fenn, Pauline was secure in the knowledge that he would be there every summer, ready to resume their friendship with few questions asked. Her relationship with Norm was unique in this sense; he was an ideal friend. While there was some romance in their relationship from time to time, it was not possessive, and both Pauline and Norm cultivated other important friendships. They talked of settling down together in the early 1970s, but Pauline never seriously entertained the idea. They simply accepted each other – though Pauline's current mission, as Norm described it, was always her first priority. He acknowledged this reality and remained her loyal and trusted friend until the day she died.

By 1959, Pauline had been granted tenure and was promoted to associate professor. In 1960 her five colleagues selected her to be chair of the department. Clearly, being hired at Carleton (which officially became a university in 1957) had been a pivotal point, not only personally but in philosophical terms as well. Many of Pauline's colleagues at Carleton were social democrats. The sociologist John Porter, one of her Constant Lake neighbours, was perhaps the most eminent of her colleagues. His book *The Vertical Mosaic* still stands as a classic critique of Canadian society in the 1960s. Like most social democrats of the day, Porter attempted to challenge the conventionally understood characterization of Canada as a classless society. Not only did he believe that there was a corporate elite in Canada, but he believed that there was also a political elite. No doubt, the Constant Lake group had many conversations about this powerful class over the years. But despite a brief intellectual flirtation with the New Democratic Party in its formative period, Pauline remained a partisan Liberal at this time, and her friends at Carleton respected her commitment to the Liberal Party.

Although writing for publication had always been a serious hang-up for Pauline as an academic, she wrote several political commentaries during these years – for the *Canadian Forum*, the *Canadian Commentator*, *Saturday Night*, and *Canadian Dimension*.[19] None of these was considered a scholarly journal; in her academic career, Pauline published just two articles in refereed journals – the defining characteristic of an academic journal. One was a 1962 article for the *Canadian Journal of Economics and Political Science* entitled "Voting in the 1960 Federal By-elections at Peterborough and Niagara Falls: Who Voted New Party and Why?" The other, which she wrote in 1966, was an article for the *Journal of Canadian Studies* entitled "The Reform of Parliament." Later, in 1968–69, she was a regular columnist for *Maclean's* magazine. But as her friend Lyn Grey noted, "She found writing to be a real chore. Her columns in *Maclean's* were always written in a crisis state. Perhaps she was a perfectionist as she never seemed to find the perfect word to describe what she wanted to say.

I remember one holiday in the early seventies – she would spend the entire day working on one sentence of her memoirs. She was at her best communicating orally, be it lecturing or on the hustings."[20]

The writing that Pauline did do was often acerbic. In a column she wrote in 1957 about C.D. Howe's political career, she made no secret of her disdain for this long-time Liberal cabinet minister. It is likely that she had formed some earlier perceptions of Howe when writing her dissertation, for he had been a major player on the Wartime Prices and Review Board. Although she documented a number of his greatest accomplishments as a minister in the Mackenzie King government, she could not hide her contempt for the man:

Certainly he has been the best friend Canadian business ever had, particularly big business. But he has also been one of the best friends the Canadian economy as a whole has ever had, as its high levels of employment and income bear witness. All of this is not enough, however, in a political democracy. Fostering the economic development of the country, no matter how successfully it may be done, is no substitute for an understanding of politics, parliament and the people. C.D. Howe unfortunately had no such understanding. He was, in fact, thoroughly at odds with the democratic process, disliking the explanations, discussions, compromises, and further explanations that are its essential ingredients. He was interested only in action and in the power that makes action possible ... C.D. Howe will undoubtedly be remembered for his many accomplishments for the Canadian economy. He will probably be remembered even more for the lesson he inadvertently taught: that a society which has had any substantial experience of self-government wants and expects its political leaders to be its servants, not its masters.[21]

Pauline's procrastination or lack of desire to publish should not be construed as a reflection on her intellect. It was a conscious choice. Pauline loved the slings and arrows of political life. She wanted to be on the front lines, not sitting at a typewriter writing about a topic so that she could be published for the sake of being published. Her friends all acknowledge that research was not a labour of love for Pauline, largely because it was such an isolating and lonely enterprise. She had experienced this isolation first-hand when she had sequestered herself for several years completing her dissertation. Pauline needed the energy of people to thrive. But of course she knew that her reluctance to research and publish would detract from her reputation as an academic.

The fact that Pauline had taken a position at a university in Ottawa was a fateful one. Her early writings demonstrate her keen interest in the workings of Parliament and a fascination with those who served in it. Since her high school days, Pauline had harboured an ambition to be a parliamentarian. The political environment in Ottawa stimulated her. On the days when she was not teaching, she was known to go and sit in the parliamentary gallery listening to the political debates of the day. While she enjoyed teaching and interacting with students, she no longer found academic life completely satisfying, and she began to entertain the idea of becoming a candidate for the House of Commons. Accordingly, she decided to be more active in the Liberal Party.

· 4 ·

The Honourable Member for Northumberland

By the end of the 1950s, the Liberal Party was in a state of disarray. It had suffered a stunning defeat in 1957 when the Liberal government of Louis St Laurent was defeated by the Progressive Conservatives under their new leader, John Diefenbaker. This defeat ended twenty-two continuous years in office for the Liberals. At the age of seventy-five, St Laurent retired and Lester B. Pearson, a career diplomat who had been minister of external affairs in the St Laurent government, was selected as the party's next leader. Unable to compete with the charismatic John Diefenbaker on the campaign trail, the Liberals were dealt a terrible blow the following year in the 1958 election when they won only 48 of 265 seats. More than half of these were from Quebec.

Pauline had begun to lean towards the Liberals when she came back to Ottawa in 1955–56. The pipeline debate in 1956 had captured her interest to such a degree that she sat in the gallery of the House of Commons throughout the entire debate.[1] She later observed, "There was a sort of rumour going around Ottawa that Mr St Laurent had said whoever made the best speech would be the next Leader of the party. Mike Pearson made by far the worst speech. He was not at all happy – that's the impression one had in the Gallery, listening – not at all happy to be defending this particular use or abuse of closure ... But in spite of that he became the next leader."[2] Although Pauline had tremendous respect for the diplomatic skills of Lester Pearson, she was less than satisfied with the political skills he had exhibited as a senior cabinet minister:

To show how strong Mike's grasp on my kind of person was, I went to the polling booth in 1957 still very angered by the pipeline debate and by what the government had done, fully intending to vote CCF because that would be my choice, my alternative, not Conservative. I even looked up the name of the CCF candidate in Ottawa West because there was very little campaigning. And I saw Mike's face just as I was about to put my "x" down. It was Mike's face, nobody else's, that came before me and said to me, "Tch." And I said to myself, "I cannot vote against the party that has Mike Pearson." It was then that I already made up my mind that he should be the next Leader if there was a change. So I put my "x" down beside the Liberal candidate, who was George McIlraith.[3]

What these two excerpts demonstrate is that Pauline was beginning to see herself as a partisan of the Liberal Party and possibly as someone who might be one of the cast of characters needed to revitalize it. As a student of external affairs and international relations, she had admired Lester Pearson for his diplomatic skills in orchestrating a settlement during the Suez Canal crisis. She was convinced that he would be a natural leader of the party. However, she was disappointed at his performance during the pipeline debate. It was one thing to read about this controversy in the newspaper, but quite another to sit in the gallery to observe the debate first-hand. Her feelings on the issue and its lack of resolution foreshadowed her concern that Parliament was not always democratic in its operation. Evidently, consensus was not always an objective of political debate. Despite her reservations about the conduct of Parliament and about Pearson himself, the above passage also reflects the loyalty that Pauline had for Lester Pearson. Mike Pearson was far from the charismatic Camelot figure that Canadians observed to the south, yet there was a certain aura that surrounded him. Political journalists typically refer to this era of Canadian politics as "Pearsonian idealism." It was a time when there was a mood of optimism among reform-minded liberal thinkers, and many of Pearson's disciples, including Pauline, truly believed that the practice of politics in Canada was poised to undergo a renaissance.

There were two other events that inspired Pauline to take a run at electoral politics. In September 1960 the Study Conference on National Problems was convened at Queen's University in Kingston. The Kingston Conference, as it became known, did much to revive the fortunes of the Liberal Party. Christina McCall-Newman described it as one of the venues providing the "intellectual background for the new Liberalism."[4] The idea of a think-tank conference was not new. In 1932 the opposition leader, William Lyon Mackenzie King, had held a conference in Port Hope "under the sponsoring spirit of Vincent Massey."[5] By all accounts, the Kingston Conference was the idea of John Connolly, who wrote to Lester Pearson suggesting a fairly small gathering of fifty or sixty people.[6] This proposal received the support of a number of prominent Liberals, including Walter Gordon, Keith Davey, and Tom Kent. Pearson was adamant in his view that the conference had to be more than a meeting of the Liberal caucus. As such, he asked Mitchell Sharp, a long-time public servant who at the time was president of Brazilian Traction, to act as chairman. Because Mitchell Sharp was not a member of the Liberal Party, Pearson believed he would be able to attract people who might hesitate to attend the conference if the invitation came from the leader.[7] One rule strictly enforced was that no member of Parliament, excepting Jack Pickersgill, was to be on the program as a speaker.[8] According to Mitchell Sharp, he had absolutely no political ambitions at the time. He accepted the invitation because he "thought the country was being misgoverned and that Pearson would make a better prime minister than Diefenbaker."[9]

It had been assumed that the conference would be organized around the Connolly model and would be rather a small gathering closed to the press. As events transpired, some two hundred delegates attended. The escalation in size and the changing nature of the conference caused some difficulty for participants who presented papers that were radical departures from current Liberal policy. The conference ran the gamut from social welfare to international issues such as the atom bomb and the Cold War. Noticeably absent were papers dealing with the "French fact" and Quebec's role in Confederation. The list of topics on which papers were presented included "External Economic Policy," "Growth, Stability, and the Problem of Unemployment," "Towards a Philosophy of Social Security," and "Defence: How Independent Can We Be?"

The two most controversial papers were delivered by Maurice Lamontagne and Tom Kent. Maurice Lamontagne advocated the creation of a special tribunal to pass judgment on price increases that occurred as a result of increased monopolization in terms of both labour and enterprise.[10] Tom Kent proposed several radical changes to Canada's taxation policy, which would have the effect of disallowing advertising expenditures above a certain level for tax purposes.[11] Both these papers were attacked by businessmen and journalists as socialist diatribes. However, according to McCall-Newman, "their general direction – toward the completion of the welfare security system that had begun under Mackenzie King – was consistent with the positive liberalism of Pearson, Gordon and the Cell 13[12] crowd."[13]

Tom Kent believed that the Kingston Conference was greatly misunderstood by both the media and the public:

Few events in Canadian politics have been as thoroughly misunderstood. Because it was originally billed as a "thinkers" conference it was regarded as a source of new Liberal policies. It was not. It produced no ideas, subsequently embodied in the 1962 platform, that had not already won party acceptance, in principle if not in detail, in the 1958 resolutions and platforms. What it did do, because it was diverted from the billed intention, was to make the media and the public more aware of those ideas. By 1960, the media were paying attention, whereas in 1958, understandably they were not. For that reason, Kingston was indeed important.[14]

Although none of the proposals went on to become official Liberal policy, the conference did accomplish several other objectives. First, it signalled that the Liberal Party was open to fresh ideas and new faces. In addition, it mobilized a number of prominent citizens to become members of the party. For example, Jean Marchand made his first appearance at this conference, and he impressed Jack Pickersgill "more than anybody else" who was there.[15] Over the next two years, Walter Gordon and Keith Davey were able to recruit a number of prominent Canadians to stand for election as Liberals. The list included Jack Davis, Hazen Argue, Maurice Lamontagne, Maurice Sauvé, Bud Drury, John Turner, Jean Marchand, Gérard Pelletier, Tom Kent, Edgar Benson, Lloyd Francis, Lucien Lamoureux, John Munro, Herb Gray, Eugene Whelan, Mitchell Sharp, Donald Macdonald, James Walker, Alastair Gillespie, Otto Lang, Ian Wahn, and Walter Gordon himself.[16] Both McCall-Newman and Mitchell Sharp included Pauline's name in the list of recruits, but there is considerable evidence that Pauline was not supported by party insiders in seeking a seat for the Liberals. The conference attracted a number of young activists to work on campaigns, and many of them later went on to political office. They included such notable Liberals as Ron Basford, David Smith, Stuart Smith, and Richard Cashin.[17] Academics, including Frank Underhill, also participated in the conference and had the effect of broadening the spectrum of participants.

The second event that stirred Pauline's newfound activism was the National Liberal Rally, an official party gathering held in Ottawa in January 1961. Paul Hellyer was the appointed chairman, and more than two thousand participants converged on Ottawa. Unlike the Kingston Conference, this one was being held specifically to discuss party policy, and its proceedings were to be completely open to the press. For each subject area, there was a working paper. The three social policy issues that were regarded as priorities were health, the skilled society (vocational training and university scholarship), and better homes and towns (housing and urban development).[18] There were also committees engaged in examining "other social security" as well as numerous economic policies. In total, there were twenty-one committees.[19] The subject of Canada's defence policy generated much heated discussion, and the resolution that eventually passed was a compromise position. As Tom Kent stated, "On one hand, it allowed for the possibility that Canadian forces under NATO command might possess nuclear weapons solely for defensive tactical use provided that the weapons were under exclusive NATO control, not that of any single member state."[20] Given what we know about Pauline's later position on NATO, American foreign policy, and the nuclear issue, it is likely that she found this resolution very troubling. Throughout her life, Pauline never wavered in her view that Canada should be nuclear-free.

The legacy of the rally was that it drummed up enthusiasm for a Pearson government and raised optimism that the Liberals would be able to unseat the Conservatives in the next election. According to Kent, "Activists began to prepare for the election, looking for able candidates and building organizations."[21] The innovations that emerged from the rally included a "campaign college." This was the idea of a group based in Toronto which ran seminars for prospective candidates on how to organize a campaign and gave advice on budgeting, advertising, projecting on television, and other useful party-building strategies.

After the Kingston Conference and the 1961 rally, Pauline was no longer a party outsider. She had become friends with some of the most influential activists in the Liberal Party, including Walter Gordon and Tom Kent, and had reached the decision that she wanted to be on the Pearson "Team" in the next general election. Many studies of legislators have begun by asking why individuals choose to enter political life. Max Weber, the well-known German sociologist, was one of the first theorists to address this question. Weber believed that politicians could, more or less, be divided into one of two groups: professional politicians and occasional politicians. He argued that occasional politicians tend to use politics for economic purposes, that politics is an avocation to be used in "the interest of gaining rents or even profits."[22] The professional politician, on the other hand, lives "for politics" and makes "politics his life, in an internal sense."[23] Weber believed that a professional politician must have three qualities: passion, a feeling of responsibility, and a sense of proportion. Passion is epitomized by commitment to a cause; to the politician, the ethos of politics is a cause. Second, the politician's responsibility to this cause "must be the guiding star of action."[24] Third, a sense of proportion should be a "decisive psychological quality of the politician: his ability to let realities work upon him with inner concentration and calmness."[25] Although Weber may not have been the first theorist to categorize politicians according to their motivations, ambitions, and economic means, his work is viewed as the *locus classicus* in contemporary legislative career theory. At one level or another, most subsequent studies on legislative careers have been based on Weber's model of political service.

Canadian political careers also have been the subject of study by a number of theorists.[26] One of the common themes from this literature is that the volatility of the Canadian electorate has resulted in a relative amateurism among Canadian parliamentarians compared with their British and American counterparts. C.E.S. Franks, the noted Canadian political scientist and parliamentary scholar, observed, "The average length of time members serve in the Canadian House of Commons is half that of British members. Canadian members are short-term amateurs, where their British and U.S. counterparts are long-term professionals. Not only in comparison, but in absolute terms, the average five-to-seven-year stint that a Canadian MP serves in the House is a brief interlude in his career."[27] Much of the literature on political careers has confusing messages. On one hand, amateurs[28] are seen as having more devotion to a cause and a more sophisticated representational role orientation. Yet the word "amateur" conjures up some notion of unsuitability or lack of skill. Canadian politicians have generally been described as "amateurish" for the express reason that there is such a high turnover during general elections.

On numerous occasions, Pauline was asked why she wanted to pursue politics as an elected official. To be sure, she was raised in a home where politics was discussed in an open and passionate manner. Her life as an academic was largely spent with colleagues and students who lived and breathed politics. However, few of the professoriate have crossed the divide between discussing and analysing politics and actually seeking office in the real world of party politics. For Pauline, talking and teaching about politics was not enough to satisfy her passion; she wanted to *do* politics.

Pauline had long had a fascination with Parliament, and she had been energized by the Kingston Conference. She was convinced that the Liberals had a new vision for Canada and for what Canada could be. She did not just want to be a witness to this revision, she wanted to be on the team that brought in the changes. In this respect, there is no question that she had a cosmopolitan orientation[29] to politics; it was the bigger picture that motivated her and not the needs of local constituents. There is also no question that Pauline's move into electoral politics was made easier by her lack of family commitments and a certain flexibility as a university professor in requesting time away from her position. These freedoms in both her public and her private life enabled her to focus and assimilate her aspirations. She had little to lose and so much to gain in pursuing political office.

In 1968 Pauline wrote an article in *Maclean's* that addressed the question of why people enter political life. She believed that politics was an honourable vocation in the true sense of its Latin derivation, *vocare*, "to call or summon" – a calling. It was true, she noted, that there might be a few who were motivated primarily by the material and patronage trappings of Parliament. In Weber's terms, these would be occasional politicians. However, she was convinced that the motives of most were inspired by the desire to serve the public – the "psychic" rewards as she called them:

The chief reason, I think, why people go into politics is that they want (or need) the material and psychic benefits that come from being an MP. By material benefits, I do not mean only the celebrated $18,000. There were just as many aspirants before the $18,000 as there have been since and there will probably be about the same number (and of about the same calibre) when the pay reaches $35,000 (as it certainly should). Nor do I think that many more than a very few candidates are anticipating a time when their efforts will be rewarded by a seat in the Senate or membership on some board or commission. What many of them do anticipate, however, are the enhanced reputations and extra incomes that their forays into politics may bring their law practices, insurance businesses, and so on. Lawyers are particularly prone to this type of anticipation, which is one reason why so many of them are always in the running … More important are the psychic rewards that come with being an MP – the prestige of having the initials after one's name, the satisfaction of performing a wide range of services for one's area or people, the public recognition that may attend one's efforts, the possibility of influencing government or party policy, of helping shape the destiny of the nation … For one candidate the dominant motive may be the desire to "run the country," for another simply the wish to serve it, and yet for another the hope of creating a better society.[30]

Of the three motivations that Pauline cited, which motivated her the most? There is little question that she had political ambitions. On a number of occasions, she was critical of Pearson's refusal to appoint her to a cabinet position after the 1963 election. Definitely, her political goals transcended being simply a good constituency person. Later in her political career, she revealed that she would like to have been the leader of the federal New Democratic Party. This suggests that Pauline was motivated by a desire to "run the country" – or, at the very least, to be in a position of authority as a cabinet minister or party leader. Although she believed that it was an honour to be a parliamentarian and serve her constituents, it is my belief (and one shared by those who knew her) that Pauline's strongest motivation for seeking political office was to create a better society. But over the years, she changed her view of what the better society was and how it could best be achieved.

The first step in Pauline's official political career began in 1961 when she committed herself to seeking a nomination for the Liberal Party. Unquestionably, the Kingston Conference and the rally had been the catalysts that Pauline needed to confirm her commitment to the party. It is also likely that she had received some encouragement from several party activists whom she met at these events. The next decision concerned the locale where this bid for nomination would be pursued. She had long been removed from her birthplace of St Catharines, and a Liberal seat in Ottawa was simply not available. She turned her attention to Northumberland, a riding halfway between Toronto and Kingston, which included Cobourg and her maternal grandparents' residence in Campbellford. The incumbent Conservative member, Ben Thompson, a lawyer from Brighton who had first been elected in 1957 and then re-elected in the Diefenbaker sweep of 1958, had decided not to seek a third term. Similarly, the previous Liberal candidate, Wesley Sweet, a garage operator in the Campellford area, had decided not to pursue the nomination. In short, the Northumberland riding was an open seat with no incumbent.

Another advantage to pursuing the nomination in Northumberland was its proximity to Ottawa. Not only was Ottawa the place where most of her friends were, but her mother was getting older and increasingly frail. A third compelling consideration was that her family had some deep roots in the county. Her grandfather Simpson had been a direct descendant of the county's first white settlers, Obediah Simpson and Mary Lord,[31] and he had been a prominent businessman in the Campbellford area. Her mother had grown up in the area, and her parents had spent the early years of their marriage in the community. Local residents are always resistant to candidates who are parachuted into their riding, and Pauline knew she had to dispel the idea that she was an outsider and that she should emphasize her close ties to the community.

In a number of important ways, Pauline's pursuit of the nomination violated several unwritten rules of political candidacies. First, although she had some ancestral roots in Northumberland, she was indeed a parachuted candidate, albeit a self-recruited one. While this was not an unheard-of practice in urban areas, it was less accepted in rural areas. Gordon Aiken, a former MP and author of *The Backbencher*, has explained why parachuting is unpopular: "There is something of a challenge to local pride if they cannot produce their own man. The parachute candidate is the stranger coming into the local society. He may not understand them. In modern transient society the attitude is mainly imaginary, but it is there. And it is a handicap."[32]

Second, empirical research on candidates for the House of Commons indicates that most candidates follow a common pattern of party participation, including local service at the constituency level. After a period of service to the party, a nomination may perhaps materialize. Not only was Pauline a nonresident of the area, but she had never worked at the grass-roots constituency level as a canvasser or party worker. Also noteworthy was the boldness of Pauline's project. As of 1962, only fifteen women had ever been elected to the Canadian House of Commons. Moreover, a number of these women, including Jean Casselman and Margaret Rideout, were widows who completed their husbands' terms. What Pauline was embarking on was clearly a most formidable task, particularly in a rural riding.

Pauline began a one-year sabbatical in September 1961 so that she could start to lay the groundwork and do the necessary networking. Admittedly, the ability to devote much of her time to a political campaign and still collect a sizable portion of her salary was a great benefit of being in the professoriate. She made her intentions known to the Northumberland Liberal Association but received what could best be described as a chilly reception. One member of the association, a pig farmer named Enid Rogers, was the lone voice of support.

For the next five months, Pauline lived in the upstairs wing of her aunt and uncle's house in Brighton, Ontario, using it as her home base. She conducted an exhaustive search for support among the rural residents of Northumberland and attempted to meet every prominent Liberal she could in order to secure the nomination: "I would go out every day in my little Dodge and I would go up and down the back forties. I would try to meet ten people a day and I would come home in the evening and memorize them, their names, their faces, and what they said. This was a rural community and a lot of them were farmers. It was really depressing. Day after day the same thing would happen. Every person I would talk to would say 'But we've never had a woman.' It was invariably the fact that I was a woman and 'We don't see how a woman could win the nomination.' They'd always find a hundred reasons why a woman wouldn't do or be taken seriously."[33]

This pursuit of the nomination was a lonely enterprise, so lonely that Pauline's closest friend was Mabel, the name she gave her Dodge. (She often used the term "we" on the hustings, much to the amusement of her friends and family.) Most people in the riding saw Pauline as an outsider despite her family's roots in the area. Moreover, her professorial rhetoric may have been unsettling to many of the rural residents. One weekend, when she was home in Ottawa visiting her mother, she told Bunny Pound, who had been John Diefenbaker's executive secretary, how discouraged she was about the way the campaign was going. Bunny told her that she had to campaign like her opponents and buy some of the locals a bottle of whisky. Pauline was aghast at this suggestion, but Bunny was serious. There was a certain way that men in rural areas campaigned, and this style was certainly foreign to a city person such as Pauline. It was particularly offensive to the campaign style of a woman candidate.

Another difficulty Pauline faced was trying to explain her single status. It was one thing to be a woman, but it was quite another to be single. Was there something wrong with this woman? Did she hate men? Was she *funny*? (Of course, in those days the word "lesbian" was not commonly used.) Time and again, Pauline had to fend off intrusive questions:

Once a farmer said to me, "You're not married?" And I said, "No, I'm not married." And he said, "Have you ever been married?" And I said, "No, actually, I have never been married." And he said, "You're sure?" They couldn't believe it. They thought there would be some wretched divorce or something that would come out in the middle of the campaign. They could not believe that a woman could survive single, that she could enjoy life, that she would want to achieve something on her own, that she would want a career. To many of them it was just unbelievable.[34]

Although Pauline was later able to laugh about the rampant sexism in her political campaign in Northumberland, it was anything but funny at the time. Every so often she retreated to the comfort of her friends at Constant Lake in order to heal from the hurtful comments that had been made. Whether or not the comments were intended to be hurtful was of no consequence. For Pauline, they were devastating. Her independent spirit and firm opinions were perceived as unwomanly and masculine; she was not seen as a "real" woman, in a feminine sense.

In seeking the nomination for Northumberland, Pauline was encountering the same kind of obstacles she had faced as a girl in St Catharines and as a young woman academic in search of a permanent appointment. In practical terms, she knew that the nomination process was a local matter and that each constituency was responsible for selecting its party representative. However, it soon became clear that behind the scenes was a well-oiled nomination committee working out of Toronto and Ottawa with its own agenda. One of the members of this group was David Anderson, the husband of her future friend, Doris Anderson. Pauline had no intention of slipping quietly into the background, and she ultimately won the nomination.

Many writers who have examined the role of women in electoral politics have concluded that winning the nomination is often harder for women than winning an election. Pauline had managed to clear the first hurdle – no small accomplishment. One of her contemporaries, Judy LaMarsh, claimed that political parties appeared to have little interest in recruiting women: "Throughout my years in the Liberal Party, I never saw evidence that any real attention was paid to seeking out and grooming women as a part of the party machinery, or as parliamentary material, except in one area and that was the importuning of fresh widows of members of Parliament to seek their husbands' unexpired terms."[35] The Royal Commission on the Status of Women also found that parties had done little to encourage women to participate in electoral politics: "There have been 134 federal and provincial elections between 1917 and June 1970, and 6,845 people have been elected. Of these, 67 were women, just under one per cent of the total."[36]

The royal commission concluded that there were two major obstacles confronting women in pursuing a nomination: the reluctance of male party officials "to take a chance on admitting women" and "the reluctance by established women's organizations to abandon their position of nonpartisanship in political affairs and to support qualified women for public office."[37] With regard to the former, the royal commission concluded, "It is at the constituency level, according to the women interviewed, that disparagement of women candidates and the belief that a woman candidate will lose votes are usually encountered. Women who have been successful at the polls confirm that winning the nomination is a more formidable hurdle than winning the election."[38]

In her book *Memoirs of a Bird in a Gilded Cage*, Judy LaMarsh wrote about the resistance of male leaders to female candidacies. She had attended the Kingston Conference about a month before the nominating convention for the Niagara Falls by-election: "As I was leaving Kingston, Mike Pearson called me out on the lawn to tell me that while it wasn't his business who was nominated (not his business to hold a seat, when he had a miserable forty-eight members!), he personally would like to see me nominated. Pearson had been pencilled in to speak to our nomination meeting. He was told by his advisors that it might be a Donnybrook, so he stayed out and sent Paul Martin instead. And that was the first time I learned how gutless Mike was, but not the last!"[39]

Judy LaMarsh had first been elected for the Liberals in the riding of Niagara Falls in a 1960 by-election, and inevitably comparisons were made between the two women as they campaigned for the 1962 election. Peter Gzowski, who was Quebec editor of *Maclean's* at the time, wrote:

Unlike Judy LaMarsh, her platform manner is quiet, thoughtful, scholarly. On the day that Miss LaMarsh was ticking off the Tories on trade policy, Miss Jewett was quietly explaining to a group of labour leaders in her riding how and why she differed ideologically from the New Democratic Party. She used, in her explanation, such sentences as, "I tend to be an emotional egalitarian." Also, by contrast, she is a Joanie-come-lately to her party. Like many other academics, she was urged – and somewhat inclined – to join the New Party[40] in its embryonic stages. But after more than a year of mind-searching, which ended sometime in 1959, she decided her sympathies were with the Liberals.[41]

Gzowski's article highlighted some issues that were fundamental to Pauline.[42] When he asked her what she thought the most important issues of the 1962 election would be,

Miss Jewett named – "not in this order" – social security, health insurance ("I favour a plan whereby all people will be comprehensively covered"), and, in her somewhat professorial phrase, "The distribution of income in society." What about nuclear arms? "That is a decision we'll make in conjunction with other nations. We have to move toward arms control and the best way, obviously, is not to get involved ourselves. But we are not the same as Africans or Asians; our set of values is rather closely connected with those of the United States and the United Kingdom. We'd be kidding ourselves to say we could become true neutralists" … "The Voice of Women? They take a very strong position. I'm in sympathy with any humanitarian position, but at the same time I'm aware of the problems of power."[43]

In a later interview, in 1974, Pauline explained why she had not been more aggressive in her comments on women's issues during the 1962 campaign. She believed that "too overt an appeal to women would probably, certainly at that time, have made it impossible [to win the nomination]."[44] In retrospect, she believed that political women in the 1950s and 1960s had made a mistake in being silent about the representational needs of women, because progress had been "so slow."[45] Pauline had probably been wise to take a low-key position about women's issues in 1962, but the "silence" that women politicians were expected to embrace likely served to delay the entry of more women into the public realm of politics. This silence was a double-edged sword, and the losers on all counts were women.

There were those who believed that Pauline's brand of liberalism was not really liberal at all. Many academics in Canada, including most of Pauline's colleagues at Carleton, had jumped on the New Party bandwagon. Pauline also thought of joining but came to the conclusion that the Liberal Party had the capacity to embrace some of the more appealing positions of the New Party. She felt more aligned with the Liberals:

I'm so undoctrinaire that I won't have any difficulty fitting in. I think the Liberal Party provides a reasonably congenial home for people who are concerned with the social and economic structure of society. I don't think, for instance, that government intervention is, *per se*, a good thing, so I'm not a socialist. My socialist colleagues, in fact, think of me as good old middle-of-the-road Pauline. But I think that some government intervention, on a planned basis, not the kind the present government uses of responding to immediate pressures, is a good thing.[46]

However, her stubborn streak and her resistance to the intentions of the party bosses may have undermined her political future with the Liberal Party:

When I first determined to enter the political arena, actively, I had a pretty difficult time persuading the "powers-that-be" that I had a hope. Even after

I was nominated I was still on trial – a great risk – in their eyes. And just the other day, when I was speaking to a World Federalist group in Toronto on the subject of Canada and Vietnam, who should the newspapers send to interview me but the gals from the women's pages. The thinking behind this, I suppose, is that women are inevitably and exclusively bound up in recipes and Ann Landers. Vietnam is for the men just as political nominations are. I find, too, that if I take a strong position on an important public question the subsequent write-ups suggest that I am being a bit too shrill. It is all right for a man to take a strong position on an issue but not quite nice for a woman to do so![47]

The difficulties that Pauline encountered in gaining the nomination in Northumberland made her far more conscious of the systemic discrimination against women that existed in the political world, and she became more outspoken as a result. As an academic, Pauline had experienced first-hand the fact that there had been little improvement in the status of women. In an article she wrote for *Continuous Learning* in 1965, she warned, "The proportion of women in professional, as compared to other, occupations is no higher today than it was in 1931 (in fact it is lower), and the proportion is very little higher than it was in 1901. Furthermore, the proportion of women in commercial and financial occupations is only moderately above what it was thirty or forty years ago."[48]

She identified the root of the problem as patriarchy, though she did not use that term. The word "patriarchy," like "feminism," had not yet reached mainstream political discourse. "The root of the problem," wrote Pauline, "surely lies in the fact that our society is not yet prepared to see women occupy positions of equality with men, let alone authority over them. Our society is prepared to see women work – even married women (who now constitute almost fifty per cent of the female labour force) – but only so long as they remain, for the most part, in the low-income, low-status jobs. There is apparently a lingering feeling that it is just not fitting for women to invade 'the world of men,' to compete with them on equal terms, to speak with authority on the subjects they speak on."[49]

After all her efforts, Pauline lost the 1962 election by 758 votes to the Conservative candidate, Harry Bradley.[50] Her defeat could not be explained by a lack of campaign funds – an argument that has been commonly advanced by women candidates and women's groups. According to the summary of election expenses that she filed on 18 August 1962, the total cost of her campaign was $11,024.00, compared with Bradley's total of $9,980.39. No candidate had outworked her or met more constituents than she had. Yet still she lost. Reflecting on the defeat a number of years later, she said, "I've said since that almost everyone ought to have one really resounding whack; it toughens your spirit a good deal. I really had the experience of thinking that you're going to make it and not doing so. My next-door neighbour in Durham County made it. Everyone thought we would be running at least about the same."[51]

Pauline was not convinced that her sex was the only reason she had lost the 1962 election. Recalling her father's advice about learning from setbacks, she embarked on an exercise to determine where her campaign had been deficient. She analysed the election by comparing the polled results of four adjacent counties (which coincided with federal election boundaries), including the one in which she had run. The constituents were more or less the same in terms of socio-economic characteristics, and the rural and semi-urban nature of the ridings were similar. The candidates in the other three ridings were men, it was true, but they were also local people. Pauline became convinced that it was the local recognition factor that was critical in her loss. She had transplanted herself into the riding, and this may have been the deciding factor.[52] She also believed that the party had done little to help promote the candidacies of women. After winning the nomination in 1962, she had received the instructions sent out to all new candidates, which directed them to have their pictures taken for the campaign and said, "Be sure to wear a dark suit, a white shirt, French cuffs and a plain tie. Be sure to be freshly shaven."[53] This kind of communication from party headquarters did little to offer support to the women candidates who were seeking election.

It did not take long for Pauline to catch campaign fever again. The Conservative minority government was in a state of disarray. The Diefenbaker cabinet was revolting against its leader, who had lost the support of a good many caucus members from Quebec. The Tory syndrome[54] had struck again! Parliament was dissolved and another general election was called. Pauline mobilized her local team into action and once again hit the hustings. She won the nomination handily, and on 8 April 1963 she won the election, defeating Harry Bradley by 505 votes.[55] Her objective had been achieved. At long last, she could take a seat in the House of Commons and start working on her vision of making a better society.

LIFE AS A NEW MEMBER

As David Docherty notes in *Mr Smith Goes to Ottawa*, "the world of legislation, committee work, caucus, Question Period, and just about every other aspect of elected life is a totally new experience ... and is tantamount to moving from a farm team to the major leagues."[56] Feeling somewhat overwhelmed, Pauline spent the first few months acquainting herself with Parliament Hill. Although no stranger to the visitors' gallery, she had much to learn, for Parliament has an entire set of rules and behavioural norms associated with how the business of the House of Commons is conducted. Legislative scholars have described these codes of conduct as institutional "folkways." Some six years later, Pauline wrote an article for *Maclean's* describing what it was like to be a new MP:

By now you will have received your free copy of Beauchesne's Parliamentary Rules and Forms and your free copy of Standing Orders and have realized why they are free ... as I recall, I broke three unwritten rules on my first passage. In the first place, you do not cross over to chat with someone on the other side unless you are an exalted personage, like a prime minister or House leader, or have been in the House for ages. Second, if you insist on fraternizing publicly so early in your career, you should at least negotiate your passage in such a way as to avoid getting between the Speaker and whoever has the floor at the time. Finally, you should bow to the Speaker twice, once as you're leaving your seat and again as you're about midway across. On the latter occasion be sure to come to a full halt.[57]

In the same column, Pauline mused about the limitations of new MPS:

Government backbenchers are not supposed to ask questions unless prompted by ministers to do so. Their job is to applaud the front bench, vigorously, although in all fairness it should be said that opposition parties are as bad about government backbenchers asking questions as governments are. Opposition parties feel that parliament is chiefly for them ... Indeed, I sometimes think that the reason MPS vote so conscientiously with the leadership of their parties is because they're not clear, half the time, what the votes are about and, after they've been around long enough to know, the habit of following the leader has become too ingrained to be shed.[58]

As one of the more high-profile members on the "Pearson team," Pauline thought she had an outside chance of being appointed to cabinet, though she was aware that she was being rather presumptious in thinking so. Certainly, she had high expectations. It was not her intention to toil indefinitely on the back benches. Turnover during every election is quite high – between 30 and 40 per cent, on average. Not only is new talent brought into the House each time, but it is not unheard-of for a rookie to make it to the front benches almost immediately. In other words, Pauline was not unusual in having high expectations; many new MPs have the same ambition.[59]

Pearson's task of cabinetmaking was a difficult one. He had an old guard within the party that had been faithful through the dark days of 1957 and 1958, and he also had a new guard of capable and enthusiastic newcomers. Walter Gordon was made minister of finance, Mitchell Sharp, minister of trade and commerce, and Paul Martin Sr was awarded the plum portfolio of External Affairs. Other returning Liberals, Lionel Chevrier and Paul Hellyer, were rewarded, as were Maurice Lamontagne and Jack Pickersgill. Judy LaMarsh was given the difficult Health and Welfare portfolio, which was a bit of a surprise. However, Pauline was not the only capable newcomer left out of cabinet. According to McCall-Newman, "Maurice Sauvé, an economist from Quebec who had been involved with organizing the provincial Liberals before winning himself a seat in Îles-de-la-Madeleine in 1962 in defiance of the Quebec old guard, was given nothing."[60]

Of course, it was most unlikely that Pauline would have been awarded a cabinet position. It is generally understood that new MPs are required to serve an apprenticeship of sorts to learn the folkways of Parliament, though there is no consensus on how long this period lasts. John Porter, in *The Vertical Mosaic*, suggests that members require at least one term to learn the ropes.[61] C.E.S. Franks indicates that a four-year apprenticeship is desirable, while Sharon Sutherland claims that two years is adequate.[62] Not only did Pauline's rookie status work against her, but Pearson had already appointed his token woman. Still, Pauline believed that Pearson's insistence of just one woman in cabinet was unfair. Others agreed. Tom Kent, the head of the Prime Minister's Office wrote:

Mike Pearson referred to "a" woman in the Cabinet. I commented that there was no necessity to have only one, which smacked of tokenism. While Judy was the only woman with claim to a senior portfolio, Pauline Jewett was more capable of assuming a junior one than were most of the new members. Mike demurred. He had to consider seniority in the party, regional balance, ideological balance. He would be personally delighted to consider Pauline, not now but later. He never did. Mike was not happy in dealing with women as colleagues. He soon came to think of Judy as a problem, and to conclude that it would be multiplied by another woman.[63]

Doug Fisher, who served as an MP with Pauline in the 1960s and later became a political journalist, suggested that Pauline's personality, particularly when compared with Judy LaMarsh, was a disadvantage: "In

1963, Judy LaMarsh was a caucus colleague of Jewett with three years more experience. At that stage Judy was a bellicose but adroit partisan warrior. She was much treasured for this by her fellows, whereas they typecast Pauline as an egghead, an Adlai Stevenson sort with lofty talk and no practicality. While this was an unfair rap, Pauline never did get untracked as a Liberal MP on the Hill or identified with any particular causes or issues … Though charming in a formal sense, she was never gushy or loud and demanding of notice. In the short run such a personality was not to her advantage in politics."

In early May 1963, Lester Pearson suggested to Tom Kent that he invite Pauline to have the honour of making the first speech in the new Parliament, the formal address that begins the debate on the Throne Speech.[64] Even though this could hardly make up for being excluded from the cabinet, it was quite an honour for a new back-bencher. On 17 May 1963, Pauline stood up in the House for the first time. As a university professor, she was no stranger to speaking in front of an audience, but there was something very different about this experience and she was excited. Her address was preceded by Question Period, which was quite boisterous that day. It is a common occurrence for many MPs to leave the House after Question Period, and that day was no exception. As Pauline stood up to deliver her speech, she was disconcerted to see in the opposition benches "a sea of retreating backs."

"Is everyone going to leave before I begin?" she thought in a panic. Prime Minister Pearson and most of the Liberals stayed, and a few of the Conservatives and NDP, including Mr Diefenbaker and Tommy Douglas, the two Opposition leaders. Mr Diefenbaker sat across from her. As she spoke, his piercing blue eyes were fixed steadily upon her, except for the odd moments when he lowered his gaze to make notes. She thought wildly, "What's he making notes about?"[65]

Later, in interviews, Pauline commented on the rambling and rather aggressive nature of this speech. It had five distinct parts. The first was a commentary thanking the people of Northumberland and extolling the virtues of her riding, though she also noted that all was not well with the economy in Northumberland and that a number of individuals and families were living in poverty.

The population has not increased very rapidly latterly because there is quite a degree of distress in the constituency. In this, of course, it is not unique. It is like many other parts of Canada. There is a great deal of unemployment and the people who are out of work are out of work not necessarily because of seasonal factors but rather because there is basic, or what we call nowadays, structural unemployment, and they cannot get work at any time of the year. Even those who are employed one finds frequently are living at or close to the margin of subsistence.[66]

The next component of the speech was, in essence, a philosophical discussion of Pauline's liberalism:

We still hear people talking about the good old days of self-reliant individualism when all an individual had to do was to get up and go. It is always very pleasant to wish we could return to those days; but the fact of the matter is, and we could see this if sometimes we were not blind, that we have moved from an individualist society to a collectivist society, a society where it is very difficult for a great many of us to make the decisions that affect our own destinies. These decisions are increasingly taken by others on our behalf, particularly by large organizations which exist throughout our whole economy. These decisions are simply beyond our control. When we are unemployed or in distress it is extremely difficult for us nowadays to do a very great deal about it ourselves on our own initiative.[67]

Next came a summary of the Liberal Party's mandate and agenda for change. There was nothing in this section of the speech that indicated any particular departure from official Liberal policy. In the fourth part of the speech, Pauline highlighted three domestic policy areas which she considered to be key priorities: biculturalism, the state of public health, and the role of government:

I am particularly pleased that we have emphasized, as indeed the Liberal party has always emphasized, the fundamentally bicultural character of Canada. What we hope to do is to promote and develop this bicultural character of this country ... I am still concerned about the state of public health in this country. I do not see how anyone can run for parliament and not be concerned about it. This, too, is a subject with which we shall be dealing as soon as we possibly can ...
Since the kind of measures which will be necessary in this country from now on must inevitably increase the role of government and lead to a greater degree of government regulation and intervention, may I say how glad I am to see toward the end of the speech from the throne a provision for the establishment of a committee on procedure over which you, sir, will be presiding. Certainly, as the positive state becomes more positive and as we

move further and further into the era of government regulation, as I suggest we must do in the collectivist society in which we are living, it becomes essential that we should devise the means whereby we can control executive action through this house – a means whereby we ourselves can understand what is going on and make useful contributions, as well as of seeing that what is being done at the administrative level is being done justly and fairly. I expect it will be the function of this committee to look into these matters, as well as, I hope, revamping the whole committee system of this house realigning its tasks in such a way as to bring its work more closely in line with the various responsibilities of government. Perhaps after that, in order to ensure the greatest degree of fairness and justice in the administration of complex public policy, we might give consideration to the question of reforms in administrative procedure.[68]

The concluding part of Pauline's inaugural address related to Canada's foreign policy, an area in which she had tremendous interest:

It is not only the western world which is undergoing change. It is not only the countries of Asia and Africa, even, which are undergoing change. We should also bear in mind that central and eastern Europe, too, are undergoing change – that the whole system of international communism is undergoing change. Indeed, the tendency toward the bipolarization of power which we have known since the second world war may be undergoing change. I hope we may encourage our trading, cultural and other relationships with some of these countries in the communist world. I hope we may do this, because it is in this way more than any other, possibly, that we can be sure of peace. There are tendencies toward incipient pluralism in international communism and this, I think, is something of which we should take advantage. The best way to do it is by expanding our trade and cultural contacts with the rest of the world, and not simply with the western world. This may also lead – and I believe it should lead – to diplomatic recognition being given where it is not now extended.[69]

It was this part of her speech that proved to be a bombshell. Many sitting members were likely taken aback by Pauline's knowledge of international affairs. After all, this was a portfolio that was considered a man's world, just as the Finance ministry was. This part of the speech was also startling because of its substance. The world was at the height of the Cold War. The Cuban Missile blockade had occurred only one year earlier, and the United States continued to be fiercely anticommunist. Perestroika, glasnost, and the fall of the Iron Curtain were decades away. Canada had consistently taken its cue on foreign policy from the United States, and there were no indications that anticommunist rhetoric would be abating anytime soon.

In later interviews, Pauline said she had received a rather icy stare from Pearson when she single-handedly recognized Red China! Although her speech does not specifically refer to China, this was her message. By suggesting a thawing in Canada's relations with communist countries, Pauline clearly intended to put recognition of China on the political agenda or, at the very least, to open the matter up to public debate. This passage also illustrates Pauline's views on Canadian foreign policy. She firmly believed that Canada should be autonomous in setting out its own position and should not blindly and unquestioningly follow the American lead. She held these beliefs throughout her political career.

On the Sunday following her first speech in Parliament, Pauline was invited to have lunch with the Pearsons and Kents at Harrington Lake, the prime minister's retreat in the Gatineau Hills. According to Tom Kent's recollection of the day, Pearson uncorked a bottle of champagne before lunch and proposed a toast to the Throne Speech: "Words by Kent, music by Jewett."[70] Pauline was thrilled. She had pleased the leader and his chief staffer with her first speech and was now enjoying lunch at the prime minister's country retreat. How could life be better?

Pauline worked hard during the next two years. While part of this time was spent learning the rules and behavioural norms of Parliament, she also spent time trying to raise her recognition level. One of these forays into elevating her profile occurred in 1965. The CBC was broadcasting highlights of a national conference held by the Canadian Society for the Abolition of the Death Penalty, an organization that had approximately two thousand members, though it was only one year old. Although the death penalty was still on the statute book, all death sentences had been commuted and there had been no hangings since 1963. The issue of capital punishment was morally charged and the government was having difficulty resolving it. According to a Gallup poll taken several months earlier, 56 per cent of Canadians were in favour of retaining capital punishment. Of the 265 parliamentarians, 101 were in favour of retaining it, 96 were in favour of abolishing it, 61 had failed to reply to the questionnaire, and 7 were undecided. The leader of the abolitionists was Arthur Maloney, a former Liberal MP and a practising Toronto lawyer. A spokesman for the retention side was René Lévesque, who at the time was a Liberal minister with the government of Quebec. When Pauline was interviewed about her position, she said:

There is a good deal of feeling of encouragement that the Canadian public is becoming more and more convinced that there should be abolition. Indeed, the opinion of the Canadian public right now is a good deal more in favour of abolition than, say, the British public when the act was passed by the House of Commons there not very long ago. And all of us are pleased about this. All of us who are abolitionists are particularly pleased. There are still a large number of MPs and senators who haven't made up their minds. But I have a feeling that things are going fairly well from the point of view of seeing the abolition of the death penalty.[71]

Pauline was then asked whether the 56 per cent figure of support for retaining capital punishment should affect the consciences of MPs. "Well," she said, "MPs are perhaps more likely to look at the enormous change that there has been during the years. The fact that opinion is so fluid on the subject. There are still a large number of undecideds – you didn't mention those, and therefore we're fairly convinced that if it comes to a fifty-fifty division, then the exercise of their own conscience and their own view on the matter is entirely justified.[72]

Between 1963 and 1965, there were only four women members in the House of Commons, and life was not made easy for them. For instance, there were plans on the books to construct a penitentiary in Northumberland, so Pauline requested to be appointed to the Penitentiaries Committee of the House: "The guys who were selecting people, the Whip and the Parliamentary Assistant to the Minister of Justice and so on, said they thought this would be awkward because we'd be having to examine things that would offend my sensibilities, and perhaps even have to go into a men's washroom or something. Incredible. Maybe they wanted me off for other reasons, but these were the ones that were given."[73] As Pauline later observed, "You have no idea how this separate facilities thing was used as an excuse to keep women out."[74] She was also quoted as saying, "Women are still in a position where they are not thought of when an important position is vacant."[75]

As an increasing number of public women write their memoirs, more stories surface about the male culture that permeates the House of Commons. Judy LaMarsh talked about the loneliness she experienced as a member in the 1960s: "The isolation I encountered at first was pretty depressing. I suppose because I was a woman, or perhaps because he'd been there so long he couldn't remember how little a first-timer knew about Parliament, our ineffectual Whip, Joe Habel, never came to see me or tell me anything – not how to get supplies, or stationery, or furniture, or secretarial help – nothing."[76] More recently, Audrey McLaughlin noted that the most visible manifestation of the male culture is the behaviour in the House of Commons itself.

I remember how amazed Marion [Dewar] and I were when we sat through our first Question Period. The posturing, the banging on desks, and the shouting made us think of school kids. And like children in a school yard, the men seemed to constantly be jockeying for territory and dominance ... As for Question Period, the abuse that is shouted back and forth, the heckling and the histrionics strike me and my women colleagues as silly and childish, sometimes wounding, and always counter-productive. These performances get in the way of rational problem solving, and make the House look ridiculous in the eyes of Canadian citizens.[77]

Judy LaMarsh recalled an incident that involved Pauline and Margaret Konantz, another woman in the Liberal caucus:

Public life in Ottawa revolves about time-hallowed institutions, both [those] of Parliament and the life that surrounds it. Across Wellington Street from the Parliament Buildings broods the haven of the Establishment, the Rideau Club. Its members are all men ... Women are permitted on the premises, but only as guests and only at the dinner hour or later ... From time to time, the Government of Canada engages a dining room in the Rideau Club for an official or semi-official function. At one of these, hosted by Paul Martin for a foreign dignitary, two women, Pauline Jewett and Margaret Konantz, both then members of Parliament, were invited as guests. But this was a luncheon, and as the two members entered the lobby and prepared to climb the winding staircase and take their seats officially, they were apprehended and barred from the Club, it being only noontime. It did not matter that they were members of Parliament; they were only women![78]

There are several theories about why Lester Pearson called an election in 1965. The official reason was that since his was a minority government, it was simply not able to govern effectively. The Liberals were prepared to risk a negative backlash from an early election call in the hope of winning a majority government. Some suggest that Pearson relied heavily on an American pollster, Oliver Quayle, who convinced Keith Davey as well as Pearson himself that the Liberals were rising in the polls and that a majority government was a strong possibility. However, the election campaign was disastrous. Pearson simply was not as good on the hustings as John Diefenbaker, and there had been several scandals involving his French-Canadian ministers.[79] Moreover, Diefenbaker was successful at tapping into an anti-Liberal sentiment that had been steadily growing in the Canadian West. The logistics of the campaign were flawed; crowds at official events were sparse, and sound systems were often defective.[80] The result of all this was that the 1965 election gained the Liberals only two seats more, and the government continued to have a minority in the House of Commons.

When the election call was made, Pauline was confident that she would receive the support of her constituents in Northumberland. She had been a high-profile activist in the debate surrounding the abolition of capital punishment and was given some credit for the development of a big construction project in her riding – the Warkworth Prison. It was estimated that this project had created two hundred construction jobs, and an additional two hundred were expected to be generated by the facility after its completion. For a relatively small riding, this was an infusion of much-needed jobs. The Conservatives, this time around, were running George Hees, a former cabinet minister in the Diefenbaker government. Described in the press as "a handsome, driving, fifty-five year old former Toronto Argonaut football player and millionaire who moved in the business world and skied in Europe,"[81] Hees packed some impressive credentials. He had previously been the MP for Toronto Broadview and was lured back into politics by Eddie Goodman, the national organizer for the Conservative Party. Goodman had discovered that Conservative members from Northumberland had gone quietly to Mr Hees, asking him to stand in that constituency.[82] Hees claimed to be a native son, born and raised in the riding, who continued to own a farm in the riding (though the farm was only a weekend and vacation property).

After winning the nomination, he stepped down from his position as president of the Montreal Stock Exchange in order to seek election. The voters of Northumberland had been loyal supporters of Diefenbaker in 1957 and 1958, and Pauline believed that Hees's public criticism of Diefenbaker and his abrupt resignation from the cabinet in 1963 would not sit well with many of the Conservative supporters in her riding. Attempting to capitalize on this disloyalty, she broke into a song at her nominating meeting: "Hees knifed him before; Hees will knife him again."[83] As usual, she ran a good campaign, yet she was defeated by Hees by 563 votes.[84] The defeat plunged her into a long period of despair. What had she done wrong? Why had she been betrayed by her constituents?

There are several explanations for Pauline's defeat. In the first place, it would probably be more accurate to say that George Hees won the election than that Pauline lost it. As stated previously, the rural voters had been hesitant about supporting a woman candidate in 1963, especially one running for the Liberal Party – and Hees was a dashing figure with great appeal. There was also the fact that as a former cabinet minister he had considerable stature. Pauline, on the other, hand may have lost popularity during the flag debate of 1964. She had supported her leader in his quest for the new Maple Leaf flag, though the Red Ensign was beloved in her riding. As Doug Fisher noted, "One can still drive through the region and spot lots of Red Ensigns flying."[85]

After her loss, Pauline spent a considerable time thinking things over, and she came to the conclusion that life as a politician was just too hard and defeat too devastating. The year 1965 had been a tumultuous one on all fronts – Pauline's mother had died after a long illness. With the small inheritance she received, Pauline took a trip to Europe, where she spent some time recharging her batteries. She visited England and France, took a French course at the Sorbonne, and then had a holiday with Lyn Grey (whom she always addressed as Baby). The two had arranged to meet in Venice and spend four days there before going on a cruise of the Greek Islands. Lyn stayed up until 3 AM on a rainy morning, drinking tea while awaiting Pauline's arrival. At length PJ appeared – soaking wet and roaring with laughter. She had entered a room on the third floor instead of the second, and as she opened the unlocked door and walked in, she had given her normal "Baby" greeting. She found herself facing a sleepy American couple, who rose up in bed and stared at her in amazement.

On returning to Canada, Pauline resumed her teaching position at Carleton, but she maintained her connection with the Liberals, and in 1967 she was appointed one of the four vice-presidents of the Liberal Party. At this time, both of Canada's mainstream political parties – the Conservatives and Liberals – were undergoing leadership changes. Diefenbaker was forced out as Conservative leader, to be replaced by Robert Stanfield; and after three lacklustre elections, Pearson announced that he was resigning from the Liberal leadership. Almost immediately, several candidates came forward. Mitchell Sharp, a long-time Liberal with a background in the public service, cast his hat into the ring. He was seen as the choice of the party establishment headquartered in Toronto and Ottawa. The press dubbed his advisers "the group of eight"; it included Jean Chrétien,

Michael McCabe, Jack Birkenshaw, Robert Wright, and David Anderson. Several members of this group were among those who had been so negative about Pauline's nomination in Northumberland. Paul Hellyer, another Toronto-based candidate, also entered into the leadership stakes. A young, politically ambitious member of the caucus, John Turner, representing a riding in Quebec, was next to follow.

As ambitious as these candidates were, they were well aware of the Liberal Party's long-standing convention of alternating anglophone and francophone leaders. At this point in the contest, the only declared candidate who could claim to be francophone – albeit a Franco-Ontarian – was Paul Martin Sr, who represented the Windsor-Walkerville riding in southwestern Ontario. However, despite his long and distinguished service to the party, Martin was seen as a party relic who would be unable to give the party a new look. After a considerable period of soul-searching, a candidate with strong connections to the business community, Robert Winters, came forward. Winters had been a member of the House since the late 1950s, representing a Maritime riding, but had abruptly resigned in 1965. Although strongly supported by business, his candidacy was viewed with suspicion by some members of the Liberal caucus.

The candidates were all expecting a francophone from Quebec to launch a bid, and they knew that it would probably be one of the "three wise men" who had been elected in 1965. At the time, it was speculated that the candidate would be Jean Marchand. He had impressed many of the party insiders at the Kingston Conference. One evening, when Tom Kent and Marchand were discussing his leadership prospects in Marchand's small bachelor apartment in Ottawa, Marchand asked, "If I were prime minister, could I go on living here rather than move to 24 Sussex?" Kent said no. "That's it," replied Marchand. "If I could live here, I would run. Obviously I couldn't. So I won't." According to Kent, Marchand simply did not have the temperament required of a prime minister, and he was too sensible to be seduced by the power of a position.[86]

The other most likely Quebec candidate was the flashy and provocative minister of justice, Pierre Trudeau, who had been aligned with the party for a relatively short period but was seen as Pearson's candidate of choice. Trudeau brought with him some impressive credentials. His keen intellect and his knowledge of the law were widely acknowledged. His academic credentials were impeccable, and his ability in both official languages exceeded those of any other candidate. At the same time, there were many questions raised about this relatively unknown figure from Quebec. His bachelor status had provoked considerable rumour and innuendo. His background of privilege was viewed suspiciously in some circles as being somehow antiliberal, and his flirtation with socialism and the organized labour movement in Quebec was well documented. In many respects, Trudeau entered the leadership race in 1968 surrounded by polarized opinions in much the same way as he left politics in 1984.

Mitchell Sharp dropped out of the race before the leadership convention. The official reason: a currency crisis affecting the Canadian dollar required his attention as finance minister. Before he left the race, Sharp endorsed the candidacy of Pierre Trudeau. This was viewed as manipulative and coercive by several of the other candidates. Meanwhile, all this activity revived Pauline's political ambitions. She longed to be actively engaged in the House of Commons once again, participating in the debates and media scrums, and in the battlefield of Question Period. But it was imperative that she support the candidate who would be anointed king during the leadership race. At first she supported a leadership bid by Jean Marchand, but she was also one of the early backers of Pierre Trudeau. Her ability to read the leadership situation accurately and gauge popular opinion in the Liberal Party was finely honed. It was her prediction that Trudeau would be the eventual winner and that he would spearhead a rejuvenation of the party. The Liberals were in great need of a Kennedy-style leader, given the increasing influence the media were having in election contests. Plugged into a university campus, Pauline was sensitive to the fact that young Canadians in particular needed to have a reason to support the Liberals. Trudeau's flair would attract a good deal of positive media coverage, and his intellect would bring in large numbers of young, well-educated people. Pauline considered that this infusion of new energy and enthusiasm was critical to the renaissance of the Liberal Party.

Her attraction to Trudeau's candidacy was based on other considerations as well. First, she strongly believed that Canada needed a leader from Quebec who was committed to federalism and constitutional change. It was her view that the separatist fires continued to smoulder in Quebec and that only a francophone with a federalist vision could extinguish them. Second, her strong commitment to civil liberties was shared by the young justice minister. Last, she shared an affinity with Trudeau in that he too came from an academic background and was not a member of the Liberal establishment. He was a thinker and not a party hack, and this appealed to her.

Above all, Pauline was a strong believer in democracy, maintaining that the men and women elected to Parliament should have the greatest influence in establishing both domestic and foreign policy. Trudeau, like Pauline, believed that too many unelected and unaccountable people, especially the public-service mandarins, wielded excessive control in policy making. His commitment to re-establishing accountability and political control over both the agenda and the machinery of government appealed to Pauline. She believed that he was the candidate who could restore the sense of idealism that had surrounded the early Pearson years; and she was convinced that he would continue to stake out the social welfare side of liberalism as the territory of the Liberal Party, resisting those within the party whose objectives were to move it into the realm of business liberalism.

During the leadership campaign, an article in the *Globe and Mail* speculated on the type of cabinet Trudeau would build and mentioned Pauline's name as a possibility: "Outside the Commons – she was defeated by George Hees in the 1965 election – is Pauline Jewett … an early Trudeau backer. A suitable Senate appointment could open up a seat for her in the House, and perhaps a place at the Cabinet table."[87] But after Trudeau won the leadership and Trudeau-mania swept the country, nominations were extremely competitive. Hees was firmly ensconced in Northumberland and would be difficult to unseat. There were no openings in Ottawa-Carleton. In all likelihood, the party elite was not interested in Pauline's desire to run for office. Without the promise of a winnable riding, she would have to go it alone again. Did she want to put herself through the grind of yet another nomination race and election campaign? Pauline had never made a secret of the fact that she found campaigning thoroughly draining. In a column for *Maclean's*, she wrote, "There are easier ways of spending six or seven weeks than getting up at dawn, standing at factory gates and bus stops, ringing doorbells, attending coffee parties, giving speeches and pep talks, saying the same things over and over again, glassy-eyed, bone-weary."[88]

The Liberals had the prospect of a majority government, and many favours were owed to loyal party men. Despite Pauline's faithful service as vice-president, her obvious desire to run again, and her early support of Trudeau's leadership bid, she was left out in the cold. Another rejection, another rebuff. Clearly, she had not endeared herself to the party establishment. Perhaps they were worried that she might be a maverick and not toe the party line. Some of them carried the memory of Judy LaMarsh and her vitriolic comments about Trudeau. Maybe the Liberal Party was simply not interested in women such as Pauline who had strong opinions. The final straw came two years later at the 1970 Liberal convention when she lost out as vice-president. She believed that Trudeau was partially responsible, since he had not backed her candidacy.

Pauline had made a concerted effort to remain active within the party after her election loss in 1965. Not only had she been vice-president of the party since 1967, but she had become a regular panel member of *Crossfire*, a popular program on CTV. As a television personality, she had developed a knack for a catchy phrase. For example, she once described the economy under Diefenbaker as "the four D's ... Debt, Deficit, Diefenbaker, and depression."[89] In spite of these efforts, she was dismissed by the new Liberal Party establishment under Trudeau. She felt betrayed by both the leader and the party.

There is another plausible explanation. Throughout Pauline's political career, she had enormous confidence in her own abilities. And while few would deny her understanding of policy issues, questions have been raised about her ability to "read the political landscape" correctly. This weakness occasionally led Pauline to miscalculate a political situation (which happened several times when she was later a member of the New Democratic Party). She was so convinced of the talents she could bring to the Liberal Party that she failed to see that the party insiders had little interest in her candidacy.

At the age of forty-eight, Pauline had come crashing full force into a second glass ceiling – Canada's political system. Escape to the comparative security of academia would have been easy, but PJ was never one to abdicate in the face of rejection. In fact, adversity served to buoy her up. Ten years later she reflected on how she handled her setbacks:

One of the things that's probably saved me from depression, or some feeling of rejection, is some little monitor inside me that helps me move on and almost deflects the negative. Like, when I'm told I can have one more year teaching at Queen's, I say "To hell with it," and move on. I think that there is a constant process of toughening one's spirit as it goes on through every rebuff – at least in my own life – and also through every success. You toughen yourself in a sense not to be hurt and not to lie down and you can become quite sharp, and even resort to sarcasm to protect yourself against those rebuffs. Similarly, when you have successes you have to toughen yourself to face the almost inevitable decline. The expectations are just so great when you have a first, like being the first woman to be a university president.[90]

Over the next year or so, Pauline's enthusiasm for the Liberals and the world of party politics began to wane. She was convinced that the Liberal Party was not the egalitarian one she had considered it to be. Women were not taken seriously, and their candidacies were not being encouraged. Some ten years of her life had been committed to a party that no longer seemed receptive to her ideas or appreciative of the considerable skills she had to offer. It was time to move on.

· 5 ·

The Institute of Canadian Studies and Moving Left

THE INSTITUTE OF CANADIAN STUDIES

The 1970s were tumultuous times on the campuses of Canadian universities. All across the continent, traditional values and mores were under siege. Fuelled by the virulent anti-Vietnam peace movement and attacks on American imperialism, all authority structures were being challenged. Middle-class values on marriage, lifestyles, sexuality, capitalism, and consumerism were all under attack. Not only were students challenging the lifestyles and values of their parents and other authority figures, but they were openly defying economic, political, legal, and moral norms. Activists claimed that administrators in the ivory tower were remote and had lost touch with students, that progressive currents in scholarship were absent in course curricula, and that tenured instructors were not exploring innovative pedagogical techniques. At the same time, progressive young instructors were being denied tenure. Far from being an instrument of academic freedom, tenure was viewed as an excuse for academic inertia. Multinational corporations were targeted as well and charged with pillaging the environment in their quest for even greater profits. Juxtaposed against this radicalism were new alternative lifestyles. It was a time of free love, Woodstock, long hair, sexual liberation, and widespread drug use. Rock and roll had been replaced by acid rock and protest music, with messages sung by Bob Dylan, Janis Joplin, Jimi Hendrix, the Doors, John Lennon, and the Rolling Stones.

This was the mood and these were the times on the Carleton University campus when Pauline was appointed director of the Institute of Canadian Studies for a two-year term (1969–70 and 1970–71), the third director in its history. The institute was associated with the Faculty of Graduate Studies; eleven departments in the humanities and social sciences had cooperated to offer an MA in Canadian studies. Beginning in 1962–63, a visiting fellow was invited to collaborate with the director in leading the core seminar. The visiting fellows had included Professor Mason Wade, former CCF leader M.J. Coldwell, journalist Douglas Fisher, poet Alfred Purdy, and Harry J. Boyle, vice-chair of the Canadian Radio-Television Commission. In the first year of Pauline's stewardship of the institute, the visiting fellow was Professor Edward J. Miles, director of the Canadian studies program, University of Vermont. The Institute of Canadian Studies also sponsored and provided editorial supervision to Carleton Library, a series of paperback reprints and compilations of classic material relating to Canadian history, law, economics, politics, anthropology, sociology, geography, and journalism. By 1969–70, forty-three volumes had been published. In addition, the institute sponsored a variety of public lectures and seminars.[1]

Although none of the full-time faculty were affiliated with the institute, the position of director was considered a prestigious one because the institute's creation spoke volumes about Carleton's "mission" and the priority given to Canadian studies. It had been the first graduate degree offered at Carleton in 1967 and was considered the flagship program at the university. A mandatory core course could be supplemented with any other graduate course provided the theme and content were Canadian. It was one of the first interdisciplinary courses of its kind in the country, and it was hoped that Carleton would develop a national reputation for being a progressive campus. As such, it attracted students who were interested in the "new" Canadian nationalism associated with the progressive student left in Canada.

In the second year of her appointment, Pauline taught the core seminar together with the well-known sociologist and Quebec nationalist Marcel Rioux, a visiting professor from Université de Montréal. Enrolled in the Canadian studies graduate program was an eclectic group that included Ron Graham, who later wrote *One-Eyed Kings*, Steven Langdon, who later became a federal MP for the New Democratic Party, Pat Armstrong, who authored *Double Ghetto* and in 1995 was appointed director of the School of Canadian Studies at Carleton University, and Sheila Milner, who became a professor of psychology at McGill University and co-authored *Decolonizing Quebec*.

Pat Armstong recalls the first seminar convened by Pauline. There was an air of informality. Pauline insisted that the students call her by her first name, and she made the open-ended offer to "talk about anything they wanted." A number of students expressed an interest in exploring the topic of American imperialism, but Pauline quickly dismissed this as an overarching topic for the seminar. In her opinion, it was "too political" and not academic enough. Undeterred, the first seminar presentation by Steven Langdon was entitled "The American Presidency as American Imperialism." Clearly, this was a direct challenge to Pauline. Recognizing that there were those in the group who had passionate beliefs about the United States and Canadian sovereignty, Pauline ultimately capitulated and allowed this theme to be pursued by a number of students.

One of the other themes investigated was Quebec nationalism. Students in the class vividly recall the banter that went on between Rioux and Pauline, with Pauline arguing that socialism and nationalism did not dovetail and Rioux arguing the opposite. On one occasion, Rioux said to Pauline, "Oh, Pauline, nationalism without socialism wouldn't be any fun!" The juxtaposition of these two instructors was dynamic. Pauline was well acquainted with the fact that Rioux was a radical sociologist as well as an ardent Quebec nationalist. She knew that they would have areas of disagreement and would be foils for each other. In inviting him to help lead the seminar, she had made the conscious decision to demonstrate to the students that there was a wide philosophical divide between the federalist view of Quebec and the nationalist position espoused by so many Quebec intellectuals. It was clear that she wanted a "stimulating stew" for students enrolled in the Canadian studies program. By having someone whose views diametrically opposed her own, she was inviting students to stretch their intellectual horizons.

The selection of Rioux could have been a recipe for disaster, but although they challenged each other from time to time, it was never done in a mean-spirited way. The entire seminar worked on a model characterized by respect between the instructors, between the students and professors, and among the students themselves. Pat Armstrong recalls, "She actively engaged with us and made it a safe place to do that. The most important thing a professor can do is make it safe to have those kinds of discussions while ensuring that they are discussions about academic projects as opposed to personalized attacks."[2]

Although some of the women graduate students were involved in consciousness-raising groups associated with the women's liberation movement, feminism was not a topic explored during the core course that academic year. This was somewhat surprising in view of the fact that the *Report of the Royal Commission on the Status of Women in Canada* was released that September. Until the release of this report, complaints about the status of women and gender discrimination "had been mostly anecdotal."[3] Along with Sylvia Ostry, June Menzies, and Flora MacDonald, Pauline served as a consultant on the commission.[4] While no area was left uninvestigated, two dominant themes emerged: education and family life. Pauline presented a brief to the commission on women in Canadian faculties. The ideological current of feminist thought directing the commission was liberal feminism, calling on the government to institute changes to laws and policies that were discriminatory to women. Many women believed this was all that was necessary in order to achieve equality. The women's liberation movement, on the other hand, was much more radical in calling for the dismantling of patriarchal structures such as the family and capitalism.[5] It was this current of feminist thought that was primarily embraced by progressive women students across campuses in Canada and the United States. Since Pauline was decidedly in the camp of liberal feminism, it is not surprising that she avoided radical feminism as a theme for the core course.

Students recall that PJ held strong views on issues, yet she was remembered as an objective listener to another point of view. Although not regarded as a profound theoretical thinker like John Porter, she was considered to be "plugged in" to the issues of the day and well versed on them. She held regular social get-togethers with graduate students at her apartment at 150 The Driveway, revealing that her involvement and interest in her students transcended the classroom. This interest was particularly evident in her association with a progressive book collective.

A number of the more radical students in the institute and at Carleton had banded together to form a book collective. Modelled on a number of similar collectives on campuses in the United States, the mission of the store was to carry progressive literature that was not available in conventional Ottawa bookstores or in the university libraries. Many of the titles which the students wanted to purchase were American and British books about such topics as the new political economy, neo-Marxist analysis, radical feminism, civil rights, and American imperialism. Secondarily, the group wanted to have a venue where like-minded people could meet and discuss issues of mutual intellectual interest.

As a collective, the students needed some seed money to develop an initial inventory. The collective was organized in such a way that people would join for a modest fee, and this membership fee would be converted to a credit to be used at the store. However, in order to get going, the group needed to find some benefactors who would be prepared to invest money immediately but would delay their book credit until later. The students approached Pauline for an investment, and by all accounts she asked some tough questions about the organization of the collective and established several conditions. In the end, she came through with five hundred dollars, the largest contribution received by the group. Rather than just giving the collective this money, Pauline supported the principle behind the project and gave her tacit approval to the distribution and sale of radical and progressive literature to students. For the students, here was an authority figure at the university who supported their enterprise. It was empowering. Pauline's contribution was critical to the survival of the collective, and the Octopus Bookstore remained on the vanguard of progressive bookstores for a number of years. It has since relocated to a site in the Glebe area of downtown Ottawa. Privately owned and operated, it now distributes more conventional fare.

Inspired by her students and by progressive faculty members at Carleton, Pauline's views about Canadian nationalism continued to evolve. She grew increasingly convinced that continued American penetration into our economy and cultural institutions constituted a real threat to Canadian sovereignty. This menace could only be counteracted by aggressive Canadian policy in terms of foreign ownership and increased government regulation in the area of culture. Her growing conviction that an aggressive response was necessary began to put her at odds with official policy of the Liberal Party.

MOVING LEFT

In 1971, to the shock of some of her friends, family, and students, Pauline officially announced her candidacy for the nomination of the federal New Democratic Party in the riding of Ottawa West. She had been increasingly vocal about her displeasure with a number of policies pursued by the Trudeau-led Liberals, yet there is no consensus on exactly why she left the Liberal Party. One of her friends suggested that she had become disillusioned with the federal Liberals because they had been dragging their feet on passing legislation limiting election expenses. This friend said that Pauline was convinced that candidates were being financed by American corporate interests and, once elected, were engaged in influencing the passage of legislation that would further these same interests. The "capture" of the federal Liberal Party by American corporations was not a novel idea and had been advanced by some theorists at both ends of the political spectrum. George Grant's classic *Lament for a Nation* was the best known of the conservative critiques on this notion of capture. While this conspiracy theory may have been Pauline's private reason for leaving the Liberal Party, she never cited it publicly. If she had publicly announced that her defection from the party was premised on her belief that some Liberal MPs and candidates were being financed and controlled by U.S. corporate interests, she would have summarily been dismissed as a neo-Marxist radical from the ivory tower. She had witnessed that kind of marginalization all too often. Pauline was too politically astute to use this as her official explanation.

Another unofficial explanation cited to explain her defection was her growing disaffection for Pierre Trudeau. It had become clear to her that he was not the visionary leader she had hoped for when she came out in support of his candidacy for leader in 1968. She had been convinced that he was an "idea" man when he came into politics, and she had been optimistic that under his leadership more "idea" people would be attracted to Ottawa. In 1968 she had written:

Pierre Elliott Trudeau was himself a candidate of this type in 1965. As Minister of Justice after 1967 he vigorously pursued his policy goals and when he became leader of the Liberal Party in 1968 he was still a policy-oriented man, particularly on the constitutional question. It was widely anticipated, therefore, that he would attract into the party a number of people who were as concerned about policy as he was. Indeed, he had already done so in his run for the leadership. The universities, at least in English-speaking Canada, were hotbeds of Trudeau Liberalism.

Trudeau did not, in fact, attract a new group of idea people. There was Eric Kierans, of course, an idea man through and through, but one got the impression that Trudeau was not very keen on Kierans' running, even though he was by far the most exciting newcomer in the party. Other idea candidates – Mark MacGuigan and Martin O'Connell in Ontario, Otto Lang in Saskatchewan, Lloyd Axworthy in Manitoba – had, for the most part, been drawn into politics during the Pearson years and had run (albeit unsuccessfully) either federally or provincially or both, during those years.[6]

Pauline also had reservations about Trudeau's treatment of women in the party. Later in his leadership, it was understood that he had a quota in terms of the number of women he was prepared to promote to the front benches.[7] However, as early as 1968, Pauline concluded that Trudeau was not particularly enlightened as far as the promotion of women was concerned, and she knew that her prospects for a cabinet position were unlikely with him as leader. Moreover, it appeared likely that his appointment of women would be premised more on geography and language considerations than on ability. As a white anglophone woman from the national capital area, Pauline's prospects were limited at best. It was also evident that the Liberal Party was being run not by the caucus and the extraparliamentary wing but by a small group of advisers in the Prime Minister's Office.

This disenchantment with "her" party was evident in a column Pauline had written for *Maclean's* in November 1968. In this article, she reflected on the various options that Canadians had open to them in having their voices heard by government. Clearly, Pauline was an advocate of inclusiveness and strongly believed that more people should participate in politics. Beyond actually running for Parliament and transferring power to the people by the frequent use of referendums, she posited a third option – a reoriented and reorganized party system. She presented the case that the extraparliamentary wings of the parties should "have voices of their own."[8] If they were independent entities, several benefits would materialize. For example, it would become impossible for the caucus, and more particularly the cabinet, to ignore the opinions of these extraparliamentary wings. Another benefit would be that while parties would continue to be important representational vehicles during elections, they would avoid the doldrums they habitually fell into during non-election times. Best of all, Pauline claimed, the reorganized parties would attract more people. Reading between the lines, it was evident that Pauline believed that the Liberal Party had become an exclusive institution, closed to average Canadians.

Increasingly, she had gained the impression that Trudeau had a raging ego and enjoyed playing the role of benevolent dictator. Aside from his small group of political advisers, he had little interest in consulting with members of his caucus or with the party as a whole. His statement, made years later, that away from Parliament Hill MPs are "nobodies" underscored his disdain for parliamentarians. Pauline had suffered some unpleasant experiences with him when she was vice-president of the party. There was the occasion, for example, when she was speaking to party members at a public forum and Trudeau walked in, held a scrum of sorts, and disrupted the proceedings. There were no apologies, and Pauline saw this as just another example of Trudeau's disdain for his colleagues.

Trudeau's attitude towards women also displeased her. Pauline was friendly with Madeleine Gobeil, who had enjoyed a relationship with Trudeau for some time. For reasons that were never clear, he stopped dating Madeleine and soon afterwards announced his engagement to Margaret Sinclair. This confirmed Pauline's suspicion that Trudeau was less than loyal. In her view, his behaviour towards women sent the wrong message to impressionable young people. Although she never cited her dislike of him as an official reason for leaving the Liberal Party of Canada, there appears to be little doubt that Pauline was less than enamoured with Trudeau and his policies.

Pauline's official explanation varied over time, and it is this inconsistency that lends some credibility to these other reasons. In an interview with Mia Stainsby of the *Vancouver Sun* in February 1989, Pauline stated that she left the Liberal fold and joined the NDP because she "admired that party's dedication to life, liberty, and the average person."[9] However, in her last public interview in the spring before she died, she told Charlotte Gobeil of CTV that she left the Liberals because of her disagreement with the imposition of the War Measures Act and other Trudeau policies. She described the War Measures Act as a "draconian" measure.[10] The act had the effect of suspending civil rights, and Pauline considered its imposition in 1970 to be unwarranted, an overreaction by the government.

Pauline never regretted her decision to leave the Liberal Party, and as time passed she pointed to a variety of reasons why the New Democratic Party was better suited to many of her political stances. She spoke often of her admiration for NDP leader Tommy Douglas, recounting the story of how Tommy passed her a note after her inaugural speech in the House in 1963 which read, "You sound like a New Democrat to me!" Like Pauline, the NDP had opposed the War Measures Act. Public opinion polls taken in 1970 indicated that an estimated 85 per cent of the Canadian public supported Pierre Trudeau's use of the act, yet when the time came to vote in the House, members of the NDP stood up, one after another, and cast their vote against the government's position. Pauline stated on a number of occasions that she thought the NDP had been very courageous in taking this stand.

By 1972, the progressive element of Pearsonian idealism within the Liberal Party that had initially attracted Pauline had all but disappeared. Pauline remained convinced of the need for an autonomous foreign policy, yet the Liberal Party had all but abandoned its position on Canada's sovereignty. In other words, it was not that Pauline had changed her political views; rather, the Liberal Party had retreated to its pre-Pearson platform in the areas of foreign investment and foreign relations. Pauline had also become disenchanted with the level of democracy within the party. It had become increasingly important to her that her party be democratic, led by its members and not by a small group of backroom elite. She felt that the *esprit de corps* which had been so evident in the Pearson Liberal Party no longer existed.

Pauline knew that there was only an outside chance of winning a seat for the NDP in Ottawa West, given the pervasiveness of a conservative public-service ethos. Four years later, however, the honeymoon was over for Trudeau. The press and other organizations had become increasingly critical of his leadership. So even though the national capital region had been strongly influenced by Trudeaumania in 1968, Pauline thought she had a slim chance of winning the riding if she worked hard on the hustings and assembled a good campaign team. There was also the possibility that the Liberal and Conservative candidates might split the mainstream vote, allowing her to win. But despite running a spirited campaign and receiving relatively favourable media coverage, Pauline lost the 1972 election, coming in third behind a local television personality, Peter Reilly, of the PCs and Liberal Lloyd Francis, who placed a close second.

Although she was obviously disappointed by the election result, Pauline was convinced that shifting left had been the right decision. First and foremost, the NDP was far more democratic in its internal workings than the Liberal Party. The NDP leadership was obliged to listen to what its grass-roots members thought, since policy had to be supported by party members at conventions before being adopted. This accountability factor strongly appealed to Pauline, because it ensured party control of policy matters. In her view, accountability had been sadly lacking in the Liberal Party. In addition, New Democrats were strongly committed to the protection of civil liberties and the Canadianization of our economy. These stances had always been central to Pauline's political belief system. As an added bonus, the NDP had a much more friendly climate for women. Women were not only encouraged to be candidates but were promoted to leadership positions within the party. Pauline was comfortable in her choice, though she recognized that any future she might have in the House would be as a member of the opposition. But she could live with that.

Pauline had a third choice, of course, which was to abandon party politics altogether and become an independent. However, she continued to believe that political influence in Canada was waged largely through party politics. She probably suspected that she would be seen as a Liberal turncoat and as a "Joanie-come-lately" to the NDP, but she was resolute in her belief that she could handle whatever fallout there might be from the switch. For the first time in a number of years, Pauline felt that she was surrounded by a group of people who shared the same views as she did on civil liberties, the need to Canadianize our economy and universities, a commitment to the advancement of women, and the importance of world peace. Meanwhile, she busied herself with party activities and was one of the founding members of the Participation of Women (POW) group within the NDP. She also became an active member of the Committee for an Independent Canada.

COMMITTEE FOR AN INDEPENDENT CANADA

The alarm bells about the domination of Canada's economy by foreign interests were originally set off when the Royal Commission on Canada's Economic Prospects, chaired by Walter Gordon, released its report in 1958. Ten years later, the Task Force on the Structure of Canadian Industry, chaired by Mel Watkins, issued its report. While both these reports warned of impending crisis and recommended government action on their policy proposals, the Liberal government in power for much of this period chose to ignore their recommendations. Ultimately, Mel Watkins and Walter Gordon joined other economic nationalists (among them, Abraham Rotstein, Gary Lax, Mel Hurtig, Peter Newman, John Trent, Jim Conrad, and Bernard Bonin) to form an ad hoc group called the Committee for an Independent Canada (CIC). This group, headquartered in Toronto, included former politicians, academics, economists, business people, and political analysts. Pauline joined the group after her electoral defeat in 1972, at which time there were some two hundred members.

The policy proposals recommended by the CIC were adopted at policy conferences. Foreign ownership of the Canadian economy was the group's prime concern. Industrial strategy, technology, entrepreneurship, the independence of trade unions, book publishing, and the CBC were also areas of intense focus. At their annual conference held in Edmonton in 1972, CIC members adopted a resolution recommending that "universities and colleges should establish committees to ensure that adequate emphasis is placed on Canadian Studies in all areas, especially in the presently deficient areas of teacher training, English and French literature, sociology and native studies."[11] The CIC was very aggressive in its resolutions concerning faculty citizenship in Canadian universities. Its first recommendation demanded that provinces pass statutes requiring that all future administrative officers of Canadian universities, including presidents, deans, and department heads, be Canadian citizens. Its second recommendation required that all members of hiring committees be Canadian citizens. In all appointments, Canadians were to be given preference. Foreign nationals could be appointed only when no qualified Canadians were available. Moreover, only Canadian citizens should be granted tenure.[12] The rationale for such a strong position on the Canadianization of university faculties was clearly spelled out:

Strong intellectual leadership is a crucial factor in the development of an independent nation-state. Without this base of knowledge, it is difficult to plan and implement necessary policies, such as a national industrial strategy. Since the universities are our main source of intellectual power, it is imperative that these institutions remain under the control of Canadian scholars who are aware of, and sympathetic to, the issues which confront this nation as it emerges from the shadow of dependence.[13]

The CIC acted as an interest group that scrutinized legislation being considered by the House of Commons. For example, on 21 June 1973 it submitted a brief to the Standing Committee on Finance, Trade, and Economic Affairs concerning Bill C-132, An Act to Provide for the Review and Assessment of Acquisitions of Control by Canadian Businesses in Canada by Certain Persons. Many of the themes presented in this brief have a resonance today. For instance, the CIC argued that unless Canada gained more ownership of its economy, it would continue to lose out on meaningful employment. It talked about the dangers of inaction and stated, "As obeyers-of-orders and second-level managers Canadian businessmen have increasingly lost their sense of creativity, independence and entrepreneurial initiative."[14]

The CIC was very clear about its mandate: "It is not a question of race or nationalism or claims that we are any better than any other community in the world. It is much more a question of dignity and self-respect – a question of having the capacity to have a real influence over our own destiny and to play a meaningful role in the world."[15]

In the meantime, Pauline had earned another sabbatical, and she spent from January to April 1973 at Radcliffe College. She later described this period as "a terrible four months." She was trying to write a book on politics for Macmillan Publishers, and it was not going well. When she was back home, relaxing at her cottage on Constant Lake, she managed to complete three chapters. Due to go back to Carleton in the fall, she asked for leave without pay to finish the book, but the familiar pattern of writer's block still plagued her, and she was unable to complete the project. An embarrassed Pauline was obliged to return the advance she had received from the publisher for this book. This was Pauline's last attempt at writing an academic manuscript.

Pauline was restless. She had taught for fifteen years at Carleton, and the thought of going back to the classroom did not excite her. As an active member of the Committee for an Independent Canada, she had become alarmed at the state of Canada's universities and the continuing barriers obstructing the promotion and advancement of Canadian academics. As a faculty member in a department at a small university, there was little influence she could bring to bear on the important issue of the Canadianization of the country's universities. She recognized that the role of universities, both as cultural institutions and as facilities for higher learning, was reaching a crossroads, and she began to believe that the most effective way to influence the hiring practices of universities and their role in the broader community would be to become president of one.

The question has often been asked why Pauline wanted to become a university president. She had never held a major administrative post at a university, so it could not have been a love of being a manager or a deep desire to be an administrator. While part of the answer may be prestige, status, and power, she told a number of people that her key motivation was to set a new landmark for women in the academic world. Pauline believed that a woman president of a Canadian public university would open the envelope of opportunities for women even further, and she was determined to be the first. She had heard through the academic grapevine that several Canadian universities had launched presidential search committees.

Pauline applied for the presidency of the University of Prince Edward Island, a new university forged out of two junior colleges, St Dunstan's and Prince of Wales. Simultaneously, she applied for the presidency of York University. According to one of her friends, she blew the Prince Edward Island job when she lit up a cigarette during the interview and, in response to a question from the Catholic members of the search committee about her religion, said (truthfully but rather unwisely) that she was an agnostic. Pauline's spontaneity and honesty – two characteristics of her personality that endeared her to so many of her friends and family – did not serve her well in this interview. As for the York position, both Pauline and Sylvia Ostry had been short-listed but were ruled out by the male members, according to a member on the search committee. By all accounts, the committee was mesmerized by Ian Macdonald, a former hockey player and Rhodes Scholar, and a high-ranking Ontario bureaucrat in the Davis government. Whether or not the short-listing of two women demonstrated enlightened thinking or tokenism is not known. However, this second rejection did not deter Pauline. She had made application for one other position – the presidency of Simon Fraser University in Burnaby, British Columbia – and in December 1973 she was contacted by the university and told she was on the short list.

· 6 ·

Life on Burnaby Mountain

In 1975 John Mills, an alumnus of Simon Fraser University (SFU), wrote a provocative essay that characterized the various factions that had developed on the campus by the late 1960s and early 1970s. In the following passage, he describes these groups.

When I arrived at Simon Fraser in the summer of 1965 it was still possible, for those who enjoy such polarities, to divide academics up into the "old guard" on one hand, and the "skin-headed" on the other. Skin-heads were publication and administration conscious – they spoke of the PH D being the absolutely minimum requirement for the job, of "resumes," of "curriculum vitae." They believed, very strongly, in publish-or-perish and in hiring and firing. The old guard saw them as a dreadful threat, for your old style teacher is essentially an Oblomovic niche man, half in love with easeful mediocrity, whose need to intimidate students is topped only by his inability to impress those students with his scholarship ... Harmless stuff and yet, suddenly, into their imaginary cloisters and hallowed courtyards strut these shiny-suited, nylon-shirted Aliens with their plots, caucuses, points-of-order, and mysterious in-group mutterings about bibliographies and learned journals. They were the Enemy.

They were *Americans!* The rivalry that developed between these two groups dwindled by the Fall of 1966 and, by the new year, had changed into an alliance. Two other breeds of academic had arrived and both of them were inimical to the older traditions. The first, relatively harmless, consisted of the beautiful young people whose clothes were inspired by Quant and Carnaby Street, the Beatles, and the psychedelic revolution. The second breed emerged from the generation of antinomian graduate students brought up on James Dean and politicized by the Berkeley Free Speech and

Civil Rights movements. These were the militants. They dressed in combat boots and camouflage pants; wore earrings and Black Panther hairdos. They said "Right on!" and "Up Against the Wall" and they made poor McFog's [the first president at sFU was a meteorologist named Patrick McTaggart-Cowan who was known as McFog at the Department of Transport] life a misery. They believed in confronting administrations with impossible demands and, when these were rejected, in occupying the buildings. Government by quiet, low-toned, gentlemen's agreement between senior tenured faculty in secret sessions was replaced, as it were overnight, by the daily proliferation of ad hoc committees, clench-fist signs, cries of "lackey" and "fascist pig," demonstrations, and strikes ...

Most of them were members of the PSA Department [Political Science, Sociology, and Anthropology] and were squeezed out of it by an outrageous series of administrative manœuvres ... The censure of the University by the Canadian Association of University Teachers, still in force, has meant nothing, and has this year been resurrected as an issue confronting the new president.[1]

In 1963 the Government of British Columbia – and, some suggest, Premier W.A.C. (Wacky) Bennett in particular – had decided that the province required another university and had managed to find the $25 million necessary to begin construction. A picturesque site on Burnaby Mountain just north of Vancouver was found for the new campus. Building a new university for some 2,500 students from the ground up presented a real challenge for the planners and administrators. Moreover, when Simon Fraser University opened its doors in 1965, Canada was in the midst of the unruly sixties, and sFU became a mecca for some of the most radical student activists in the province. The university quickly became known as Berkeley North, though there is some debate over whether the radical nature of sFU during this time is "part of a false legend."[2] What is apparent is that the university was perceived as being fundamentally and culturally different from the more staid and established universities across the country. Over and above such issues as civil rights and the Vietnam War, which were fuelling student unrest on campuses across North America, Simon Fraser had experienced heated faculty controversies almost from the beginning. The history of these controversies is relevant because many of the problems still existed when Pauline accepted the position of president in 1974.

Simon Fraser's status as an instant university requiring an instant faculty was bound to cause growing pains. Before its third year, faculty members had become disillusioned with both the university administration and the Board of Governors. They successfully mobilized the Canadian Association of University Teachers (CAUT) and the SFU students and challenged the authority of the university's administration. There were some victories. Appointed department heads and deans were replaced by elected ones, and an economics professor, Kenneth Strand, was named as the university's second president.[3] Some suggest that the administration was heavy-handed in dealing with radical faculty members.[4] Others suggest that some faculty members were irresponsible. Whatever the truth, the result was the same – the Canadian Association of University Teachers (CAUT) invoked censure against SFU in 1968 following a strike.

THE PSA, ACADEMIC CENSURE, AND BOYCOTT

The chronology leading to the censure is complicated, but it is generally agreed that the flashpoint of acrimony between the administration and faculty was the dismissal of five teaching assistants in March 1967. The dismissal was done by the Board of Governors without a hearing. The unilateral imposition of this decision galvanized the faculty association and students into taking concerted action against the administration. Ultimately, the Canadian Association of University Teachers joined forces with the faculty, and together with the students it was able to get a reversal of the board's actions. This lone victory was not enough for the faculty association, which had been continually at war with the administration since its early days. In October 1967 the association formally requested CAUT to "investigate the breakdown in communications between the Faculty Association and the President."[5]

CAUT dispatched a three-member committee to Simon Fraser, and several months later its twenty-five-page report was approved by the CAUT executive and subsequently published in the *Bulletin*, CAUT's newsletter. In May 1968 the fifty-six-member Council of the Canadian Association of University Teachers passed, by an almost unanimous vote, "a resolution of censure against the Board of Governors of Simon Fraser University for its continued contravention of accepted principles of university governance through interference in the academic affairs of the university; the President of the University for his continued failure to carry on appropriate administration of the University; and both the Board of Governors and the President for their failure to take adequate steps to deal with the situation described in the report of the investigating committee."[6]

On 30 May, at a meeting of the joint faculty at Simon Fraser, the resolution of censure was endorsed by a vote of 121 to 60, and a recommendation was made to ask President McTaggart-Cowan to resign. The following day, the chairman of the Board of Governors announced that the president had been asked to take an extended leave of absence and that steps were being taken to appoint a temporary acting president. It is evident that the Board of Governors made the serious miscalculation of assuming that the censure would be removed as a result of bringing in a new president. CAUT was looking for a fundamental shift in administrative philosophy, not simply a change in administrative personnel, and it would revoke the censure only if a number of the other issues relating to tenure and academic freedom were resolved.

At the centre of the controversy was the Department of Political Science, Sociology, and Anthropology (PSA). From its inception, this department had been an experimental one and, as such, had received its share of commentary, both positive and negative. The PSA had always stood out as a hotbed of activism. Its faculty had been "initially attracted to SFU by the prospect of a new and exciting university, by the presence of T.B. Bottomore as PSA head and later, by the radical reputation of the department."[7] During the 1968–69 academic year, both the faculty association executive and members of Simon Fraser's administration had become concerned about a series of allegations against the PSA. These included complaints about the active participation of students in grading, the opening of confidential faculty files to students and others, and the misuse of budget money within the PSA department itself.[8]

The allegations were followed by a series of confrontations between the university administration and members of the department concerning the acting chairmanship and the appointment of outside trustees to administer the department. The flashpoint was the creation of the six-member Departmental Tenure Committee, which included only one member from the PSA. Many of the recommendations which this committee made on contract renewals, tenure, and promotion were considered too harsh. Despite widespread discontent with the committee, the administration continued in its battle with the department. CAUT then sent a delegation to the university for informal talks with members of the faculty association, the PSA, and the administration.[9]

Despite CAUT's request that direct action be avoided, the students and the PSA faculty were resolute in their decision to strike. For them, it was "the only honest act left to a department harassed and wearied by a reactionary university determined to destroy them."[10] They had been the target of harassment, they said, because of their efforts to make social science "both critical and relevant and its own internal workings both democratic and humane."[11] The PSA strike began at 12:30 AM on Wednesday, 24 September 1969, and it was followed by a week of confrontations, recriminations, and threats. The strike action came to a head on Friday, 3 October, when the new president, Kenneth Strand, initiated suspension and dismissal proceedings against eight members of the department.[12] At this point, the faculty association's executive requested CAUT to review the dismissal and suspension procedures and make recommendations on them.[13]

Over and above the CAUT involvement at Simon Fraser, there had been increasing student militancy on campus, and more than one hundred students were charged by the RCMP for occupying the administration's offices.[14] By the summer of 1969, the Department of Political Science, Sociology, and Anthropology was under a trusteeship and a committee from outside the department had been established to judge the competence of the PSA faculty. Meanwhile, the battle between the faculty association and the administration continued. According to the CAUT *Bulletin*, "After lengthy hearings and arbitrations, Dr Strand and the Board of Governors abruptly suspended, then rescinded, the university's dismissal procedures, and the eight professors were ousted; two were dismissed in August 1970, another two in June 1971, and three failed to have their contracts renewed.[15] The faculty voted 131 to 83, with thirteen abstentions, in support of Dr Strand. In November 1971 the CAUT invoked its ultimate censure on SFU, a boycott actively recommending that faculty not take positions at the university as there was no guarantee of academic freedom and tenure."[16] Despite efforts to resolve these outstanding points of disagreement, it took until 1977 to have the censure on SFU lifted.

In the fourth year of his five-year mandate, President Strand announced his intention to step down. Almost immediately, the university began a search for a new president. More than ninety names were submitted to the selection committee, which in turn submitted three to the Board of Governors.[17] Pauline was one of the three who were short-listed. The other two were the academic vice-president at SFU, Brian Wilson, and George Harrower, vice-principal at Queen's University in Kingston.[18] Of these two, Wilson was seen as the front runner and the choice of the administrators. According to Clive Cocking, department chairmen were highly territorial and very protective of their fiefdoms. The Barons of SFU, as he called them, were a clique of about two dozen top administrators who effectively held power at the university. According to Cocking, "The Barons [were]all men and they had wanted one of their number to become president, the current academic vice-president, Dr Brian Wilson, a naturalized Canadian from Northern Ireland whom they regarded as a cool, efficient administrator."[19] It has often been speculated that Pauline was recruited for the presidency, because of her involvement with the New Democratic Party. But she was not recruited, according to Jill Vickers, who talked with Pauline at the time of the competition:

I met Pauline in the coffee shop at the Park Plaza in Toronto just accidentally. I was there for something and so was she. She told me she was going for the presidency at SFU. And I said it was wonderful. But she had to campaign for it. Get people to write letters – she had to lobby and so on ... She wasn't recruited – that's my point ... She had to campaign actively and aggressively for it. She had all sorts of people writing. She got the students drummed up. So when she got there ... she found the guy who wanted it internally was in charge of the university ... And he went on sulking for the entire time she was there.[20]

As the story goes, Pauline had listed Walter Gordon, the former minister of finance in the Pearson government, as a reference. When telephoned by a member of the selection committee, Gordon was less than supportive. "Well," he said finally, "ordinarily I'd be delighted to recommend her highly, but just now I hesitate. If she becomes the president of Simon Fraser, she'll be too busy to take on the presidency of the Committee for an Independent Canada, and I want her for that."[21]

As a candidate, Pauline publicly expressed her belief that the surviving seven PSA faculty had been unjustly dismissed, as the three independent arbitrations and five academic inquiries had concluded. She therefore "could not in all conscience accept the presidency of a university under censure." Later, she only accepted the $50,000-a-year position when the university's Board of Governors gave its assurances that steps would be taken to have the CAUT censure revoked and the boycott lifted. By publicly supporting the PSA seven, Pauline had set the dynamics of her opposition within the university itself. In hindsight, perhaps she was too hasty in siding with the suspended professors; however, her support of the group had been widely anticipated.

The selection of the new president had been a contentious affair, with the eleven-member Board of Governors deadlocked at five votes each for Pauline and Wilson after two meetings (President Strand refused to vote). Despite being directed to expand the search for new candidates, the committee did not put forward any new names. Meanwhile, the students were very vocal about which candidate they supported. In a campus-wide referendum, Pauline received an 85 per cent approval rating by the student body. Unquestionably, there was an ideological split on the selection committee. Although its inner workings were never made public, it was clear that the chairman and the four members appointed by the NDP were on the pro-Jewett side; throughout her time at Simon Fraser, the perception persisted that Pauline's appointment had been political. However, many at SFU believed that the timing was right for Pauline. "What was required now was someone to make the university more favourably known in the community and build the kind of support needed for the next stage of development, someone who didn't stand in awe of the politicians in Victoria and Ottawa and who could take on any audience. 'Hell,' said an SFU staff member of Jewett's campaign for the job, 'she just charmed the pants off everyone.'"[22]

There is no question that the changing ideological component of the Board of Governors may have helped Pauline in her quest for the president's position, but there is some debate about whether she was in over her head as president of a university. In terms of administrative experience, she had been chair, once, of a very small political science department, and she had served as director of the Institute of Canadian Studies at Carleton University – a prestigious but small enterprise – for a two-year period. She had never served as a dean or assistant dean, and her only academic experience as a tenured faculty member had been at Carleton. By all accounts, she was an excellent teacher, but she was not a high-profile or research-oriented academic. Despite these limitations, a slim majority of the Board of Governors believed that Pauline was capable of performing the job. She had demonstrated that she had other skills. She had a network of academic and political colleagues across the country who could be instrumental in fundraising, and she had considerable "people skills"; her enthusiasm was infectious, and she had great rapport with students.

As well, there was a strong sense among several members of the Board of Governors that Pauline had some interesting ideas about what a university should be. Pauline herself was confident that her public-relations skills and consensual style of decision making would serve her well, and that she would be able to get the censure revoked. The confidence she exuded was not lost on the Board of Governors. More importantly, she had no history with the university or its politics. She was a fresh face, someone with a new approach. Neverethless, there were sceptics who believed that Pauline was not the right person for the job. Some of them, it would appear, devoted themselves throughout Pauline's presidency to "proving" that the Board of Governors had made the wrong choice.

At PJ's inaugural address in September 1974 she was not heckled or jeered – a rare phenomenon for a president at Simon Fraser! Although she indirectly referred to the university's history of conflict with its presidents, she made it clear that she was not an advocate of confrontational politics. Rather, "she preferred to achieve things on the basis of openness, candidness, and discussion." Further, she stated that "the university had both an intellectual and a social purpose and hoped it would lead in stamping out discrimination against women, against students, against radical thinkers, or just against Canadians."[23] Despite the courtesy shown her during her speech, there were signs in the audience urging the reinstatement of the "PSA seven."[24] There are, of course, many different versions of what happened at Simon Fraser University in its early years. However, one thing is certain. Pauline was walking into a hornet's nest.

As noted above, the controversy surrounding Pauline's appointment continued to plague her. Before her actual hiring, there had been an uproar over her salary demands. The *Vancouver Sun* and the *Ottawa Journal* had claimed that Pauline was seeking a contract worth $1 million: "It had been reported that to take up the president's position at the British Columbia university, Dr Jewett wanted a six-year contract with an average salary of about $65,000 ... On top of that the reports said she wanted a pension of almost $40,000 a year after six years and it was estimated that would total $1 million if she lived to be 75 years of age, the average life expectancy of Canadian women."[25] This $1 million "demand" looked excessive, of course, and Pauline and others were convinced that the inflated figure was a "leak" designed to discredit her.[26] Pauline attempted to shrug off the salary story by stating that she "felt like the Bobby Hull of Canadian academia," but she was deeply embarrassed.[27]

The true story was that Pauline had requested a six-year contract starting at $54,000, with an 8 per cent annual increment and a pension of half her salary on retirement. The pension was a big consideration to Pauline because she had not qualified for a parliamentary pension or for a sizable pension benefit from Carleton University. Ultimately, she negotiated a five-year contract at $50,000 per year and a pension package identical to that received by SFU faculty members.[28] In total, the value of her compensation package was $330,000 – a far cry from the million-dollar package she was purportedly demanding.[29] Although Pauline had previously been outspoken about inflated salaries, she believed that by not asking for a median salary, she would be doing a disservice to other women competing for administrative positions: "I was a woman going into this position for the first time and I really felt I would be sort of letting down the side if I didn't go in at roughly the same level as a man would do. So I asked for a salary in the middle range [for university presidents], and that's what I got."[30]

Meanwhile, Pauline was determined to get CAUT's motion of censure lifted. It had been the final straw in what had been a protracted battle over Simon Fraser's educational reputation. Much had been written about the inferiority of degrees from SFU compared with other postsecondary institutions. The following passage written by a former professor at the university demonstrates the type of malaise the university had fallen into:

I recall being impressed by SFU's seven Fellows (Woodrow Wilson Fellowships) announced in the Spring of 1969. It was a higher number than UBC and I believe, ranked SFU as third among Canadian universities. But in 1970, SFU received only one Fellowship. The abrupt drop off in Fellowships was excused as a result of an incapacitated faculty, the strike by the PSA. But this was all beside the point … The truth about SFU's sudden decline in Fellows is simple. The students who'd won Fellowships the year before were now gone, and SFU no longer attracted capable young students.[31]

It is important to remember just how serious the boycott was. The 1970s were a time of major university expansion. The baby boomers were now of university age and were entering postsecondary institutions in droves. Generous government-funded student aid programs were making higher education more accessible. There were far more teaching jobs available than qualified candidates to fill them. Increasingly, campuses were in competition with each other to attract young faculty members. By all accounts, even if you were "all but dissertation" (ABD), it was likely that you would have little difficulty securing a position. Yet the few qualified people available were being advised not to apply for jobs at SFU. Boycott was a very powerful tool. Clearly, Pauline had to get the censure removed, especially as it obstructed her goal of Canadianization; as long as it remained in place, the university could not advertise new appointments in the CAUT *Bulletin*, which went to academics across Canada.[32] The boycott was briefly lifted in November 1974 when the university adopted a new academic freedom and tenure document, but it was reimposed in July after unproductive SFU-CAUT negotiations.

An interesting aside about Simon Fraser University's hiring practices at this time was recalled by Kim Campbell in her memoirs, *Time and Chance*. According to Ms Campbell, the Department of Political Science, Sociology, and Anthropology at SFU advertised for a Soviet specialist in 1973. She immediately applied for the position and arranged to have Ole Holsti, who had been her faculty adviser at UBC, write a letter of reference in support of her application. Her curriculum vitae was impressive, yet she received no acknowledgement of her application. Upon hearing that a man from Columbia University had received the appointment, she called the department to inquire about her application. Apparently, neither her application nor the letter could be found anywhere. "If I had been interviewed for that position and not been hired," she stated, "I would have accepted the situation. The injustice of not even being considered, though, was upsetting. It is standard practice at universities to hire faculty before their doctorates are finished. Like me, the successful applicant had not yet completed his PH D. I hated to admit it, but I felt I had just been staring discrimination in the face. The following autumn, Pauline Jewett became Simon Fraser's president, but that spring, there was no one I could turn to."[33] Kim Campbell's inference that Pauline was approachable and fair-minded provides an interesting insight. Clearly, this was the type of reputation Pauline developed while at Simon Fraser University.

Meanwhile, the case of the PSA seven – who were now scattered across the country in various universities – was not yet resolved, though negotiations continued throughout the first few years of PJ's term. It became clear during this time that she could not deliver on her promise to have the censure lifted. She simply could not get the Barons and the Board of Governors to make concessions to the dismissed instructors of the PSA. Not until 1977 did an arbitration ultimately result in the lifting of the censure and the boycott.

Pauline had some very intense opinions about what a university should be. Given her own difficulties in securing an academic position at a Canadian university, she was convinced that priority should be given to hiring Canadian talent. In the documentary *Two Schools of Thought* she stated, "I feel it is the duty and responsibility of universities to seek out and hire bright young Canadian academics."[34] This was a long-held belief. In a March 1969 article for *Maclean's* she had written:

Why ... have they [Canadian universities] kept themselves so ill-informed about Canadians? Can it be that they simply haven't wanted to recruit them? There has always been a tendency in Canadian life toward a kind of intellectual colonialism, a reluctance to use one's own talents if other talents are available. For a long while our universities looked to Britain. Have they now simply shifted to the States? Only in much greater numbers since the American market is so near, so large, so efficient, so open and so interested? In short, have our universities taken little advantage of Canadian talent because they have been indifferent to Canadians? Because they have had a decided preference for others? Chilling, if true. It means that the numbers of Canadians doing graduate work at home and abroad, in the future, may well be irrelevant. They simply won't be hired. Not by Canadian universities anyway.[35]

Pauline's critics claimed that she wanted to bring about change too quickly. But since she had only a five-year mandate, her haste in undertaking progressive initiatives is understandable. She had been hired for her ideas, and she certainly was not going to procrastinate in implementing reforms. In Pauline's first year as president, 80 per cent of the new appointments were Canadians. While her "national" hiring program was applauded in a number of circles, there were those who did not agree with her objectives; they believed that the Canadianization program was resulting in mediocre hirings. Much of this criticism came from networks within the university that had developed among academics from American universities and from the Barons of the administration. One American department chairman said, "A lot of the attraction in appointing her president was in getting a woman and a politician. She's turned out to exemplify the worst aspects of the stereotypes of both. She's bitchy."[36]

There were other complaints too. From time to time, she was accused of meddling in departmental affairs. However, for the most part, the institutional resistance from the Barons was nothing more than old-fashioned male chauvinism. One critic stated, "Pauline Jewett's charisma has not packed much clout in the tough internal politics of her Burnaby Mountain campus. Nor has her knowledge of the inner workings of university administration or her political skills proved tremendously effective in the face of the Byzantine complexity of her challenge at Simon Fraser."[37] Later, after she had left Simon Fraser, Pauline was greatly amused, considering all the criticism she had endured – both academically as president and also personally – when she heard that one of her most trying tormentors had said, "We all long for the halcyon days of the Jewett presidency."

Pauline believed that the university should not be an elite bastion of intellectuals accessible to only a few select students who had the financial resources and social opportunity to attend. She believed that it was a university's obligation to be a missionary, to contribute to the community, and to bring at least some part of a university education to those who were either "unwilling or unable to climb the mountain."[38] Towards this end, cultural groups performed concerts out in the community, and extension courses associated with SFU were offered throughout the province.

Pauline was usually objective about the quality of her work, and she was the first to admit that "learning the ropes" of university administration would take time: "Like many women who come to a bureaucratic position without having been taught the skills, I have many shortcomings as a manager ... At first I exhausted myself and must have driven the men around me up the wall. I'm learning to be better organized."[39] She found the job both demanding and stressful. Her usual work day lasted about fifteen hours. Pauline had always been able to strike a balance between her work and her private life, and this had kept her grounded. But by the end of her term at SFU, this balance had been shattered. Her sister Catharine and many of her friends were concerned about Pauline's weight loss and her growing sense of fatigue.

Of course, Pauline was no stranger to patriarchal institutions. As a graduate student, she had experienced the alienation of not being taken seriously. She had weathered the snub at Queen's and the attitude of the selection committee for the public service. She had endured the male culture that permeated Parliament Hill. Yet none of her experiences had prepared her for the intensity of the "old boys' club" mentality that pervaded Simon Fraser. The Barons of SFU tried almost every conceivable tactic to block or undermine her initiatives.

There also were other instances of institutionalized sexism. An episode at the University Club of Vancouver mirrored her experience at the Rideau Club in Ottawa in 1965. The trouble began when someone at the university asked for a membership application for her following her acceptance of the president's position, and she was inadvertently sent a copy of the men-only bylaws. On realizing that women were habitually barred from membership, PJ declared that

SFU would no longer pay for the nine staff memberships it held at the club and, until further notice, any functions paid for by the university would be held at other locations.[40] At the time, Pauline refused to pursue an amendment to the club's constitution, explaining, "I don't like discrimination on any basis, whether it be sex, religion or ethnic background."[41] She also stated, "It seems to me that if the University Club was renamed the University Men's Club – because that is what it is – then it would be all right. Its name would then reflect more accurately its function."[42]

The evaluation of Pauline's administration at SFU has been mixed. Undoubtedly, she had a very clear and ambitious agenda. She wanted to be an important agent of change at the university, and she intended to use whatever influence she could to see Simon Fraser regain its academic reputation. A major part of this restoration project was to recover Simon Fraser University for Canada, since Canadians comprised only 58 per cent of the faculty.[43] However, Pauline's motives for reclaiming SFU were largely misunderstood. The Canadianization of Simon Fraser was not simply a matter of nationalism or of providing opportunities for Canadians in the academy. Pauline's vision was that SFU would become "an outward-looking, socially responsive institution reflecting largely Canadian concerns and serving the community in which it has its roots."[44]

Pauline's mission when she assumed the presidency had three clear objectives: to have the censure removed and restore academic respectability; to Canadianize the faculty and curriculum; and to reach out to the community. Even her critics had to agree that she had considerable success in each of these areas. Censorship was eventually lifted, more Canadians were hired, and a number of community-based programs were established under her stewardship. In addressing SFU's image problem, Pauline worked tirelessly to restore the university's reputation as a solid academic institution. Towards this end, she gave some eighty-two speeches in 1975 alone and entertained to the point of exhaustion. There was no doubt that she was totally committed to restoring SFU's academic reputation.

She also introduced several measures directed at restoring morale at the university. For example, she established a women's advisory committee to examine the salary levels of women faculty. The committee reported several inequities, including the fact that one woman professor was being paid $5,000 less than a man at the same level. To rectify this state of affairs, Pauline pushed through a 33 per cent salary increase for academic women. This initiative was largely triggered by her long-time concern about wage differentials between men and women faculty – a situation with which she was all too familiar.

In 1972 Muriel Uprichard, her former mentor and friend from her days with the Canadian Nurses' Association, contacted Pauline for advice about her negotiations concerning the terms of her employment at the University of British Columbia. Muriel had never been able to secure a tenure-track position teaching psychology but had developed an excellent international reputation in the field of nursing education, and she had been offered the position of professor and director of the School of Nursing at UBC, taking over from the acting director, Elizabeth K. McCann.[45] Of the thirty full-time academic staff in the School of Nursing, only one other faculty member had a PH D, most of the others having undergraduate degrees in nursing.

The School of Nursing offered both an undergraduate and a master of nursing program. Pauline advised Muriel to ask for three times the salary she was currently earning. She believed that it was critical for the future credibility of the nursing science program and for the faculty employed there (the majority of whom were women) that the director be paid at a comparable salary level to her administrative colleagues in the university. If the director of the school was paid a substantially lower salary than other departmental chairpersons, this disparity would be reflected in lower remuneration levels paid to women faculty. It was essential, in Pauline's view, to establish the professional nature of the School of Nursing and of the faculty teaching in it. Muriel ended up being paid an equivalent salary to other chairpersons at the university. She was also able to negotiate a contract that allowed her to stay on past the mandatory retirement age of sixty-five. Given her less than continuous working career, this flexibility in retirement dates was an important benefit.

After Pauline became president of Simon Fraser University, the paths of the two women crossed on numerous occasions. However, it was an event in 1976 that saw their roles change. Like many other universities, both Simon Fraser and UBC were experiencing problems with unleashed dogs on campus. Many students in residences kept dogs in their rooms, in defiance of the rules of the universities, and let them have free run of the campus at all times of day and night. Muriel was a well-known fixture on the UBC campus and was often seen walking her beloved little dog, which by then was quite elderly. One day during the winter of 1976, three stray dogs savagely attacked her pet, dismembering and killing it before her eyes. It was a horrifying spectacle, and Muriel could do nothing to stop the carnage. She was devastated. For the next three days this intelligent, articulate, and compassionate woman suffered a torment of grief that has been described by some as a nervous breakdown and by others as an alcoholic binge. Although Muriel was known to enjoy a drink or two, this uncontrolled drinking was not characteristic. Concerned by her unexplained absence, individuals from her department went to her home to investigate. What they found was a woman in a severe state of despondency and in urgent need of medical attention. Immediately, she was hospitalized.

That evening, when Pauline went to the hospital, she was told by the medical personnel that Muriel would be staying there for a few more days. But after talking things over with Muriel, Pauline – in her matter-of-fact way – advised the hospital staff that her friend was discharging herself. No doubt, Muriel was anxious to keep the lid on her collapse, since she would not want word of it to get to the School of Nursing at UBC. Pauline helped Muriel collect her belongings, and the two left the hospital together. For the next two months, Muriel convalesced at Pauline's home. Perhaps it was Pauline's long-time affection and respect for Muriel that persuaded her to share her home with her friend – a payback of sorts. Muriel thought otherwise; she saw it as an example of Pauline's compassion. Certainly, Pauline was not a fair-weather friend. She was fiercely loyal, especially when any of her friends were in need.[46]

It was not only academic women who benefited under PJ's administration. She also supported the creation of a university and college employees' union and raised the base pay of the support and cleaning staff, many of whom were women. Above all, she seemed to be genuinely well liked and respected by the student body and was involved in numerous fundraising projects. One of the student-run activities in which she participated was a swim for charity, when she swam the length of the pool to raise money for a student cause. How many other university presidents would make that gesture? However, it is also true that Pauline occasionally meddled in departmental business. She was known to get on the telephone to her academic contacts back East, inquiring about young, bright Canadian academics. This type of interference was not well received by university departments.

In the years following Pauline's Simon Fraser experience, she gave mixed messages regarding her feelings about her time on Burnaby Mountain. Several of her friends, as well as her family, have stated that she viewed her years there as four of the happiest and most fulfilling years of her life. She told others, however, that her years out West were lonely and she missed her friends and family. Moreover, the institutional resistance to many of her ideas was a major disappointment. She had no desire to pursue a second term at SFU, and in fact she ended her first term a year early in order to return to politics.

Pauline had often said that one could not live in British Columbia for long without becoming interested in politics. The New Democratic Party had always had some measure of electoral success on the West Coast, and she decided to seek a seat there. As the story goes, her sister Catharine had planned a trip to Vancouver to visit Pauline, and instead of being met at the airport by her sister, she was met by a staffer at Simon Fraser, who told her that Pauline was entering the nomination contest for the riding of Burnaby that very evening. Pauline believed that this was a logical seat to pursue because she had gained a high profile in the community as the president of the university. She had been encouraged to seek the nomination by Dennis Cocke, a senior NDP official in British Columbian politics. The nomination was contested by a brash, enthusiastic, dynamic twenty-three-year-old law student named Svend Robinson. Much to Pauline's surprise and that of her team, Svend ran an impressive campaign and demonstrated the political skills that have continued to make him the incumbent in this riding. It must have been a humiliating defeat for Pauline. How could a fifty-five-year-old political veteran and former university president lose a nomination to a student?

There was an important lesson to be learned from Pauline's nomination defeat. She had a decidedly eastern and Liberal Party bias in her views about process and how politics was done. The Liberal Party, it was argued, was largely controlled by an elite party establishment headquartered in Ontario and Quebec, which targeted prominent people in corporate Canada as well as individuals who enjoyed high public profiles. Since Pauline had cultivated a prominent community profile as the president of SFU, she had assumed that the New Democratic Party in British Columbia would welcome her candidacy with open arms. When she first contemplated contesting the nomination, she held a reception at the president's house. A number of the party faithful, who were already suspicious of Pauline's intellectualism and eastern establishment image, viewed the reception as a pretentious display. Others in the riding regarded Pauline as just another transplanted Ontarian – and a former Liberal at that – who would never fully understand the political culture of British Columbia. Svend, by contrast, held his reception at a regular haunt of the local NDP – a very ordinary restaurant that was frequented by union workers. Pauline had miscalculated the importance of labour support in B.C. politics and had failed to cultivate this constituency. Svend's success, on the other hand, can be attributed not only to his superior organizational abilities but to his talent for gauging the public opinion of his constituents.

The lessons of the nomination defeat were not lost on Pauline. She committed herself to becoming more educated about the politics of British Columbia as well as more informed about the processes of the New Democratic Party. Shortly after her defeat in Burnaby, she was contacted by an incumbent NDP member, Stuart Leggatt, who advised her that he was stepping down as the member for New Westminster–Coquitlam, the riding immediately adjacent to Burnaby. Pauline did not make the same mistake twice and was successful in gaining the party's nomination in 1978. Everyone was anticipating a general election call in 1979 and, sure enough, it was not long before the next election was announced by the Trudeau government.

· 7 ·

The NDP Years and the Turbulent Eighties: Star Wars, the Cruise, and Meech Lake

Pauline's nomination by the New Democratic Party received a mixed reaction. On the one hand, she was a strong candidate who had parliamentary experience as well as a prominent public profile. On the other hand, she was a new face in a party that demanded fierce loyalty, service within the organization, and a strong commitment to process. As an easterner and someone who had limited connections to the trade union movement, Pauline had much to learn about politics in British Columbia and the inner workings of the party. In this sense, her candidacy generated suspicion among some party veterans. It was incumbent on Pauline to earn the trust and respect of the party faithful; it would not flow to her automatically. However, in a wider sense, she had a considerable following. Despite the fact that her tenure at Simon Fraser University had been characterized by controversy and tension, many people in the party and in the community at large saw Pauline as a champion of the re-Canadianization and democratization of Simon Fraser University. She had taken on the "old boys' network," rattling the university establishment, and had won the respect of many outside the academic community who had long been critical of the university administration.

After winning the nomination for New Westminister–Coquitlam in 1978, Pauline was eager to hit the hustings for the election call that was expected sometime in 1979. It had been fifteen years since she had campaigned with her car Mabel and cultivated her "farmers"[1] in Northumberland riding, and more than six years had passed since she had compaigned in Ottawa West. Fortunately for Pauline, she was able to retain the services of Dawn Black, a seasoned campaign worker for the New Democratic Party who became her canvass manager.

Her campaign manager in 1979 was Anita Hagan, and Pauline also had the backing of Dennis and Yvonne Cocke. They were known in the B.C. New Democratic Party as the Coke machine and were integral to Pauline's political success in British Columbia. Pauline's team was able to guide her in the ways of campaigning B.C.-style. Dawn stayed on as constituency assistant after Pauline defeated her nearest competitor, Marg Gregory of the Progressive Conservative Party, by a margin of slightly more than four thousand votes – a far more comfortable margin of victory than she had received as a Liberal in the Ontario riding of Northumberland.

Pauline received 19,360 votes to Marg Gregory's 15,350. The retiring incumbent, Stuart Leggatt, had garnered 15,397 votes in the 1974 election, narrowly defeating the same Conservative candidate by only 204 votes and the Liberal candidate by 400 votes. Pauline's victory in 1979 can partially be attributed to her success in attracting a number of people who had voted Liberal five years earlier. However, the general pattern was that the federal vote for the NDP went up in the 1979 election throughout the province because the NDP was no longer the party of government in British Columbia. (This theory of counterbalance has been observed elsewhere in Canada.)[2] By the time the votes had been counted, the New Democrats had been victorious in eight ridings, up from the two seats they had captured in 1974. While personal voting and name recognition may have played some part in Pauline's victory, another factor may have been the growing dissatisfaction with the Trudeau government in Canada's western provinces. Trudeau's imposition of the Official Languages Act and the francization of the federal public service had both been viewed as pandering to Quebec by many westerners.

Pauline was thrilled to be back on Parliament Hill, though she arrived there amidst the controversy over the party's NATO policy. Since 1969, it had been the NDP's official policy to pull Canada out of NATO, a stand that was vigorously supported by the B.C. caucus. There was a strong peace movement in British Columbia, where members of the party had long been resolutely opposed to nuclear proliferation and were highly critical of the American position. In this respect, Pauline's personal position on NATO was similar to the B.C. stance. However, the NDP leader Ed Broadbent had unilaterally announced a much softer stance. This infuriated the B.C. caucus. Pauline spoke out at the first caucus meeting, upbraiding the leader for waffling on the party's position. Some members of the caucus scolded her for challenging Broadbent's authority, but her aggressive position was applauded by the B.C. contingent.[3] As Margaret Mitchell noted, "It was an interesting way to get started in the caucus."[4] The dispute led to a certain factionalization within the caucus, splitting it along regional lines.

The altercation with Broadbent set the tone for Pauline's future relationship with the leader, which has been described as chilly. To Ed Broadbent's credit, not only did he not punish Pauline for questioning his authority, but he awarded her the critic's position she requested – external affairs – as well as appointing her critic for the status of women. The appointment of critics by the leader of the NDP is based on a consultative process. Each member meets with the leader and expresses his or her preferences for critic assignments. Given Pauline's knowledge of foreign policy, her appointment as external affairs critic in June 1979 came as no surprise to those in the party, though it did ruffle a few feathers – the external affairs critic's position being a much-coveted one. However, it was generally supported by the caucus.

In 1979 there were few women in the House. Pauline and Margaret Mitchell, who represented Vancouver East, had both been elected for the first time as NDP members, and they served together until Pauline retired from politics in 1988.[5] According to Margaret, they were a good team. A social worker by training, Margaret was a long-time community activist. She was well acquainted with party process and rules governing accountability and maintained liaison both with women's groups and with antipoverty activists. Pauline, on the other hand, had a stronger background in policy and had academic connections. According to Margaret, "We were often co-conspirators. Of course being the only two women we would often have to get together on issues and, in a way, we complemented each other. She was the intellectual, much more of a thinker and better read than I was. However, I had much more experience in community organizing and was more knowledgeable about the inner workings of the party."[6]

Although Pauline and Margaret were the first women elected under the NDP banner since the retirement of Grace MacInnis in 1974, there had been a strong presence of women in leadership roles within the party structure. In 1977 the party had created a committee called the Participation of Women (POW) and appointed a paid coordinator, Judy Wascylicia-Leis.[7] POW acted as an advocacy group for women's rights and policy within the NDP and established committees in each province and territory. The national executive of the organization had representation from each geographic region. At every policy convention there was a women's caucus, involving a larger group of women who developed strategies and were engaged in proposing policies and establishing internal party practices.[8] The NDP adopted a policy of parity in the mid-1970s which required equal representation in executive positions of the party. It was official policy to have women run for every leadership position in the party. As well, the party established the requirement that at least half of all delegates at party conventions must be women. Under the leadership of Ed Broadbent, the party committed itself to the aggressive recruitment of women to run for nomination.

Even though the nomination process was a local constituency matter, Broadbent appointed Pauline to encourage the candidacies of women seeking the party's nomination in open or vacant ridings. She actively encouraged Lynn McDonald to compete for the nomination in Broadview-Greenwood (vacated by Bob Rae in a by-election held in March 1982), and she contacted Premier Tony Penikett, urging him to lobby Audrey McLaughlin to make a run for the nomination in the Yukon by-election in 1987.[9] Pauline also encouraged her old friend and campaign worker, Marion Dewar, to seek the party's nomination in Hamilton and she, too, won the by-election in 1987. Pauline implored other women to run, with varying degrees of success, and performed this recruiting role in every election after 1979. When Audrey McLaughlin became leader, she initiated a policy requiring each riding to have at least one woman declared as a candidate before the nomination date was set by the leader.[10] Although this policy of gender parity did not guarantee that women would win nominations, it was considered a valuable political experience. In addition, regional groups affiliated with POW, such as the B.C. Women's Rights Committee, were involved in running training workshops for women, based on a model that had been used effectively in trade unions.[11] As a further incentive to women, the Agnes Macphail Fund was established to provide financial support for women candidates.

By 1987, there were 29 women in the House of Commons out of a total of 282 members, and 6 of these women were New Democrats. Although this marked a significant improvement from the four women in the House when Pauline was first elected in 1963,[12] there still was not a credible presence of women in Canada's federal legislature. As Audrey McLaughlin noted, "When you stand up in the House to speak, you look out over a sea of blue and grey – the men in their club uniform, the business suit."[13] Even though several women in the Liberal Party had been promoted to the front benches, they had not become party insiders. The age-old adage of "the higher the fewer" was still an accurate description of the position of women in Parliament. Christina McCall-Newman made the following observation about the status of Liberal women in 1978:

Women knew the Liberal network was a male combine of the kind Lionel Tiger had written about in his book, *Men in Groups*, where men bonded together, choosing each other, as Tiger wrote "in processes analogous to sexual selection ... [so that] the bond generates considerable emotion ... Males derive important satisfactions from male bonds that they cannot get from male-female bonds." In other words, outside of sexual partnerships, women Liberals were still mainly thought of as understudies or back-up troops, secretaries, special assistants, even campaign chairmen and candidates, though rarely running in the choice ridings. ... Women were increasingly useful to the Liberal Party. But they were not yet central to the network.[14]

Pauline had not been an MP since 1965. Although she had maintained some of her connections in Ottawa during her time at Simon Fraser, much had changed in terms of the feel and culture of Parliament. But perhaps the fact that she had been there before minimized the mystery of the House. Also, she was now fifty-seven years old and had gained valuable administrative experience as a university president and as a member of several policy groups and committees. In 1963, when Pauline had first entered Parliament, she had been a political rookie with high expectations and progressive ambitions about a possible seat at the cabinet table. There was now a certain appeal about being free to criticize as a member of an opposition party. This time around, her expectations were far more realistic and her ambitions were simply not the same. Although the New Democratic Party was not Her Majesty's Loyal Opposition (the Liberals had that role), she would have ample opportunity to criticize Canada's foreign policies. As David Docherty has observed, while a critic's portfolio has limited influence on policy, it does allow individuals "to make their mark as opposition members and to build reputations as experts in their particular fields."[15]

OPPOSITION CRITIC ON EXTERNAL AFFAIRS (1979–87)

As an opposition critic on external affairs, Pauline's position involved two distinct subject areas: international events and peace and disarmament. She had long had an interest in both these areas, but during the course of her tenure as critic she took a particular interest in peace and disarmament. A recurring theme in the area of peace and disarmament was the ability or inability of Canada to maintain its sovereignty in the development of a "made-in-Canada" foreign policy. For Pauline, the issues of sovereignty and peace and disarmament were inextricably linked.

International Events

U.S. Invasion of Grenada. In October 1983 the United States invaded Grenada for the express purpose of rescuing American nationals, and Pauline's opinion was sought by CBC's flagship newscast, *The Journal.* Pauline was adamantly opposed to this type of military operation. When asked by Barbara Frum, "Where do we go from here?" PJ did not mince her words: "First of all, we have to ensure that Americans and other foreign troops get out of Grenada immediately. I am terrified that this is just a first step and the next thing is going to be a multilateral invasion of Nicaragua. We want them out immediately. There would be no question of doing a peacekeeping operation until they were out and until there was a commitment that the U.S. would not invade any other country in that part of the world. I myself am opposed to the kind of peace force that is operating in Lebanon. It is not a U.N. force. It must be a U.N. force or a force operating under similar rules."[16]

Apartheid in South Africa. Pauline opened a can of worms when in 1987 she rose in the House of Commons to address the issue of apartheid and growing civil unrest in South Africa. With the aim of admonishing the government for ignoring the report of a Commons committee which had advocated a series of sanctions against the Government of South Africa, she made the following statement:

Although the Government has been strong in its condemnation of apartheid in the work it has been doing with other Commonwealth countries, it has not yet responded to the resolution of the all-Party committee which met this summer. I refer to the committee which studied the matter of human rights and which, in effect, called for a complete legislated embargo on imports and exports of goods and services to and from South Africa. To my knowledge there has been no response to that unanimous recommendation of the committee.[17]

Pauline was concerned that by sitting on the committee's report and essentially taking no proactive stance, the government was sending the message to South Africa's black majority that their only option was violence. She continued:

Mr Speaker, my question is for the Secretary of State for External Affairs and concerns what signal Canada is giving to the black majority in South Africa, first relating to violent struggle. The Prime Minister has said that while we don't condone violence, we can understand why South African blacks sometimes resort to violence when violence sanctioned by the state is used to maintain the apartheid regime. In late August the Minister told Oliver Tambo, I understand, that the ANC should abandon violent struggle in return for Canadian support. What is the black majority in South Africa to believe?"[18]

Pauline then asked a supplementary question that proved to be highly controversial. The logic in her question was that apartheid, by its very nature, was a policy rooted in violence and oppression, and if apartheid was not abolished by the Government of South Africa, it was only logical that the black majority had no option but to resort to violence. In other words, violence breeds more violence. Nowhere in the above sequence or in the statement that follows was Pauline advocating violence, yet this is how her statement in the House was interpreted: "Mr Speaker, my supplementary question is for the same Minister. To make this amply clear, since we do want one message to go to the black majority in South Africa, will the Minister also agree that since the root of the violence is apartheid itself sometimes a resort to violence is absolutely essential in the struggle?"

Pauline was promptly accused of promoting violence. Clearly, this was a defensive ploy to discredit the point she was making – that the government had done nothing to implement the recommendations of a report that encouraged it to take a more proactive position in having apartheid rescinded. It did not take long for conservative news outlets to blow Pauline's statements out of all proportion. Shortly after the exchange in the House, the following appeared in the *Western Report*:

The National Energy Program underlined the cancerous nature of government intrusion into private business. But Miss Jewett's proposal for Africa is different and infinitely worse. It is as incredible as it is shocking that persons elected to positions of responsibility in Canada's parliament would express even the most tentative concurrence with violence as a response to any national problem given the death, horror and hopelessness that is implicit in such a recourse ... Human rights and freedoms get short shrift through much of Africa, including, of course, South Africa. Legislated inequity, which clearly exists in South Africa, has engendered violence throughout the country and neighbouring states. It offends decency. But to encourage additional violence to add to that which already exists is grossly irresponsible and, in my view, immoral.[19]

The journalist who wrote this commentary did, however, state that it was the message that was abhorrent, not the logic. Indeed, he argued that Pauline was probably right when she made the point that violence was imminent in South Africa. But as Gordon Gibson wrote in the *Financial Post*, her stand was likely to be disavowed by her party because it was the type of issue that Canadians did not want to hear about:

You try to choose winners for issues, and this one is a big loser. To tell a country with a horror of violence that there are times when it is okay is an uphill battle ... Jewett has a point, painful and difficult though it may be to confront. We hate violence because we see in it the potential for the destruction of some of our cherished freedoms, security of the person and property being not least of these. We forget – because we weren't there – that our current freedoms were won by violent times in the past. The end result will be violence. The South African government and the African National Congress argue over who is killing more people, the prize apparently being, like golf, for the low score. The truth is the volcano is building. Jewett, you are quite right. You can't make an omelet without breaking eggs. For a socialist to accept this concept attracts my admiration. Her party, of course, will repudiate her thought.[20]

Shortly after the exchange on South Africa, Pauline was replaced as external affairs critic. It was speculated that relieving her of the position was some sort of disciplinary action taken by the leader, Ed Broadbent, because of her statements on South Africa. However, Pauline denied that this was the case and in fact indicated that she had asked to be released from these duties so that she could concentrate on her other position as the critic responsible for the constitution. When asked whether she had any regrets about her position on South Africa, she replied, "Oh, no not at all. Nor may I say that there were any differences with the leader of the party or other members of the party that I am aware of ... It was purely coincidence that it coincided with my stepping down as critic. I had worked all summer on the Meech Lake Accord. I was on the constitutional committee and had therefore gotten involved up to my ears with Meech Lake. In fact, the deterioration in my health is likely due to the fact that I ended up overworking. I had asked Ed if I could continue as constitutional critic and be relieved of my role as external affairs critic. It was my wish to do this."

Peace and Disarmament, and Sovereignty

Pauline's interest in peace and disarmament dated back to her attendance at an international conference in Connecticut while she was a student at Queen's. In reflecting on her political career after she retired, she believed that this was the policy area in which she made her most important contribution. Pauline's appointment as critic overlapped with Ronald Reagan's term as president of the United States. From the time Reagan took up residence in the White House in 1981, his rhetoric was decidedly anticommunist, and the American people admired him for his aggressive, right-wing stance. The Reagan administration pursued a strategy of new weapons technology – "smart weapons" – and the Americans assumed that their allies, especially Canada, would cooperate and support this new strategy. Pauline, as the NDP's external affairs critic, was not prepared to accept that Canada had to acquiesce to American pressure. To do so, she believed, was giving in to coercion and would ultimately result in Canada's loss of sovereignty over its external affairs:

What has happened in Canada is that we have so consistently over the past few years simply said yes to whatever request the U.S. Defense Department makes of us. We have never examined the request. We have never exercised lately the kind of nuclear restraint that we did exercise at one time. Canada has taken independent initiatives in the past. She hasn't always said we'll do what you want. And I'm just puzzled to know why the government this time didn't say no. There are states in the U.S. that refuse to test cruise missiles. They seem to have more sovereignty than we do.[21]

On this same theme, Pauline wrote the following two years later:

While Canada from time to time has diverged from enthusiastic support for specific U.S. policies – by maintaining trade with Cuba, and of late, muted criticism of U.S. bombing in Cambodia, for example – Canada has never taken a fully independent course, or a course in concert with countries other than the U.S., on any fundamental foreign or defence policy issue. Lost opportunities range from Pierre Trudeau's dismissal of the neutron bomb as a "European matter," to Mark MacGuigan's "quiet acquiescence" on Central America, to Erik Nielsen's "prudent" acceptance of Star Wars research and Brian Mulroney's "benefit of doubt" support of U.S. policies in general.[22]

A third argument PJ invoked against the escalation of the arms race was that it had a human cost in terms of human rights and the distribution of wealth:

Willy Brandt has called democratic socialism "the humanitarian ideal of this century." Internationalism is part of that ideal. Arms spending must be diverted to human needs. The division of wealth between societies, as well as within them, must be attacked in bold and imaginative ways. The preservation and extension of basic human rights must be a constant struggle. Such views, coupled with a continuing call by the NDP for greater independence, offers Canada a real alternative to old party foreign policy.[23]

Rather than accepting the formal position of the Canadian government on weapons testing, Pauline became the spokesperson for an alternative strategy – a strategy of peace, common security, and disarmament. This vision was outside the mainstream of popular opinion in the 1980s, and Pauline and members of her party were at times labelled socialists and communists by American authorities. However, since perestroika and the fall of the communist regime, Pauline's vision for peace and disarmament had gained new credibility. She summed it up during an interview on *The Journal* when she said:

We all want peace. I disagree entirely that the way to get it is to fuel the nuclear arms race with an unverifiable generation of nuclear weapons such as we have with the cruise [missile]. We'll simply send the Soviets back to their laboratories where they will develop a cruise with a stealth technology and so on. What we've got to do is recognize that there is a rough balance when you count both theatre and intercontinental nuclear weapons between the two sides and that now is the moment that we have a rough balance. Not for one side to try to get superiority but rather have a freeze so we can stop the new and very destabilizing weapons such as the cruise from being deployed or tested or developed and get into genuine arm reductions following a freeze.[24]

The first disarmament issue to arise during Pauline's tenure as critic had involved the testing of cruise missiles over Canadian territory. The issue was never discussed in the House of Commons because it formed part of a "framework agreement" that Canada had negotiated with the United States, which included a wide range of weapons testing. The agreement was signed in Washington on 10 February 1983. Pauline registered her concern about Canada's complicity in testing the cruise missile in a debate about the value of such tests which appeared in *Reader's Digest*:

Cruise testing implicates Canada in the nuclear race as never before, and at a particularly dangerous time. Because the cruise is small, easily transported and easily hidden, its numbers and locations are unverifiable. It has been said the cruise will make nuclear arms control impossible. Going contrary to public sentiment and foreign-policy tradition, Canada is thus contributing not only to the nuclear arms race but also to a dangerous escalation in the ability to wage nuclear war. Refusal to test would also be a practical and symbolic return to Canada's traditional no-nuclear-weapons policies.[25]

The perceived advantage of the air-launched cruise missile was its high degree of accuracy. Ironically, its guidance system was made in Canada at Litton Systems Canada Limited. The Red Lake area in northern Alberta was selected as the test zone because of the similar terrain and climactic conditions found in various regions of the Soviet Union. Negotiations soliciting Canada's support for the testing had begun with an exchange of letters between President Reagan and Prime Minister Trudeau in March 1981. By December of the same year, an approval in principle had been reached on the framework agreement.

There were all sorts of things about the decision to test the cruise that were of great concern to Pauline. First, the decision had been made in a very undemocratic way. Parliament was not consulted and the Canadian people had been denied an explanation from the government about why the testing of the cruise was seen as such an important exercise. At the very least, Pauline believed, the Canadian people were owed some sort of statement from the government about the country's commitment to peace and deterrence, though she felt that such a statement would fall within the realm of propaganda. On *The Journal* on 10 February 1983, she stated, "This is not a Canada–U.S. agreement. It's a President Reagan–Prime Minister Trudeau agreement. And it's to assist the United States in its intercontinental strategic force and it has nothing to do, in my view, with decisions being made in NATO."[26]

Pauline also spoke out vehemently against Star Wars, the strategic defence initiative (SDI). In her view, it is was not just another weapons program; it was the largest military venture ever proposed. If it was deployed, its cost would be an estimated trillion dollars. Over and above such a huge expenditure, the question Pauline and others were asking was, Will the Soviet Union develop its own Star Wars? Although SDI was sold to the American public as the ultimate "defence" system, it threatened to escalate the proliferation of a new round of weapons build-up.

Pauline became the NDP's self-appointed watchdog in this area. In 1980, for example, she went on the attack when the American Defense Preparedness Association, an alliance of military, industry, and government officials, chose Ottawa as the site of its conference on Trends in Large-Calibre Gun Systems. Although the federal government claimed it was not the official host, Pauline and others associated with the peace movement believed that Ottawa could hardly have been more accommodating. For instance, the meeting was held in the government's Conference Centre in downtown Ottawa. Pauline raised the matter in the House of Commons and denounced Canada's involvement. In particular, she targeted the participation of the Canadian-based multinational Space Research Corporation. (In June that year, this firm had been convicted in the United States of selling arms to South Africa.) According to an article in *Maclean's*, Pauline received an unexpected phone call during the conference. "It was a government official inviting her to drop in at the symposium. When she arrived early Wednesday morning, she was met by nervous federal government officials who escorted her to one morning lecture but refused to issue her a *carte blanche* to wander at will. Her verdict on the basis of one morning inside: "Jargony as hell. Boys' games."[27]

Special Joint Committee on Canada's International Relations

Perhaps Pauline's greatest accomplishment in the peace and disarmament field was her participation in the Special Joint Committee of the Senate and the House of Commons on Canada's International Relations, which was struck in June 1985. The committee's first task was to report on the government's green paper entitled "Competitiveness and Security: Directions for Canada's International Relations," which had been tabled in the House of Commons on 14 May 1985.

There were twenty members on the committee, including six senators.[28] Pauline's two colleagues from the New Democratic Party were Jim Manley and Steven W. Langdon. Representing the Liberal Party were Lloyd Axworthy and Jean Chrétien, and from the Progressive Conservatives, Tom Hockin (joint chairman), Jim Caldwell,

Patrick Crofton, and Suzanne Duplessis. In total, there were sixty-two sittings of the committee, beginning on 28 June 1985 and finishing on 25 April 1986. The committee's mandate was "to consult the Canadian people on the full range of Canada's international relations" with the "objective of elaborating on a framework within which Canadian external policy should operate."[29] In total, almost seven hundred individuals and organizations filed written briefs, and well over three hundred witnesses appeared at public hearings in Halifax, Montreal, Vancouver, Calgary, and Winnipeg. The committee criss-crossed the country, beginning in January 1986, with scheduled meetings every two weeks until April. Each province and territory was visited during this process. Two of the major issues raised during these consultations were bilateral trade with the United States and SDI – Star Wars.

For Pauline, her involvement in this committee was one of the greatest challenges she ever had as a parliamentarian. She took her work very seriously and gave up most of the summer to attend the public meetings. The volume of paperwork and briefs was enormous. According to some outside observers, she was one of the hardest workers on the committee. Although she was a veteran of committee work, cognizant of the fact that in the end the government line would rule, she nevertheless worked tirelessly to give voice to dissenting opinions. She was particularly concerned about SDI and Canada's participation in NORAD and wrote, "Public concern about Star Wars was so widespread and the testimony against participation so overwhelming that the committee, despite the Conservative majority predilection, could not in any honesty recommend an enthusiastic 'yes' to Star Wars. The committee report on Star Wars on 23 August paved the way for Mulroney's qualified 'no' to Star Wars on 7 September 1985."[30]

From the beginning, the Conservatives on the committee showed that they had no intention of seriously examining NORAD, the strategic questions of the 1980s, or the future of Canada-U.S. defence arrangements; and the government soon demonstrated that it had no desire to share necessary information for such a review or to weigh public opinion about militarization of the North or of space. In the end, the Conservatives prevented the expression of dissenting views from opposition parties in the committee's recommendations.[31]

To counter the one-sided nature of the committee's report, Pauline became one of the chief architects of the NDP's policy on peace and disarmament. Marion Dewar went so far as to suggest that it was Pauline's drive, intelligence, and analytical skills that brought the

NDP's *Common Security* document to the fore. Common security was not a made-in-Canada idea. It had gained prominence in 1982 with the release of the report of the Independent Commission on Disarmament and Security Issues entitled *Common Security: A Blueprint for Survival*. The chairman of the commission was Olaf Palme of Sweden, and there were sixteen commissioners, including Gro Harlem Brundtland (Norway), Giorgi Arbatov (USSR), Cyrus Vance (United States), and Robert A.D. Ford (Canada). The cornerstone of the commission's report was that the doctrine of deterrence was a very fragile protection against the horrors of nuclear war and that the most appropriate alternative to mutual deterrence was common security.[32] As described by the commission, "the principle of common security asserts that countries can only find security in cooperation with their competitors, not against them."[33] The report's many recommendations included advocating a stronger role for the United Nations, designating large parts of Central Europe as nuclear-weapon-free zones, and emphasizing the importance of regional approaches to security.

The approach set out in *Canada's Stake in Common Security* became official NDP policy in 1988. As defined in this report, common security could best be understood by the idea that "the security of one nation is dependent on, and contributes to, the security of others."[34] In some respects, the world had become safer and the nuclear threat less evident in recent years. However, the report concluded that our global security was threatened "by unfair trading arrangements, violation of labour laws, unemployment, regional conflicts, environmental destruction, resource depletion, human rights abuses, and global inequalities."[35]

There were three key components to the NDP policy. First, it recommended that the United Nations be given greater support by Canada and others so that it could become a more representative and effective institution. Second, the federal government should commit itself to improving both trade with and official development assistance to developing countries. Third, the Government of Canada should take steps to claim the "peace dividend." The NDP put forward several initiatives towards achieving this end, including closing redundant military bases, reducing the size of Canada's forces, and ending Canadian participation in NATO and NORAD. According to the NDP report, Canada spent eleven dollars on its military for each dollar spent on the environment.[36] What was unique about the NDP report was its strong endorsement of the Independent Commission's recommendations and its proposals for downsizing the military.

Its position on withdrawing from NATO and NORAD had been a long-standing NDP policy but was expressed in a slightly different context in this report.

CRITIC FOR THE STATUS OF WOMEN
(1979–81)

Pauline's primary interests associated with the status of women related to economic position, education, and training and not grass-roots issues such as day care and poverty. Although she made statements in the House and asked questions on a number of issues that were of particular interest to women, there is little question that her role as a critic for the status of women focused on the constitutional aspects of the subject.

In 1980 Pauline's old nemesis, Pierre Trudeau, declared his intention to repatriate the constitution, a process that culminated in passage of the Constitution Act, 1982. This project occupied a considerable amount of Pauline's time in terms of ascertaining the implications of proposed constitutional provisions for Canadian women. It was during this time that PJ developed an enduring friendship with Doris Anderson, who was then serving as president of the Advisory Council on the Status of Women. It was becoming increasingly apparent to Pauline that Canadian women had much both to gain and to lose from the negotiations over whether a sexual equality rights provision should be entrenched in the Canadian Charter of Rights and Freedoms. This debate was energized by the experiences of American women, who had witnessed the defeat of the Equal Rights Amendment when it failed to be ratified by the extended deadline date of 1982. Canadian women and women's groups looked southward for strategic clues on how to avoid failure in their own pursuit of constitutional guarantees of sexual equality.

The advisory council called for a meeting of women to convene in Ottawa for the purpose of discussing the implications of constitutional negotiations for women. The conference was to take place just before the First Ministers' Conference, which was scheduled to be held in the fall of 1980. Early in the process, the government and the minister responsible for the status of women, Lloyd Axworthy, "enthusiastically supported" the initiative.[37] Constitutional experts across the country, including Mary Eberts, Beverley Baines, and Audrey Doerr, were assigned topics on which to write reports. However, enthusiasm for the conference was muted, and the media appeared uninterested. To compound the problem, just before the conference, federal translators went on strike. Ultimately, the executive decided to cancel the conference.[38]

That October, when the government released the proposed Charter of Rights and Freedoms, it confirmed the worst fears of women's groups: "The language in Section 15 which dealt with discrimination in race, religion, sex, and ethnic origin, was exactly the same wording as in the 1960 Canadian Bill of Rights. That bill had been tested ten times in the courts between 1970 and 1979 and had been found to be a useless legal tool to help women."[39] The Advisory Council on the Status of Women decided to hold a conference the following February – but after the Christmas holidays, Lloyd Axworthy sent a message to the council saying that he wanted regional conferences instead of a national one.[40] Doris Anderson was flabbergasted that the minister would dare to interfere in the council's business. To maintain the credibility of the council, she was determined that the national conference proceed. But the other members of the executive – all Liberal appointees, as she herself was – believed that this would further alienate the government, and they outvoted Anderson by five to one. She then did an end-run around the executive by lodging an appeal to the full council; and she gained the support of the two opposition critics for the status of women: Flora MacDonald of the Progressive Conservatives and Pauline.

The battering Axworthy took over this issue made for good press, and the coverage was "rarely off the front pages or television screens."[41] During one exchange in Question Period, which was carried by *The National*, both Flora and Pauline accused Axworthy of stacking the advisory council with Liberal patsies. Pauline charged the Liberal government with placing a "mole" on the Advisory Council on the Status of Women to keep an eye on its president, and she proceeded to name the mole – Hellie Wilson – adding that Wilson was "an otherwise very agreeable person except in this connection."[42] The NDP member who sat next to Pauline in the House was Bob Rae, and he and those around her all had broad smiles on their faces during this debate. Although it is likely that the alleged espionage surrounding this constitutional conference was slightly overdrawn by Pauline, the encounter illustrates some fundamental facets of her personality. Her loyalty to her friend Doris Anderson and her commitment to supporting a constitutional conference addressing women's concerns were unshakable. Her conciliatory nature and good humour also emerge – in this case, she even had a kind word for the mole.

Ultimately, the council voted in favour of cancelling the conference, and Doris announced her resignation as president on 20 January

1981. Within twenty-four hours, five members of the council had resigned and nine staffers resigned over the next several weeks.[43] Although the council was now leaderless and in a state of disarray, networking succeeded in thrusting the conference back onto the rails, and on 14 February 1981, 1,300 women from all across Canada arrived in Ottawa to hold what came to be known as the Ad Hoc Conference. According to Anderson, the Saturday morning session opened with "an inspired speech from Pauline Jewett."[44]

At one point, there was concern that the women would reject the Charter outright. Certainly, the Conservative women at the conference took this position. Describing a panel discussion on the resolution, Anderson wrote: "Towards the end of the afternoon, Maureen McTeer, a Conservative law student and wife of Joe Clark, berated the audience for not condemning the Charter out of hand. Pauline Jewett countered by pointing out that it could be an important tool for women, and since the government was hell-bent on getting it through Parliament, it was probably going to be passed. McTeer lost her temper – and the vote."[45]

As a politician familiar with Trudeau's obsession with having a charter of rights included in the constitution, Pauline was convinced that taking on the entire package would be unwise. It would be too easy to dismiss the women's demand of pulling the entire Charter as "outrageous." Women had to demonstrate that they were prepared to be conciliatory, she argued. It simply made more sense to request an amendment that would strengthen the clout of section 15 and increase its potential as a tool for women. An intransigent government had much to lose during this debate as well. Like the women's groups, it wanted to be seen as conciliatory, consensual, and democratic. Although Pauline cannot be given credit for the ultimate inclusion of section 28,[46] she was one of the voices – a clear and credible one – heard not only by the women who attended the conference but also by omnipotent government officials.

Later in 1981, Pauline was replaced as critic on the status of women by her colleague Margaret Mitchell, but this did not mean that she stopped taking an active interest in issues that were of particular interest to women. There were many matters, commonly described as women's issues, that Pauline strongly defended as a member of Parliament and a member of the NDP. During her parliamentary career, she concerned herself with such diverse issues as day care, pay equity, employment training, and the plight of women in the Third World. On the contentious issue of abortion, she was clearly more concerned about accessibility to therapeutic abortions than with the moral overtones of the debate. This position was not popular. As a British Columbian, Pauline was well aware of the strength of the Pro-Life movement in that province. In the 1984 general election, anti-abortion organizations targeted the ridings of Pauline, Margaret Mitchell, and Svend Robinson, among others.

Although abortion was no longer a violation under the Criminal Code, a number of provinces had thrown up barriers that served to constrain large numbers of women from gaining access to a therapeutic abortion. In her reply to the Speech from the Throne, made on 6 October 1986, Pauline commented on this problem of accessibility: "In practice, we are rapidly coming to a position of denying access to women to therapeutic abortions. It is shocking that in Prince Edward Island it is not possible to get a therapeutic abortion, and it is practically impossible in Newfoundland. In a letter received from a Dr R.C. Gustafson of Kamloops, he points out that it is becoming clear that women in the whole of the southern interior of British Columbia are going to be denied access to safe therapeutic abortions." Pauline went on to say that by continuing to erect obstacles for women seeking access to abortion, the lives of women would be placed at risk and democratic freedoms would be abridged. "Let us not return to abortion on the back streets. Let us think again of Tom Harpur's words: 'To compel a woman to bear a child against her will or to force her to abide by what others define as adequate or inadequate reasons for an abortion, is a form of naked, authoritarian violence.'"[47]

CONSTITUTIONAL CRITIC (1986–88)

Special Joint Committee on the Meech Lake Accord

Pauline had long been a student of Canadian constitutionalism. There is a certain classic symmetry in Pauline's legislative career that she would spend her last two years in the House as a member of a joint committee of the Senate and the House of Commons studying the constitution. As an academic, she had an intellectual interest in the constitution, particularly in the area of human and civil rights. She had been a persistent advocate of recognizing the "French fact" in Canada, regretting that she had never become bilingual. Pauline knew that her remaining days in Parliament were numbered, and she had a strong desire to resolve the impasse and to bring Quebec into the constitutional fold. Given her keen sense of nationalism and her strong belief in the power of Parliament, it is evident that her last political objective was to see the constitutional "problem" resolved.

The joint committee was struck in June 1987 to examine the Meech Lake Accord and make recommendations about it. Five senators[48] and twelve members of the House of Commons were appointed as permanent members. Lorne Nystrom and Pauline were the NDP committee members. The committee was to report its findings on 21 September 1987. Over the course of the fifteen hearings, which officially began on 4 August, the committee heard 133 oral presentations and received countless briefs, letters, and submissions from various groups and individuals. The individuals who presented oral evidence included prominent academics and legal scholars, among them Gérard Beaudoin, Ramsay Cook, Deborah Coyne, Raymond Hébert, Al Johnson, William Lederman, Peter Leslie, Wayne MacKay, J. Peter Meekison, Richard Simeon, Ronald L. Watts, and John D. Whyte. Several current and former politicians, including Lowell Murray, Frank McKenna, Robert Stanfield, Jack Pickersgill, and Pierre Trudeau, also presented evidence.

In reading the transcripts of the hearings, it is apparent that Pauline relished the academic tenor of many of the oral presentations. Several times, she referred to herself as a political scientist when addressing questions to presenters from universities. On the one hand, she may have been indicating to these presenters her familiarity with legal jargon and constitutional history, but she may also have been warning them not to patronize parliamentarians. On one occasion she referred to the "rich intellectual life at Queen's University." Clearly, the Queen's connection, though a thorny one in the past, remained dear to her heart.

Although three of the seventeen permanent members of the committee were women (Yvette Rousseau and Suzanne Blais-Grenier were the other two), Pauline saw herself as the principal scrutineer of briefs relating to women's issues. She agreed with the objections expressed by a number of women's groups, especially with regard to the potential conflict inherent in the distinct society guarantees and the sexual equality provisions of section 28. However, she decided to support the accord for several reasons. Intrinsic to the argument that the Province of Quebec might override sexual equality guarantees (section 28) in the cause of promoting the distinct society was the assumption that the women of Quebec would be unable to mobilize opposition to such an initiative. Pauline was sufficiently convinced that the women of Quebec were capable of this resistance. Her confidence was largely inspired by the testimony of Richard

Simeon, then director of the School of Public Administration at Queen's University: "I personally do not think there is very much of a likelihood that something that Quebec might try to do, and justify by 'distinct society,' would directly threaten say women's rights, but if they did, it is worth thinking through what the process might look like. It seems to me first of all it would embody a huge debate within Quebec, and we know that the Quebec progressive movements would fight tooth and nail. It seems to me that Quebec is probably more advanced than most other provinces are in terms of the strength of the women's movement and its responsiveness to it."[49]

It also appears likely that Pauline was persuaded by the testimony of Norman Spector, secretary to the cabinet for federal-provincial relations. On 1 September 1987, in response to a question from Pauline about how the final agreement had been reached, Spector replied, "In the course of the discussion at Langevin,[50] the issue of the impact of the distinct society on the Charter did come up, and it was a point on which First Ministers called in outside advisers, a number of very prominent constitutional authorities. The consensus of those discussions was that the clause should have meaning, and its meaning should not be such as to threaten rights or take away rights, but to shed light when courts review legislation in specific circumstances."[51]

Spector went on to state that the provisions regarding aboriginal people and multiculturalism were the "weakest provisions of the Charter"; section 28, on the other hand, was considered the "strongest section of the Charter."[52] According to Spector, the chief negotiators during the Langevin discussions had been women. Implicit in this statement was the notion that the compromise was seen as an acceptable one to the key constitutional advisers, several of whom were women. Although there had been some discussion about exempting the Charter from the distinct society clause, this proposal, according to Spector was not acceptable. The decision made by the first ministers to include aboriginal and multicultural rights in section 16 (and therefore beyond the reach of the distinct society clause) but not to include sexual equality rights was the best deal possible. The inclusion of section 28 – sexual equality rights – within section 16 was simply unacceptable to Quebec.[53]

To be sure, the debate surrounding the Meech Lake Accord was difficult for Pauline. Although she had the strong support of Ed Broadbent and others within the federal caucus, some members were reluctant supporters. Many women's groups, especially the National Action Committee on the Status of Women, were taking a hard line in opposing the Meech Lake Accord. The B.C. Women's Rights Committee of the New Democratic Party was infuriated with PJ and accused her of not consulting them.[54] This fissure within the NDP cost Pauline future support. Nevertheless, she was not prepared to alter her position. She understood that there were some problems in the fit between the distinct society clause and the equality provisions of sections 15 and 28, but Simeon's view that the Quebec women's movement was one of the more progressive in the country and Spector's stance that the inclusion of section 28 within section 16 would have been a deal breaker convinced Pauline to capitulate and give her support to the accord. Being the astute politician and constitutional scholar that she was, she knew that there was a very small window of opportunity for a constitutional resolution. As far as she was concerned, Meech Lake needed to be passed to circumvent the very real risk of a permanent constitutional impasse. Pauline supported the passage and ratification of the Meech Lake Accord for political reasons.

As a member of the Commons committee for the constitution, Pauline continued to support the accord. In the wake of a feminist backlash, this took courage. Most women's groups, as well as her good friend Doris Anderson, believed the accord to be a setback for the equality rights project, particularly for their sisters in Quebec. While Pauline understood the logic of their criticism, she took off her feminist cap and donned her nationalist one. The needs of the country for a constitutional peace took precedence over feminist demands that ran the risk of upsetting the entire constitutional agreement. Pauline could have exercised the face-saving tactic of abstaining. In fact, the Liberal members of the committee did just that. But she was not one to back down in the face of pressure. While her stance was both difficult and controversial, in many respects this may well have been Pauline's finest hour as a parliamentarian.

Despite her support for the accord, there are several passages in the transcripts of the hearings which indicate that Pauline had a number of serious reservations about the constitutional deal. The prime example was on 8 August, when she stated, "So, when you sit and listen and read you have the awful feeling that the First Ministers forgot women, forgot minorities, forgot the aboriginal peoples and never even thought about the Yukon and the Northwest Territories as coming in as provinces."[55] The final report of the committee contains an addendum outlining the recommendations of the New Democratic Party. The first two proposed amendments relate to what the NDP referred to as "fairness for Canada's Northern citizens": that a clause be included providing for territorial appointments to the bench; and that changes be made to the requirement for unanimity of the provinces to allow for the creation of new provinces. These two items had been long-standing NDP positions, and Lorne Nystrom included them in his opening comments before the committee.[56]

A third amendment related to equality rights for women. The niggling question of whether sexual equality rights as set out in section 28 of the Constitution Act, 1982, could be suppressed or superseded by the linguistic duality/distinct society interpretation clause (section 2) arose time and time again in the briefs presented by numerous women's groups. The NDP agreed that this ambiguity could be resolved if the sexual equality clause was folded into section 16 – a clause guaranteeing that neither Canada's multicultural heritage nor aboriginal rights would be affected by section 2 of the accord. This was consistent with the position taken by a number of women's groups, including the National Action Committee on the Status of Women. The NDP addendom also called for repeal of the override clause (section 33 of the Charter) because of the "potential consequences for the rights of visible minorities, who have pointed out the dangers it presents to them and to others." Finally, the NDP recommended that the process of constitutional review and change was in need of revision. Towards this end, it recommended that public hearings be held before as well as after first ministers' conferences and that links be developed with provincial legislative committees.

The Meech Lake committee hearings were a major drain on Pauline. They went on for much of August 1987, often continuing well into the evening, which meant that she had little opportunity to relax at Constant Lake. There was a tremendous volume of reading material, and Pauline was extremely conscientious about studying it. On occasion, she became irritated with some of her committee colleagues when they did not seem to be taking their work so seriously. During the presentation of Al Johnson, the former president of the Canadian Broadcasting Corporation, Robert Kaplan and Suzanne Blais-Grenier were apparently chatting. The exchange went as follows:

Ms Jewett: I am sorry to have to say this, but my concentration has been seriously impeded by the constant conversation carried on by two government members throughout the presentation of this really brilliant brief. If the government members have decided they are not going to listen to briefs any longer, then I think they should be replaced.
Mr Daubney: Oh, come on …
Ms Blais-Grenier: I am sorry if I have disturbed you, Ms Jewett. It was not my intention. We were discussing the brief, but this is not an excuse.

Mr Kaplan: I would like to register that I thought that remark by Ms Jewett was totally uncalled for. I think it is a serious deterioration of the –
Ms Jewett: Well, I am sorry, Mr Kaplan –
Mr Kaplan: – collegiality around this table.
The Acting Joint Chairman (Senator Cogger): Maybe we can leave it at that. It has been a long week, and we will adjourn shortly. We can all reflect upon it.
Ms Jewett: I rely on listening very carefully, particularly to a witness like Dr Johnson, who has enormous experience, both provincially and federally.
The Acting Joint Chairman: Thank you very –
Mr Kaplan: I am not finished, Mr Chairman.
Ms Jewett: I think I have the floor.
Mr Kaplan: I have a point of order. I simply wanted to indicate that I could hear perfectly well.[57]

LIFE IN THE NEW DEMOCRATIC PARTY

When Pauline won the election in 1979, she was a relative newcomer to NDP politics in British Columbia. She knew few party insiders and did not meet Margaret Mitchell until both had won the nomination for their respective ridings. They started to meet regularly before they left for Ottawa and a good chemistry developed, as Margaret later observed: "Being the only two women elected, we soon became pretty good friends. She always referred to us as 'pals.' That was probably the best way of describing the relationship."[58] Jim Fulton, known as the joker in the caucus, promptly assigned nicknames to the two new women. Pauline was given the nickname PJ and Margaret became Maggie. Since party discipline mitigated against the practice of sisterhood across party lines – as indeed it still does – PJ and Maggie would in any case have gravitated to each other, and in fact they often had dinner together during their years in the House.

Between sessions of Parliament, the NDP held retreats to discuss party performance and future strategies. Pauline and Margaret shared a room on many of these occasions. Always a heavy smoker and night-time drinker, Pauline was not the easiest roommate. However, the two women enjoyed many laughs, often at the expense of their male colleagues in Parliament. Margaret recalls that they took particular pleasure in ranking the honourable members on their sex appeal. Their talk sometimes lasted into the early morning hours. After consuming several drinks, Pauline would start to sing cowboy songs in her husky, gravelly voice. Her affinity for cowboy songs was noted by several friends and seems a surprising paradox for a woman who was such a connoisseur of classical music. She would start in on one of her favourites and bellow, "Can I Sleep in Your

Barn Tonight, Mister?" Things would then quieten down, and Margaret would just be drifting off to sleep when suddenly Pauline would spring up in bed and come up with the next line: "'Cause it's cold lying out on the ground." The two of them would then burst into gales of laughter. When Pauline was in one of these moods, Margaret said, you simply could not help but love her.[59]

In her second term as critic, after the 1980 election, Pauline was a very productive member of the caucus. A hard-working committee member who was aggressive and spontaneous in her questions to ministers, she was well respected by her colleagues, including those who did not share her enthusiasm for this part of a legislator's work. They admired her attention to detail and her commitment to spending hours staying on top of the voluminous reading required by committee members.

After her re-election in 1984, there was a discernible change in Pauline's behaviour. When Ed and Lucille Broadbent held gatherings for party members at their home, Pauline often made excuses not to attend. She also missed several parties hosted by members for their staffers at Christmas. This began to worry her friends, many of whom suspected that Pauline was going home to her apartment to drink. Several of her colleagues had noticed that the ever-punctual Pauline often came in late and was increasingly passive during Question Period and in debate. When questioned about her behaviour, Pauline told Margaret she drank because she was lonely.

Pauline was by no means unique in feeling lonely in Ottawa as a parliamentarian; the "loneliness factor" has been experienced by many women who have served in electoral politics. Rosemary Brown, describing her days as an MLA in British Columbia, wrote: "Much of the time in Victoria I was desperately lonely; I began eating and drinking too much."[60] Similarly Sheila Copps, reflecting on her life as an MPP in Ontario, commented: "That feeling of loneliness haunted me throughout my work in the provincial legislature, the feeling that after a particularly heated caucus debate, you can't always share a beer with the boys."[61] And Kim Campbell, at a conference in 1992, spoke of her life in Ottawa as sometimes having been "unspeakably lonely."[62] Nevertheless, it is likely that there were other factors besides loneliness that contributed to the escalation in Pauline's drinking. She may have become disillusioned with her role as critic; she may have regretted that she had not had the influence she had so desperately wanted. Or perhaps she felt that she had failed to make a difference. It is also possible that she simply was not feeling well. Likely, it was a combination of a number of factors.

Even though Pauline had been a heavy drinker for years, not all her friends believe she was an alcoholic. They claim that drinking at night was PJ's way of dealing with the stresses of a very busy life. However, there was no doubt that she had begun to drink more heavily. At one NDP meeting, a prominent party insider described her as a "lush." A reporter from British Columbia related this to some of the B.C. members, who promptly scolded the party insider; even if PJ did have a problem with alcohol, this kind of character assassination would not be tolerated. However, it was clear that Pauline could no longer conceal the fact that she had crossed the line from being a heavy social drinker to a problem drinker. Margaret and others credit Marion Dewar and reporter Marjorie Nichols for confronting Pauline and cajoling her into seeking treatment, though she did not enter a rehabilitation centre until after she retired from politics. Marjorie and Pauline became friends during the Meech Lake meetings. Marjorie herself was a recovering alcoholic, and it became her project to reform her friend. With her encouragement and through her contacts, she finally convinced Pauline of the need to stop drinking, and she arranged for her to enter the Betty Ford Centre in December 1989.

Pauline's problem with alcohol, while evident to some, rarely interfered with her parliamentary work. As noted above, she developed a well-earned reputation as a hard-working and conscientious member of the NDP caucus, though because she gave top priority to committee work, she had only limited involvement in the internal governance of the party. She apparently got on very well with the other B.C. members of caucus, including Svend Robinson. Despite their rocky beginning when contesting the Burnaby nomination, over time the two of them established a good working relationship.

THE HOME STYLE OF PAULINE JEWETT

"Home style" is a term referring to the approach a legislator develops to the management of his or her constituency. Empirical evidence suggests that Canadian voters do not believe a member's home style is as important at election time as American voters do. Nevertheless, the way in which a member fields problems for her constituents and the manner in which she performs the ombudsman's role is often very important at election time.[63] Pauline had assembled a highly effective campaign team and constituency staff. In the nine years she served as the sitting member for New Westminster–Coquitlam, she was never known to dismiss a single staffer. Her trust in her team was empowering to those who worked for her, and she received considerable satisfaction when she saw any of them take on a new role and do it well.

Dawn Black had had little personal knowledge of Pauline when she agreed to manage her campaign in the 1979 election, and in fact she was a little suspicious of this intellectual easterner. "When she first asked me to work for her, I thought how can I work for this woman, the Company of Canadians, President of SFU, a big Liberal, from the establishment clique in eastern Canada? But she had this presence about her, that's the only way I can describe it. When Pauline was in a room, you knew she was in a room. And I can remember younger women saying, I could just sit here for hours and listen to her. So I had these feelings of insecurity and awe."[64]

Over their nine-year association, Dawn and Pauline developed a strong relationship, characterized by mutual respect. "When I got to know her at a personal level," recalled Dawn, "I was surprised how easily she could relate to me. She was a woman some twenty-five years older than me, a woman who had lived an entirely different lifestyle than I had ever lived or could imagine ever living. And yet we bonded in a way that was real and all those other things that I thought about her before no longer mattered."[65] One of Dawn's favourite stories was about Pauline's campaigning. Although Pauline always worked hard at it and took direction well, she was not a natural campaigner, nor was she strong in the area of community outreach. Dawn recalled:

During the 1983 provincial election, Pauline came out to help a little in her own riding for the provincial candidate and she did some door-to-door canvassing. On election day, she appeared in the campaign office. As you can imagine, on election day things are a little frenetic with last-minute canvassing and organizing. So suddenly Pauline appeared with her handbag and her strand of pearls [her classic trademarks] and Pauline always had a presence about her – there has never been a question about that. And at this point, people were still allowed to smoke at campaign offices, and there was Pauline with her handbag and smoking a cigarette and she said, "Well dear, I'm here. What would you like me to do?" And I thought to myself, what am I going to do with her? And I thought, the seniors' residence. I'll get her out to do the seniors' residence. And I said, "Pauline, you could pull the vote[66] in the seniors' residence." And she said, "Pull the vote? What on earth does that mean?"[67]

Although Pauline had been involved in three election campaigns as a Liberal and several as a New Democrat, she was still not well acquainted with the painstakingly difficult work in the trenches associated with managing and operating a political campaign. What is endearing about this exchange is her candour in admitting that she had absolutely no idea what this well-known electioneering expression referred to. It was typical of her that she did not try to dissemble.

Another favourite "Pauline" story involved a skit during the 1984 election. Early in the campaign, her riding decided to have a mid-campaign party with various skits as entertainment. This kind of thing had been done in other NDP campaigns, and on this occasion it was decided to base the skits around the theme of an all-candidates' debate. The person playing Pauline picked up on her habit of ending a sentence with "ya know?" Pauline was in the audience of course, and later that night, recalled Dawn, "she came up to me very quietly and said, 'Dear, I need to ask you something. Do I really say "ya know" so often?' And I was honest and told her that yes, she did use the phrase quite a bit. And do you know, I never ever heard her say it again. She eliminated it totally from her speech. To me, it was the most dramatic thing."[68]

Although Pauline left the affairs of the constituency largely in the hands of her staff, there were a couple of local matters to which she gave particular attention. One case involved a young woman in Coquitlam whose parents came to see her:

Their daughter had some kind of degenerative eye disorder that, if left untreated, would lead to blindness. The only known successful treatment for this disorder was a surgical procedure, available only in Russia. This sounds bizarre, but it was true. Pauline made a number of inquiries. This family did not have enough money to fly the daughter to Russia for the surgery. This was 1983, I think. Pauline loaned the family money out of her own pocket. It was a loan, though, and Pauline had them sign an agreement undertaking to pay her back as soon as they could. There was something about this young woman and her family that touched Pauline. There was no fanfare, nothing public. It was several thousand dollars. I don't think she was ever paid back. The daughter was helped by the surgery, though.[69]

Pauline's constituency style and the way she engaged people was admired by many. The residents of New Westminster–Coquitlam are a diverse group, and many are unionized workers. Although Pauline's style in Ottawa may have been perceived as an intellectual approach to politics, her local style was very different. Dawn Black stated it best: "She had this ability to reach people. It had nothing to do with ideas, or being an intellectual or member of Parliament or any of these things. Her style was to listen to someone and engage with them. She respected people, no matter what their educational background or occupation."[70]

In 1984 and again in 1985, Ed Broadbent asked Pauline to chair a committee that travelled across Canada soliciting views from party members about the party's position on foreign affairs. This committee was to provide input to the NDP members who were subsequently appointed to the joint committee on Canada's international relations. As critic for the party, Pauline was expected to take the lead in this exercise, but she was having some minor health problems which detracted from her effectiveness. For some time, she had been suffering from arthritis in her hands, and her swollen knuckles made it painful to shake hands. The stiffness had begun to spread to her legs, and walking and climbing stairs became increasingly difficult; she was forced to miss the Peace March in Vancouver because she was too stiff to walk.

In January 1985 she took a trip to Stockholm for an interparliamentary committee meeting. When she left, she was suffering so badly from a sore throat and earache that her friends advised her not to attend. But she insisted on going, and by the time she arrived home her condition was far worse. On a trip back to her constituency she experienced such intense pain in her ear that she became panicky and demanded that the plane descend to a lower altitude. Descend it did, but the pilot and crew of the Air Canada flight were not at all pleased with this imperious passenger and advised Pauline that she would be permitted to fly with the airline again only if she could produce a medical certificate. Pauline felt sheepish when telling this story because it smacked of special treatment – something she had always disdained.

In fact, Pauline was on the brink of exhaustion. Her committee work had extended into the past two summers – a time of year she had always carefully reserved for relaxation at Constant Lake. In the spring of 1985, she began to talk to her friend Doris Anderson about retiring: "Later that same weekend I had one of the most depressing conversations I ever had with P. She said she wasn't enjoying the House of Commons anymore. She felt that she was having to take too many trips, which was hard on her health – particularly her ears which had been giving her more and more trouble, and all that spring she had a bad cough."[71]

As Pauline headed into her sixty-fifth year, she was beginning to feel a sense of weariness. It was highly unusual for such an upbeat person to be so downcast, and her friends began to worry about her. Meanwhile, Pauline herself was worrying where she would live. She had grown attached to her apartment in Burnaby but was undecided about retiring there. She had lost touch with many of her former colleagues from Carleton and was not sure if she wanted to return to Ottawa. According to Doris Anderson, she did not enjoy Toronto and would not consider living there either. She perked up a little by the summer, but by spring 1986 she again seemed quite unlike her usual buoyant self. Doris recalled: "When I visited her in the spring, during Expo in 1986 she seemed quite tired and without much energy. On May 24th, we attended a commemorative ceremony in her riding called the 'Anvil Battery' – part of the New Westminster Hyack Festival. I was surprised at how passive and quiet she seemed. She wasn't greeting people, shaking hands, etc. and when she was recognized during the ceremony, I thought she looked almost apologetic standing there in her raincoat, not even waving at the public. I was shocked to see her so subdued – and not her usual exuberant, outgoing self."[72]

In December 1987, Doris and Norm Fenn hosted a party for Pauline at the Park Lane Hotel in Ottawa in celebration of her sixty-fifth birthday. Afterwards, there was a sing-song at Pauline's flat. This party was an eye opener for Pauline – none of her Constant Lake friends were getting any younger. At the time, Pauline had a very sore hip, Norm was waiting for bypass surgery, Rusty Wendt had suffered a heart attack, and the whole crowd were comparing their aches and pains.[73]

Pauline treated herself to a Jaguar in celebration of her sixty-fifth year. This was quite a departure for someone who has been described as frugal for most of her life. Although she was spending more money on clothes than she used to, she recycled many of her dresses for years and was notorious for her antiquated pots and pans and other kitchen appliances. At the age of sixty-five, she began to receive some pension income and was accumulating quite a considerable sum of money. Pauline had always had an accountant in Ottawa because she was not particularly astute when it came to financial management. Except for the cottage, she did not own any property or have any major assets. When she got to the point of retiring, she decided to give each of her nephews and her niece a considerable sum of money. Bob Jewett expressed an interest in her cottage, and her accountant strongly encouraged Pauline to buy something meaningful for herself. Margaret Mitchell tells the story of what happened next:

Pauline said that she didn't really need anything. Once again, he [the accountant] asked her, is there not one thing that you would *really* like? And she thought about it and finally said, "I would like a Jaguar." And he said, "You have got to get yourself a Jaguar." So he really talked her into it. So she got the Jag. We were never even allowed to look at it for some months. She kept it under guard. So we would tease her and call her the Jaguar Socialist all the time. It was a joke with her NDP friends. She kept it covered because she was afraid it would get scratched.[74]

Pauline's hardiness, which had sustained her through many stressful and demanding times, seemed to be under siege. Finding time to relax had been difficult. It was time to gear down and try and regain her health. She decided that she would not run in 1988. The party held a retirement party for Pauline and her colleague Jim Manley, who also was retiring, at a restaurant in downtown Ottawa. Apparently, there were many laughs, a few cowboy songs from Pauline, and many reminiscences, including the unofficial Mitchell-Jewett sex-appeal survey of Canada's male parliamentarians.

Although Pauline was still reasonably young at the age of sixty-five, she had sensed that it was time to leave politics and give someone who had more energy a chance. The frequent cross-country travel back to her constituency had become a real ordeal, particularly after the airlines banned smoking. (Pauline was apparently outraged by this decision.) Also, there had been a realignment in electoral boundaries, and her riding had been renamed New Westminster–Burnaby. She encouraged her long-time constituency assistant Dawn Black to pursue the nomination for the NDP. Dawn had gained the political experience through years of service to the party, her sons were launched, and she was well acquainted with the constituency. She won the riding by a plurality of almost 7,000 votes in the 1988 election.

After the poor showing by the NDP in the 1988 election and the growing criticism that Ed Broadbent had mismanaged the campaign, there was widespread speculation that he would be stepping down as leader. Had this occurred four or five years earlier, there is little doubt that Pauline would have given serious consideration to contesting the leadership. Both Margaret and Dawn believe she would have been a very strong leader. Although Pauline was tempted by the idea, she simply did not have the energy to mount a bid for the leadership. However, as the party member who had been responsible for seeking out women candidates, she believed it was imperative to have a woman contest the leadership, especially as the NDP had long championed the principles of equality and gender parity in the party.

Furthermore, PJ believed that the time was right for a woman to be in a position of national leadership. The only question was which woman. Margaret Mitchell was not interested, and Marion Dewar had lost her seat and insisted that the woman who pursued the leadership had to be a sitting member of Parliament. Thus, Pauline, Marion Dewar, and Margaret Mitchell, among others, threw their support and all the networking and resources they could muster behind the new MP from the Yukon, Audrey McLaughlin. In the end, she emerged as the winner in a hard-fought and somewhat bitter leadership convention, with Dave Barrett finishing a close second.

Try as Pauline might, she could not get the political bug out of her system, and she put her name forward as a candidate for the presidency of the New Democratic Party. In her eagerness for the position, she failed to read the political landscape correctly. No one had encouraged her to run; in fact, most of her friends and colleagues thought it a mistake. Her home base of British Columbia had been badly divided by the leadership contest between Audrey McLaughlin and the native son Dave Barrett, and by coming out so aggressively for Audrey, Pauline had alienated many B.C. members. Moreover, her strong support of the Meech Lake Accord had led to considerable criticism by women's organizations across the country. Lacking the support of her own provincial caucus and women's groups, it is remarkable that Pauline thought she could win the presidency. At times, her supreme confidence in her own abilities was certainly not tempered by good political judgment.

Behind the scenes, those closest to Pauline were quietly trying to discourage her from entering the contest, but to no effect. The election for president was held the day after the leadership convention, and Pauline was ready for the fray – but her colleague Jim Fulton, who was supposed to be nominating her, did not show up or even call. He was still angry about Pauline's lack of support for Dave Barrett. Even though PJ knew by this time she would not win, she was astounded by Fulton's personal betrayal. It was an indication of the anger felt by many of the men in the NDP who had supported Barrett. Sandra Mitchell, a long-time member of the federal council of the NDP, won the election by a considerable margin. Publicly, Pauline claimed she was motivated to re-enter politics because "Canada is currently going through a critical moment in its history,"[75] but in fact she was at a loose end with too much time on her hands. It was unfortunate that Pauline's departure from active political life was so negative, though in many respects it typifies the spontaneity that was such a feature of her character.

Pauline's retirement from public life did not last long. During the winter of 1989, she was asked to assume the chancellorship of Carleton University. She felt very honoured and relished the thought of returning to the institution for which she had so much loyalty and passion. There was a certain symmetry to taking on this new position. She had come full circle. The one university in Canada that had given her a chance to teach was calling on her again, and on 30 June 1990 she was installed as chancellor. Although the role is largely symbolic and ceremonial, Pauline took the position very seriously. She went in regularly to an office at Carleton and was well informed about the state of affairs at the university. Clearly, her interest in the university transcended a superficial involvement in the convocation exercises. Typically, she wanted to be a "hands-on" chancellor who would leave an indelible mark on the university. Unfortunately, she was to have less time than she anticipated to tackle this new mission, for her health was seriously deteriorating. She was suffering from cancer.

· 8 ·

Lovers, Mentors, Friends, and Relations

Gertrude Robinson and Armande Saint-Jean have claimed that the first modern generation of women politicians, which included Pauline, Judy LaMarsh, and Flora MacDonald, were subject to certain media stereotypes relating to their marital status and personal lives. According to these "typologies," they were spinsters, women of easy virtue, or club women.[1] Women garnering the spinster label were "portrayed as serious, preachy, competent and hard-working because they [lacked] household responsibilities."[2] This was the manner in which Pauline was frequently portrayed in the media. Indeed, she was often placed in the position of having to explain her single status, especially early in her political career. The truth of the matter is that Pauline did not fall into any of these traditional stereotypes.

Pauline could be an intimidating force. She had strong opinions and, on occasion, was intolerant of those who held divergent views. Some of her contemporaries in Parliament believed that she was not always a good team player because of these qualities. As has often been observed in this biography, Pauline had a presence that commanded attention, and, she could be tough and aggressive in dealing with other people. She certainly had her detractors, though she was generally well liked by both men and women. Self-confidence in her abilities, a strong grasp of political issues, and many diverse life experiences added to her appeal. Douglas Fisher, a newspaper columnist and former MP, told the following story about Pauline in an interview in 1974, when attempting to dispel the spinster myth surrounding women in Parliament: "One night after a meeting in Toronto that ran late, we found ourselves together at the Westbury Hotel trying to get rooms for the night. There was only one room left so I said I would park for the night in the lobby. Pauline said, 'The hell you will. You'll use one bed and I'll use the other.' And that's what we did. I gave her time to get to bed and in the morning she was showered and dressed when I woke up. She's no prude."[3]

Most of Pauline's working life had been spent in "a man's world," and many of her interests reflected this – her interest in politics, her love of sports, and her passion for cars. Her exposure to the world of men in academia and Parliament could not help but extend to the way she conducted herself, both in her private and public life. When provoked, she could be abrupt and demanding, as the Air Canada episode revealed, yet she had a passionate side to her character and enjoyed a number of significant love affairs with men and some intense nonsexual friendships with women.

LOVE AND ROMANCE

Whether or not Pauline ever seriously contemplated a traditional role as wife and mother is questionable. Few of her acquaintances could visualize her as a housewife in the traditional sense. In an interview with Charlotte Gobeil, Pauline stated that by the time she was in her late thirties, she recognized that only an "exceptional guy" would have the courage to marry her.[4] Although she often talked about adopting older children from the developing world, most of her friends thought this was wishful musing rather than a serious intention. There is no question that Pauline relished spending time with young people, but given her ambitions and her lifestyle, it is hard to imagine that she harboured a fervent desire to be a mother. Many men found Pauline attractive, and it is likely that if she had truly wanted to pursue a traditional lifestyle, she would have done so.

However, Pauline's ambition to pursue a different course in life should not be construed as indifference to or a lack of interest in men. In truth, she was very emancipated in her views about men and sexuality. Pauline had been socialized in a traditional home, where her mother performed the conventional roles of homemaker and supportive spouse. Moreover, her mother had been brought up with Victorian views about morality and sex. This home environment with its social and moral norms must have been a strong influence on Pauline during her teenage years. But after she left home at the age of seventeen, she never returned to her home environment for any lengthy period. Meanwhile, as a university student at Queen's and Harvard, she was exposed to alternative lifestyles that were far less conventional. By her own admission, she loved to dance and party and was a free spirit. She basked in the erotic writings of D.H. Lawrence and clearly went through a period of personal introspection, questioning the old-fashioned social and sexual conventions espoused by her parents and many other women of her generation.

As a result of this self-analysis, Pauline's views on love, romance, and sexual pleasure were relatively emancipated. Her first love affair was with a fellow student at Harvard who turned out to be a rogue. Other sexual liaisons followed. A certain lustiness – and her surprising candour in talking about it – initially came as a shocking revelation to many of her friends. At the same time, this spirited and passionate side of Pauline was a quality that many of her friends and acquaintances found engaging. The rebelliousness she had demonstrated in her philosophical and intellectual thinking as a young woman growing up in the 1930s and 1940s was evidently matched by a certain defiance of the dominant sexual mores in the 1950s and 1960s. In certain respects, Pauline lived a bohemian lifestyle long before a generation of young people popularized it in the late 1960s and 1970s. It seemed such a paradox to the staid and rather sexually neutral image she projected.

Pauline had one passionate and enduring love affair, which lasted for many years. There is little question that this man was the love of her life. She also enjoyed other relationships. But it is important to recognize that Pauline was not searching for a husband or long-term partner in these liaisons. She was seeking companionship and pleasure, often in the arms of dynamic and influential personalities. It is not difficult to understand why men found Pauline attractive. She was intellectually curious, passionate in her views, and fiercely independent. Witty and confident, she was a wonderful conversationalist and fun to be with. She had many interests, including classical music and art, in which she was very knowledgeable. And despite having a lifelong insecurity about her appearance, Pauline matured into a striking-looking woman with a slim figure.

Although Pauline was a heavy smoker, she took reasonably good care of herself and routinely exercised; she was a strong and powerful swimmer, and regularly enjoyed swimming at her cottage. By the time she was in her late thirties her brown hair which she characteristically brushed back, had begun to turn a salt and pepper colour, giving her a distinguished look. As she became older, she began to pay closer attention to her clothes and to choose fashionable eyewear. (One CBC reporter went so far as to say that there was a certain majesty about Pauline Jewett and the way she carried herself.) It is clear that Pauline was not indifferent to the idea that the woman within her needed nurturing. Equally clear is the fact that she constantly needed reassurance about her femininity. Despite her crusty, aggressive exterior – and whispers about her sexual orientation – Pauline most certainly had a passionate side, but she tried not to reveal it because of her status as a public figure.

MENTORS

The life of Pauline Jewett provides a rich illustration of the role of mentoring in the occupational and intellectual evolution of an individual. As an undergraduate, she was encouraged by Jean Royce, the registrar at Queen's University, and by Alice Vibert Douglas, the dean of women. Without their encouragement, Pauline would probably not have pursued graduate studies. Other mentors, including Alec Corry, had an important role in prodding her to complete her doctoral work. Several disappointments, including the termination of her position at Queen's and her frustration in gaining a permanent teaching position, eroded her confidence, but Muriel Uprichard saw great promise in her "student" at the Canadian Nurses' Association and provided considerable direction in helping PJ complete her report on the restructuring of the CNA. Having been the beneficiary of these mentors, Pauline recognized the importance of such relationships and in turn became an influential person in the lives of many young people and younger women politicians.

There is little doubt that the person who most strongly influenced Pauline's view of the world was her Carleton colleague and cottage neighbour, John Porter. Wallace Clement, a former student and colleague at Carleton, described Porter as "Canada's premier sociologist."[5] Unlike Pauline, John Porter grew up in a family ravaged by the Depression. He was born in Vancouver, but his British-born parents took the family back to England when Porter was fifteen. He did not complete his high school education and had several odd jobs until he found work as a journalist for the London *Daily Sketch*.[6] His career was interrupted by the Second World War, during which he joined the Canadian Army. After his discharge, Porter took advantage of the education benefit for veterans and entered the London School of Economics (LSE). The ideological culture at the LSE had a profound influence on his thinking. According to Frank Vallee, "LSE was dominated by a spirit of optimism about the chances of reconstructing a world that was badly out of joint. Social democracy was the prevailing ideology, a kind of socialism without revolution which had been advocated by two generations of Fabian scholars and writers."[7]

Porter returned to Canada in 1949 and began teaching at Carleton in September of that year. Those who knew him and studied under him claim that his academic career had two distinct phases. In the first phase, his key research interests were the themes of power and class, which culminated in his greatest publication, *The Vertical Mosaic* (1965), a work that was accepted as his DSC thesis at the London School of Economics.[8] Dennis Forcese said of this book, "It was angry; it was attention getting; it was consciousness raising."[9] Later in his career, Porter conducted research on the subjects of education, occupational mobility, and ethnicity.[10] He saw education as an important means through which inequalities in society could be ameliorated.

When Porter began his work on class and inequality in Canada, "there was virtually no strong 'leftist' or 'Marxist' tradition in Canada, although there was a social democratic tradition in which Porter felt at home."[11] Porter rejected Marxism because it saw power only in economic terms; for Porter, power also existed in bureaucratic, social, and political structures. His views on class were nearer to Weber's ideal; he believed that classes could be defined according "to the 'objective' criteria of income, education, and occupation."[12] Although Porter has often been labelled a neo-Marxist, this was not the case. It was British socialism he embraced, not Marxism.

The great strength of Porter's work was its scope. It went beyond criticism of Canadian society and offered a prescription for change. Porter truly believed that his work had the potential to make Canadian society more just. Yet he was not naive. He understood "the inherent frustration, if not futility, in seeking an egalitarian society, and therefore devoted himself not to revolutionary panacea, but to manageable intervention and change."[13] For him, the expansion of educational opportunities held the promise for a new egalitarianism. Claims by others that education tended to institutionalize inequality led him to question these prescriptions at the end of his career, though he continued to believe in the importance of equal educational opportunity for all.

There is little question that Porter's view of the world influenced Pauline. She too believed in equality of opportunity in education, and it was partly this belief that drove her to seek a position as a university president. However, there were significant points of difference in their political beliefs. Pauline embraced the idea of a cultural mosaic and strongly supported Quebec's position to be recognized as a distinct society. Her support of the Meech Lake Accord is reflective of this view. More importantly, she was an ardent

Canadian nationalist. Porter, on the other hand, had a deep respect for American society and has been described as a proponent of assimilation. He preferred the American melting-pot vision to the mosaic view held by most Canadian political parties. To Porter, "ethnicity was ... primordial, a throw-back, a challenge to rationalism, moral progress, liberalism. Public educational institutions were the means to assimilation and to social mobility for ethnically stratified Canadians."[14] As support for his position, he pointed to the proportionately higher percentage of Americans who were university educated. Porter credited the massive American education system and the dominance of liberal ideology for its superior performance.[15] He was ambivalent about Canadian nationalism, which must have been a serious point of contention with Pauline. In part, this ambivalence can be explained by his detachment from Canada as a teenager and as a young man living in Britain.

In 1963 John Porter suffered a massive coronary while attending the Congress of Learned Societies meetings in Calgary. According to his daughter, this attack was so serious that there was grave concern he would not survive. Marion, his wife, was summoned from Ottawa and stayed out west for a month until he was well enough to return home.[16] Immediately, he stopped smoking and began to walk as a way to exercise. Over time, he recovered and was well enough to travel abroad, accepting the position as a Canadian fellow in the International Institute for Labour Studies in Geneva (1966–67),[17] but he had a second heart attack seven years later. In the mid-1970s, both John Porter and Pauline began to pursue a life away from Carleton. Porter became the Canadian chair at Harvard (1974–75) and spent a sabbatical year in Paris (1975–76). Pauline, of course, went out west in 1974 to accept the president's position at Simon Fraser University. Although they continued to stay in touch at the lake during the summer months, they saw each other far less from the mid-1970s onwards.

The week before John died, the Porters visited Pauline in Vancouver by way of the University of Saskatchewan, where the 1979 Learned Societies meetings were held. After taking a long walk on a Saturday afternoon with his daughter Anne, who had rented a cabin north of Vancouver, John was exhausted and felt decidedly unwell. He and Marion returned home to Ottawa on 15 June 1979, and John succumbed to a final heart attack during the night at the age of fifty-eight. Living in Vancouver at the time, Anne Porter was notified of her father's death in an early morning telephone call. The first person she called was Pauline. Pauline was devastated. She flew back to Ottawa a short time later and gave one of the eulogies at a memorial service. People recall that she was so emotional that there was some concern she would be unable to complete her tribute. Pauline had lost not just a friend and colleague but her intellectual mentor. It was a crushing blow.

Pauline had an eclectic circle of friends – political colleagues, academics, feminists, and journalists. As time marched on, she lost some of those closest to her by untimely deaths. However, in talking to those who remain, I have the sense that Pauline was generally positive and energetic in her approach to life. Her great passions were debating political issues, both domestic and international. Throughout her life and in various chapters of it, different friends played different roles. Although Pauline enjoyed the friendship of both men and women, it was her relationships with other women that sustained her in the latter part of her life.

The Associates

In her early days at Carleton and throughout most of her adult life, the Constan Associates were, in almost every respect, Pauline's "family." In the early days, there were nightly bonfires at Constant Lake, and after the children had been tucked into bed there were nightly get-togethers over drinks. Originally, the associates were both Pauline's intellectual mentors and her colleagues. As noted above, John Porter and his views on Canadian society profoundly influenced her personal dogma. The unique intellectual intimacy they shared was an enduring cornerstone for Pauline. She had always sided with the underdog, and Porter's work and his philosophy of life lent an intellectual impetus to her altruistic inclinations. Like Porter, other associates, including Marion Porter and May Beattie, are now deceased, but not all of them are. One of Pauline's last functions as chancellor of Carleton University was to confer an honorary degree on her old friend and Constan Associate, Norm Fenn. Norm proudly showed me a picture commemorating this event. By then, Pauline knew that her days were numbered, yet the smiles they exchanged mirrored the love and devotion which these two shared. Norm had a difficult time trying to explain the exact nature of their friendship:

It's hard to describe. The relationship was always there. I always felt that we were significant to each other. There was never any doubt in my mind on that score. In terms of our being together, it seemed to depend on circumstance more than anything else. When she came back to Carleton to be chancellor, I suppose our relationship returned to what it was in the old days ... She was a very important part of my life. And much of my desire to be at the cottage has decreased since her death. My cottage life and Pauline were one and the same. I don't feel the same desire to spend time at the cottage. I haven't spent a night at the cottage since her death.[18]

Doris Anderson

A very significant friendship in Pauline's life was the one she shared with Doris Anderson, former editor of *Chatelaine*, women's activist, and author of several books. Unlike her friendship with Marjorie Nichols, which developed late and was predicated on their mutual passion for politics, the relationship between PJ and Doris had much deeper foundations. Both women were the same age and thus shared the bond of history. Both had been career pioneers in male-dominated spheres. Although Doris had initially chosen a conventional home life that included marriage and children, she was divorced and an "empty nester" by the time their friendship developed. The two women did not become close friends until the early 1980s, though they had been aware of each other for years. Doris had known of Pauline and her candidacy for the nomination in Northumberland in the early 1960s. She admired Pauline's courage in taking on "the backroom boys" in competing for the nomination. In her autobiography, *Rebel Daughter*, she wrote:

Occasionally the best-laid plans of the male members of the party went astray. One evening in 1962, David [her then husband] told me he was on his way to Northumberland riding in eastern Ontario for a nomination meeting. "There's a young professor from Carleton University running," he said. "She's a great candidate, but she'll never win in a riding full of farmers. We're backing a local man who'll have a much better chance." I remember arguing with him about the heavyweights in the party ganging up on a woman. That night the professor, Pauline Jewett, won.[19]

As Doris recalled, she and Pauline "officially" met for the first time at a party hosted by Bernard and Sylvia Ostry in the mid-1960s. After that, they often ran across each other at various functions. Doris has indicated that it is likely they would have become friends earlier had geography not been a factor. Doris's life was centred in Toronto, while Pauline's was in Ottawa and Vancouver. Like Pauline, Doris was a candidate in the 1979 election; she ran as a Liberal in the

Eglinton riding in midtown Toronto. However, she failed to win the seat, as did most Liberals in the Metropolitan Toronto area. The next year she was appointed president of the Advisory Council on the Status of Women and moved to Ottawa. Pauline had been away from Ottawa for a long time and was no longer part of any particular social circle. Similarly, Doris, who by then was single, did not know many people in Ottawa, since most of her career had revolved around literary circles in the Toronto area. Their social paths crossed frequently, and a deep and lasting friendship developed.

Between 1980 and 1982, Pauline and Doris met at least twice a week, often for dinner. Both were strong-willed intelligent women who had firm opinions about politics and life in general. I asked Doris what drew them to each other, and she suggested that their mutual concern about social justice formed the basis of their friendship. But they had much else in common. Doris would blow off steam about the advisory council, and Pauline would blow off steam about Parliament. "Oftentimes, our beefs would fly past each other, but somehow we both felt better," Doris commented. After she resigned in 1981, she moved back to Toronto, but over the next ten years Doris was a regular guest at Pauline's cottage on Constant Lake, and when Pauline travelled to Toronto she usually stayed with Doris. As well, they talked frequently on the telephone. For several winters they spent a week's holiday together in February – at a Florida spa or a resort in Mexico, or in Barbados. Doris claimed that Pauline was always reluctant to go sight-seeing or shopping on these occasions, but once involved in any of these expeditions, she became the life of the party. It was generally Doris who suggested these holidays, because of her concern that Pauline drove herself too hard:

What I admired so much about her was the fact that she was so principled without being either cynical or naive. I could never get over how much energy and time she was willing to put into her parliamentary committee work. When Mulroney was in power, she spent most of two different summers toiling away on a committee report. Since she was always outnumbered heavily by Conservatives on the committee, I would shake my head at her efforts. Pauline would toil over each clause and phrase to make the report as good as possible – usually with a lot of opposition from her Conservative colleagues. When she felt particularly frustrated, I used to urge her not to work so hard, and, if necessary, bring out a sizzling minority report of her own. But she never did.[20]

For her part, Pauline enjoyed Doris's enthusiasm for life and her spirit of adventure, and she respected her friend's dedication to the

Canadian women's movement. Like Pauline, Doris had been a trail-blazer for younger women. The field of journalism was every bit as much a men's locker room as Parliament was. Not only had Doris made it as a journalist, but she had gone against the current and had a family as well. Indeed, she was one of the early superwomen who proved that women could combine a rewarding career with a family.

An essential bond linking these women together was their shared history as young, bright, ambitious women attending university in the 1940s and choosing careers that were largely untraditional for the time. Their interest in politics was another shared concern, though they did not always espouse the same view. They clashed keenly over the Meech Lake Accord. As discussed earlier, Pauline believed that Meech Lake was a compromise necessary for national unity, while Doris argued that some of its provisions – notably, the distinct society clause – threatened the sexual equality rights that were enumerated in section 15 of the Charter of Rights and Freedoms. Doris was also a strong advocate of scrapping the single-member plurality electoral system in Canada and replacing it with proportional representation. Pauline was not convinced that proportional representation was a less flawed system; she believed that it would spawn more political parties and thus be even more divisive to a country already divided along regional and linguistic lines.

Despite having opposing views on some political matters, each woman respected the other's stance. There were never any bitter schisms between them. During Pauline's illness, Doris was often in Ottawa keeping her friend company and attending to her needs. Pauline's sister Catharine told me that Pauline's eyes would brighten at the sight of Doris. During the last ten days of Pauline's life, when she was hospitalized at the Elizabeth Bruyère Centre, Doris returned to Ottawa. She was one of the three principal caregivers who stayed with Pauline in her final days and was with her when she died. In a column Doris wrote about her good friend several weeks after Pauline's death, she said, "She fought for everything she believed in. She wouldn't brook sloppy thinking or offhand arguments. No one could nail me faster than she could when she disagreed with me. I guess that's one reason I valued her so much as a friend. Her final fight against cancer was the one she fought the hardest."[21]

Marjorie Nichols

Marjorie Nichols was a highly respected political journalist for the *Vancouver Sun* and *Ottawa Citizen*. Although the friendship she and

Pauline enjoyed was relatively brief, lasting only five years, it was an intense and close relationship. There were those who believed that Marjorie was without equal at her job and that she wielded tremendous influence in the newsrooms where she worked. In an article written in *Western Living*, she and Pauline were described as "Thelma and Louise," though they referred to themselves as the "Cancer Kids." Many of Pauline's friends could not quite understand the dynamics of this relationship. Pauline was usually so tactful, controlled, and polite; Marjorie could be abrasive and downright rude. It was not unusual for Marjorie to hang up the phone in a fit of anger. She did so to Pauline on a number of occasions. To say the least, she was a highly volatile woman.

Pauline was in her sixties, and Marjorie was in her forties, so a bond of history and shared experiences did not form the basis of their friendship. Although both women were single and without children, their lives appeared to have few other parallels. Marjorie's had been filled with late-night parties and drunken binges. Allan Fotheringham, a long-time friend, said, "She wasn't an alcoholic, she was a lonely-holic." But as Jane O'Hara noted, "It's a nice turn of phrase, but he was wrong: she was both."[22] Marjorie had long battled alcoholism but had gone clean and sober in 1982, long before she and Pauline became friends. They were even at opposite ends of the spectrum ideologically, Pauline being left wing and Marjorie right wing. So what was the attraction?

Both women were totally obsessed with politics. Although Marjorie was a journalist by profession, her passion was politics, though she was very grudging in her respect for politicians and Parliament. Marjorie had been in and out of Ottawa on several occasions but moved back in the fall of 1987 to be the parliamentary correspondent for the *Vancouver Sun* and the *Province*. Marjorie's first position on the Meech Lake Accord had been that it was a bad deal for Canada and a bad deal for Canadian women. However, after attending all the sessions on the accord, she began to have a change of heart – a change largely inspired by an articulate, well-spoken woman member of the NDP, Pauline Jewett. Marjorie thought Pauline's defence of the accord put the deal in a totally new context, and over time she began to change her views. At the end, much to the criticism of her journalistic colleagues, she wrote in favour of the accord. Some journalists even accused Marjorie of having fallen to the Irish charm of Brian Mulroney. PJ argued that this simply wasn't true: "She changed her mind on Meech well before she got sick ... I know because I was one of the people who persuaded her it was a pretty good deal. Marjorie came to all the hearings when there was hardly another news person there. She was dedicated to finding out about it. She was curious. We had the experience of talking about Meech constantly for a couple of months and she changed her mind just after the summer of '87. Mulroney hardly knew her then. She barely knew him."[23]

Pauline saw Marjorie as one of the few journalists who was conscientious enough to make the effort to attend the committee hearings on the accord and to take partisanship out of the debate. She respected Marjorie's professionalism. From that time forward, Marjorie and Pauline enjoyed a great friendship. They dined together, went shopping together, and even drove across Canada together. Marjorie often came to Constant Lake for the day but rarely stayed over. Unbeknownst to them both, their lives would take on an eerie parallel. In February 1988, Marjorie was diagnosed with inoperable extensive small-cell lung cancer, which had already spread to her liver and lymph glands.

The doctors did not recommend chemotherapy, essentially saying that the cancer was terminal and nothing could be done. Marjorie credited the determination of her friend Pamela Wallin for pushing her to seek treatment. She was administered an experimental combination of three chemotherapies, during which time she was kept company by her three P's as she called them – Pamela Wallin, Pauline, and Peter Cowan, a long-time friend who at the time was special assistant to Constitutional Affairs Minister Joe Clark. For three weeks, this eclectic group performed round-the-clock nursing duties while Marjorie was in Ottawa General Hospital.[24] "I wasn't always easy to handle," Marjorie wrote in her memoirs. "One time in my treatment, I remember Pauline coming with me when I was to be admitted to hospital. I had asked for a private room, but when we got there, there was no private room. I said I wasn't going to check in. So Pauline and I had this absolute battle sitting in the waiting room. Pauline said to me, 'Just be bloody glad you're not in Mozambique.' I replied, 'I am not in Mozambique and I don't give a shit. I am going to have a private room.'"[25]

Pauline described her friendship with Marjorie as an odd one: "To be quite honest, I was worried she was becoming too dependent on me, that I was becoming almost indispensable to her. Some of my friends were worried she was eating me up. She was phoning me constantly, but no one person could take the brunt of both her cancer and her writing."[26] Certainly, Marjorie was extremely possessive of Pauline's time during the days of her illness, and the friendship was very important to her. In the preface of her book *Mark My Words*, Jane O'Hara paid the following tribute to PJ: "Pauline Jewett, whom Marjorie admired as one of this country's finest intellects, cared for and cajoled her friend in a way that nobody else could."[27]

In many respects, the common bond uniting Pauline and Marjorie was cancer. They were of tremendous support to each other, and both were optimistic they could beat the disease. In the fall of 1989, Marjorie decided to buy a house in Ottawa but had only enough money for a small down payment. To help her, Pauline put $60,000 into the house, and they struck what a friend described as a "macabre arrangement": the first one to die would leave the house to the other. Marjorie strongly believed that Pauline's chances of surviving the cancer were compromised by her heavy nighttime drinking. Like Marjorie, Pauline was perhaps a "lonely-holic." No doubt, Pauline was worried that news of her admission to the program at the Betty Ford Centre might tarnish her reputation. Moreover, the treatment program had a price tag of $10,000. Given Pauline's well-known frugality, her agreement to admit herself was quite a statement.

By all accounts, Pauline made the best of her time at the centre. She enjoyed the group seminars and even made the men's volleyball team – an accomplishment she later boasted about. Meanwhile, she stayed in telephone contact with members of her group, many of whom were from the Vancouver area. Doris Anderson recalls PJ phoning her from the clinic in January 1990 with a lot of questions about how Doris thought Pauline handled anger, her attitude to her siblings, and similar issues. Clearly, group therapy at the clinic encouraged Pauline to enter into a period of personal introspection. The fact that she did so with enthusiasm reflects a vital facet of her character and her optimistic and energetic approach to life.

Despite the fact that Pauline was not convinced she was an alcoholic, she never drank again. Her friend Lyn Grey recalled Pauline's first encounter with Alcoholics Anonymous in Vancouver. Lyn was visiting Pauline, and PJ wanted her company for moral support at a meeting on East Hastings Street, since she was somewhat nervous about going alone. (By way of backgound, the East Hastings neighbourhood in Vancouver is typically described as the lowest per capita income area in the country.) It was not Pauline's egalitarianism that motivated her to choose a meeting in this neighbourhood; it was simply the one closest to her apartment. Pauline and Lyn arrived there in Pauline's Jaguar, and as they quietly walked towards the building they could see through the window a dingy room occupied by a few elderly men (who could best be described as looking pretty down on their luck) and a young facilitator. Pauline and Lyn looked at each other and ran for the Jag – but the facilitator saw them and gestured to them to join the group. Thoroughly embarrassed, they took off and laughed all the way home.[28] However, Pauline eventually became active in an AA group in North Vancouver.

Marjorie succumbed to cancer on 29 December 1991. By then, Pauline had been diagnosed with her second site – cancer of the ascending colon – which would eventually prove fatal. Marjorie's death was an enormous blow to Pauline because they had been able to give each other such comfort during these dark days. Pauline was too upset to attend Marjorie's funeral in Alberta or even the memorial service in Ottawa. The disease they both shared had taken her good friend and now her own health was quickly failing.

The "Sisters" in the NDP

When Pauline was first elected as an NDP member in 1979, she was one of two NDP women in the House of Commons. Two general elections and two by-elections later, the group had expanded to five: Pauline, Margaret Mitchell, Lynn McDonald, Marion Dewar, and Audrey McLaughlin. According to Audrey, Pauline used to joke, "When women can fill up a table in the parliamentary dining room, that's when the men will really start to worry!"[29] Although Pauline was only to be in caucus with Audrey for one year, they had great respect for each other. When Ed Broadbent stepped down as party leader in 1988, Pauline supported Audrey's candidacy because of "her understanding about the whole of Canada, her concern about world issues, her concern for Third World issues" and because she was "a strong New Democrat ... a caring person who wants to bring people into the party in a very meaningful way."[30] At the time, Pauline sounded a little wistful that she had never had the opportunity to serve as leader. In an interview she stated, "At one time, I thought it would be terrific to be leader of the party. It's sad in a way that I didn't get the chance to try for that. But then, I've had such a terrific go at politics."[31]

Marion Dewar and Pauline met for the first time in 1972 when Pauline was running for office in Ottawa West. Marion worked as a volunteer on Pauline's campaign and organized a number of coffee parties in the riding. This was Marion's introduction to the world of federal party politics. She went on to serve as a controller for the City of Ottawa and later as its mayor. In addition, she won a by-election for the NDP in the Hamilton area in 1987 but lost the seat months later in the 1988 general election. Of her first acquaintance with Pauline she said, "In many ways she was my role model and mentor. Her thinking about what women should do and could do was very much an inspiration. I remember thinking 'Now here is Dr Jewett talking to little old me, mostly suburban housewife, asking me what I think.' It was extremely empowering."[32] Audrey McLaughlin believes that Pauline's greatest role in the party was to promote the candidacies of other women. Despite her prestigious appointments, Pauline did not play the queen bee,[33] disregarding the abilities of others. Dawn Black said much the same thing about Pauline: "This country is full of women like me she encouraged. She somehow empowered people. She had this gift to make people believe in themselves."[34]

Family

Pauline used Constant Lake as the venue to ensure that the Jewetts stayed in touch. Her brother Fred, his wife Eleanor, and their two sons usually came to the guest cottage at Constant Lake for two weeks each summer. Although Fred was seven years Pauline's senior, the two enjoyed a good relationship. Like most people in the banking industry, Fred had never been a supporter of the NDP, but politics was probably not a topic of conversation during these visits. Both Pauline and her brother were great students of Canadian history, were avid readers, and enjoyed talking about family genealogy and finances and investments.

Although Fred made a comfortable living as a bank employee, there was not always money for extras. On several occasions, Pauline gave unsolicited gifts of money to family members. Fred describes her as being very generous – he recalled the time she gave him five hundred dollars to buy a television set. Her nephew Robert S. Jewett said that Pauline received considerable pleasure from presenting cash gifts to friends and family. During the 1980s, she gave sizable cash gifts to her family at Christmas. Elizabeth Moore, who is currently a PH D candidate in political science at the University of Toronto, also had a story about Pauline's generosity:

In 1985, I served as a page in the House of Commons. Being a resident of New Westminster–Coquitlam, I introduced myself to Pauline and had several conversations with her. She always was curious as to how my studies at Carleton were going and seemed genuinely interested in what I had to say. She treated me as an equal, which was inspiring to me as a young woman, coming from someone so accomplished. I also did some volunteer work in her office on several occasions. On my last day, she gave me an envelope and wished me well with my future studies. I thought maybe the envelope might contain one hundred dollars. To my surprise and amazement, there was a cheque for one thousand dollars inside. I remember feeling quite overwhelmed by her generosity.[35]

Pauline and her sister Catharine also enjoyed a good relationship, though it was best if they avoided talking about politics. Catharine's husband was a physicist at the Chalk River branch of Atomic Energy of Canada, and his views about the value of nuclear energy were very different from Pauline's. Although Pauline was fond of her brother-in-law, she was never one to defer to his position on the nuclear issue, nor he to her. Pauline's activism in the women's movement was also occasionally a source of tension with the Kushneriuks. Catharine had spent her adult life as a wife, mother, and homemaker, and in her view, feminists had been overly dismissive of women like herself. However, the two never battled about such things. It was a conscious decision not to engage in argument because, above all else, family harmony was important to both of them. Some of Pauline's friends thought Catharine too deferential to Pauline at times, but as Catharine points out, it was her deliberate decision to avoid having an argument that neither could win. Her silence was a way of ensuring continued harmony. No issue was important enough to risk a falling-out with her sister.

One very important family relationship was the one that developed between Pauline and her niece "little Pauline" – Pauline Kushneriuk Coupar. As the story goes, little Pauline had just been born but not yet named when in bounded Aunt Pauline with a fifty dollar cheque for the baby. Had the baby been a boy, it was Catharine and Steve's desire to name him Paul after Pauline. So although a girl's name had not been decided beforehand, there was a certain logic in calling their baby daughter Pauline (though the family joke was that PJ had used a bribe to have the baby named after herself). Little Pauline always admired her famous aunt because she was so alive, so funny, and so energetic. The two Paulines often went shopping together and would spend hours talking about the challenges facing young women.

Young Pauline went on to Carleton to study journalism and political science, later taking women's studies courses at the University of Toronto. Despite having a young child at home, she became one of her aunt's caregivers in her final days. Pauline Coupar has retained many of her aunt's personal things including her tapes, scrapbooks, and boxes of political notes and memoirs. The relationship the two shared was very special. In some respects, young Pauline was the daughter PJ never had, a link to a younger generation. For young Pauline, her aunt was not only fun to be with but she was a source of inspiration, a person who had had the courage to pursue her goals in the face of seemingly insurmountable odds. She was a wonderful role model.

Pauline had greatly encouraged her four nephews as well as her niece in their education. When they finished grade eight, each of them received a hundred-dollar bond from Aunt Pauline. Every subsequent grade that was completed earned an extra fifty dollars. While Pauline's gift may only have been a slight incentive, all five graduated from university – an accomplishment that made Pauline a very proud aunt.

· 9 ·

The Final Battle

Chemotherapy's the pits, but it beats being under the sod.
Pauline Jewett, 17 January 1992

Perhaps it was inevitable. As Pete McMartin said in the obituary he wrote about Pauline in July 1992, "She liked her smokes, loved her scotch."[1] Although Pauline knew that she had not taken good care of her health, it was not until 1989, when she had a routine physical examination, that a small growth was discovered in her lung. Unlike Marjorie's cancer, Pauline's was considered treatable. A lobectomy was performed in 1989, and the prognosis was so favourable that neither chemotherapy nor radiation treatment was recommended. Pauline and her doctors were confident that she would have a full recovery.

At long last, Pauline had given up smoking, a habit acquired during her undergraduate days at Queen's. Following her stay at the Betty Ford Centre, she had also given up drinking. Unfortunately, these lifestyle changes came too late. About a year later, while visiting her sister Catharine in Deep River, Pauline complained of a "stitch" in her side that did not seem to want to go away. She made an appointment with a doctor in Ottawa, and it was discovered that she had cancer of the ascending colon which had spread to her liver. This time, the prognosis was poor, but Pauline kept up her spirits and decided to follow an extensive course of treatment. This decision took great courage. Pauline had witnessed first-hand, with Marjorie, the nausea and fatigue associated with chemotherapy, but Pauline clearly wished to prolong her life. She had a radical course of chemotherapy and, like Marjorie, had the support of a group of women throughout her treatments and in her final days. It is ironic that when she was admitted to hospital for her chemotherapy, Pauline and her friend Marion Dewar had an argument about a private room much like the one Pauline and Marjorie had had – except that whereas Marjorie had insisted that she have a private room, Pauline was insisting that it was not necessary.[2]

Between the time Pauline received her first diagnosis in 1989 and her chemotherapy treatments in the spring and summer of 1991, she and Marjorie were of great comfort to each other. When one was downcast, the other would offer encouragement. The illness they shared was a bond that strengthened their friendship. When Marjorie underwent chemotherapy treatment, she chose not to wear a wig; she preferred to wear turbans and floppy hats. For convocation exercises at Carleton during the spring of 1991, Pauline donned a floppy black velvet hat lent her by Marjorie. Lyn Grey's son Marcus gave Pauline an antique gold pin to place on it, and much time was spent getting it to look just right.

Pauline was inconsolable when Marjorie went west in December 1991 to spend her final days with her family. Intellectually, Pauline knew that Marjorie's cancer was terminal, though she refused to admit it; she felt that if Marjorie succumbed, it would just be a matter of time before she, too, lost the battle. In many respects, Marjorie's death was not simply the loss of a dear friend; it was the end of Pauline's dream that both of them would somehow be able to survive the ordeal. The day after Marjorie Nichols died, Doris Anderson took Pauline to the hospital for an appointment with her doctor. Despite a poor prognosis, Pauline, in her optimistic way, pleaded with the doctor to try something else. Doris remembers feeling devastated as he bluntly announced that it would be a matter of weeks, or a few months at the most, before she would die: "It wasn't so much the finality of what he was saying – we had all been prepared for months for what seemed inevitable. What I couldn't bear was to watch all that unquenchable positivism that was so much a part of Pauline. I cried my eyes out."

That winter, Margaret Mitchell tended to Pauline, cooking for her and occasionally spending the night. On weekends, Doris made the long, often difficult drive from Toronto to tend to her friend. In the spring of 1992, it was announced that Pauline was to receive the Order of Canada, an honour that greatly pleased her. But would she survive long enough to make it to the ceremony in April? On the day of the presentation, Pauline was a shadow of her former self, thin and fragile. Nevertheless, she walked proudly to the front, made her bow, listened to the citation, and received the medal from Governor General Ray Hnatyshyn. Several weeks later, she asked Doris to drive her to her beloved cottage on Constant Lake one last time. In fact, she drove herself to the cottage twice more. It was clearly so difficult for her to say that final goodbye to the place that had become such an important part of her life.

Lyn Grey visited PJ that April and was amazed by her positive attitude: "Even after a sleepless, pain-filled night, she would comment on how beautiful the sky was, how good life was, and how Mozart's music was so magnificent."[3] Pauline had never been one for gift giving or demonstrative displays of affection, but Lyn realized that this would likely be the last time they would see one another, so she made certain to take Pauline a gift, to hug her, and tell her how much she loved her. Pauline's last words to Lyn were, "I'm okay, kiddo, I'm okay." Pauline had always used the word "kiddo" to emphasize a point.

Despite being so sick, Pauline continued to have an insatiable appetite for news and politics. She frequently walked to the local convenience store to stock up on newspapers, and she made a point of watching the parliamentary channel and various newsmagazine programs. Pauline remained in her own apartment until the last week in June. There she was tended to by her team of friends and her niece Pauline Coupar. Calling themselves the Caregivers Union, little Pauline, Doris Anderson, Audrey McLaughlin, Dawn Black, Anita Hagan, and Marion Dewar ministered to Pauline in those final days. Recalling their team approach, Marion Dewar said, "It says something important about women but more important, I think it says something about Pauline ... Maybe we feel it's almost a privilege to be able to share and give something to her."[4]

Pauline spent the last ten days of her life at the Elizabeth Bruyère Centre in Ottawa, and it was there she received an honour that thrilled her, bringing recognition to a political career begun some thirty years earlier. Prime Minister Brian Mulroney phoned to tell her he was planning to breach protocol by inviting her to become a member of the Privy Council. The Privy Council is largely an honourary body comprising former prime ministers, chief justices, cabinet ministers, certain members of the Royal Family, and other notables. It was the ultimate honour. In fact, Mulroney telephoned Pauline on several occasions to let her know he was thinking of her. As Audrey McLaughlin noted, he didn't need to do that; it was something he chose to do. Pauline's spirits were always improved after his calls.

Privy councillors are allowed to place the word "Honourable" before their names and the letters PC after. Audrey McLaughlin stated that Pauline "was very excited about it ... It was really meaningful to her and I was terribly pleased for her."[5] The official swearing-in ceremony was to take place on 1 July in Rideau Hall. Queen Elizabeth II was to attend as was the governor general, the prime minister, and others. Unfortunately, Pauline's health had deteriorated to such a point that she was unable to attend. Guy Coté, the assistant clerk of the Privy Council, offered to come to the hospital to administer the oath, but Pauline was too ill to speak. Audrey placed the document in a frame and presented it to her with Marion Dewar, Doris Anderson, and Pauline Coupar present.

During those last days, Pauline was slipping in and out of consciousness. One day, when Doris and Audrey were discussing something about the constitution, Pauline suddenly sat up in bed and was ready to participate in the conversation. On the Friday morning before she died, there was one hour when PJ seemed her old lucid self. Doris Anderson called it a miracle. Pauline was advised that a scholarship had been established in her name at Carleton University and that it had been bolstered by a bequest of $125,000 from Trans Canada Pipelines.[6] Pauline insisted that Doris get her a pen and paper. "We must thank them appropriately," she said with touching formality. However, soon afterwards she lapsed into a comalike state.

Pauline died on Sunday morning, 5 July 1992, five months short of her seventieth birthday, with Doris Anderson at her side. Her niece and Marion Dewar had left only minutes before. Pauline was cremated and her ashes scattered in front of her cottage overlooking her beloved Constant Lake. Some time later, a memorial service was held at Carleton University, attended by her friends and family, and by former colleagues and students from Carleton. Marion Porter contributed to the ceremony with remembrances from the cottage, Marion Dewar talked about Pauline's years in the NDP, Steven Langdon spoke of her life as a teacher, and Kenneth McRae and Jill Vickers highlighted her association with Carleton University. There were glowing tributes to this woman who had had such an influence on the lives of others and had established several significant landmarks for women. It was a deserving tribute to such an important Canadian.

There was also a memorial service in New Westminster, at Douglas College, on 9 September 1992. Dawn Black welcomed the guests, and the speakers included Anita Hagan, MLA, John Cashore, MLA, Dennis Cocke, and Pauline's old friend from the federal NDP, Margaret Mitchell. Margaret made the following speech:

Pauline Jewett, PH D, Order of Canada, winner of the Persons Award, and member of the Privy Council, established many firsts. She was the first female president of a major university – Simon Fraser University – the first Liberal MP to turn her back on the War Measures Act and join the NDP. In 1979, she was elected to represent New Westminster–Coquitlam. She was a great feminist and actively recruited women to run for public office. She was a role model for many more.

I recall her tough defence of our own anti-NATO policy in 1979 when we were elected as the only two NDP women MPs. She was a citizen of the world who worked for peace and was a strong defender of the United Nations. As critic for the status of women, she worked in the struggle to have section 15 and section 28 included in the Charter of Rights and Freedoms. She was an expert on constitutional matters for our caucus.

Pauline retired from the House in 1988 but continued to give us all advice from the sidelines. She continued to be a fighter as she suffered cancer and she died with dignity in July 1992.

Pauline had a brilliant intellect and academic training that at times was awesome. While most MPs used the round file to get rid of stacks of paper that pour into each office, I am sure Pauline read every item. She loved committee work, where she could dig into research and policy and work in a nonpartisan way. Usually she convinced the government members to side with her, probably because she bamboozled them! I used to occasionally kid her about being an abstract academic and would bring her back to the grassroots reality of community politics. She would laugh and agree.

This wasn't hard because Pauline loved people – and she loved this riding. She especially enjoyed visiting older folks and talking to young people, who responded to her warmth and sincere interest. She stimulated young people to look beyond the present and think of future goals and she worked for equality for all of them.

Pauline will go down in history as an outstanding Canadian who was also a citizen of the world. She was a student of Canadian history. She could always be relied on to remember obscure political details with a perceptive analysis. As a constitutional expert she spent hours of study and work on constitutional developments over her years as a parliamentarian, and this continued until her death. Some may not have agreed with her stand on Meech Lake, but no one would doubt her broad knowledge of constitutional law and of the dynamics of Canada's complexity. When she was convinced she was right, she would not compromise, despite opposing opinions within our own party.

As an internationalist and the NDP external affairs critic, Pauline's major interests were in promoting peace and disarmament. She was a strong supporter of the U.N. and she attended sessions each fall. She visited many countries and spoke eloquently in Parliament on many issues. Les Benjamin always complimented PJ on her speech on the Crow Rate – the only topic on which she had zero knowledge.

I will remember Pauline as a close and cherished friend. We were elected together in 1979 and we soon formed the women's caucus of two. We became close "pals" as Pauline would say, with nicknames of PJ and Maggie given us by Jim Fulton. We shared many laughs together and gossiped about the old boys' network that dominated our lives. We both came from small-town southern Ontario and shared tales of growing up during the Depression and war. Ed Broadbent always said that the most parochial BCers came from Ontario.

Pauline had a great sense of fun. She was addicted to hockey and baseball to the end and refused to allow visitors to interrupt her game. She enjoyed her family – particularly her niece and nephews, to whom she left a legacy before she died. She also established a scholarship fund to assist potential school drop-outs to complete their education. With her early Carleton University colleagues, she owned a cottage property on a beautiful lake near Ottawa. There she spent many happy summers. I drove out with her at the wheel of her silver Jag for a final visit just before she was hospitalized. Over the past year, PJ was surrounded with loyal sisters, including Dawn, Anita Hagan, Marion Dewar, Doris Anderson, and myself, who took turns being caregivers. As shop steward for the caregivers' union, I can tell you one had to take orders and do things the Jewett way!

Pauline told me several times how happy and peaceful she was over the past year of her life. She never gave up hope and never complained. She said she woke up each day to enjoy the sunshine, music, the view from her windows, and the many friends who called or visited. She couldn't wait to read several papers each morning to check up on what Brian was up to. She was in control to the end, deciding when it was time to go into palliative care. She died with great dignity and will be remembered with great respect.

· 10 ·

The Political Philosophy of Pauline Jewett

When individuals change their party allegiance, they are accused of being fickle, turncoat, opportunistic, and inconsistent. In Pauline's case, there is considerable evidence to suggest that while her partisanship changed, her ideological thinking did not. There is no question that her beliefs and attitudes continued to evolve; she was never a static thinker. Her view of the world can be categorized into two distinct periods. Her younger years as a university student and young professor at Carleton University were structured by her belief in reform liberalism and the policies of her political hero, Lester Pearson. Towards the end of this period, certain events occurred which shook these beliefs and caused her to question whether or not her evolving political thought could be accommodated in the Liberal Party of Canada.

By the late 1960s, Pauline had reached a number of conclusions that influenced her decision to change her partisan allegiance. Her growing disaffection with the slow and incremental nature of liberalism had been fermenting since the late 1960s and her decision to support the NDP was not hastily made. It is my opinion that Pauline's political philosophy about the three core values of liberalism – egalitarianism, the pre-eminence of the individual, and the limited state – had undergone a metamorphosis. While this change was hastened in part by several short-term factors, there had been some longer-term influences at work that help explain this shift. First, and most important in my view, was Pauline's evolution into an ardent nationalist. As a young girl, she had never questioned that nationalism and liberalism were incompatible belief systems. By the time she had been at Carleton for several years, however, she was no longer convinced that the two could coexist – at least within the vision of liberalism espoused by the Pearson- and Trudeau-led Liberal Party of Canada. Unlike some of the members of the Committee for an Independent Canada, who were alarmed by the proliferation of American multinational corporations, Pauline initially concentrated on the foreign control of intellectualism and of universities in Canada. Later, her apprehension about foreign influence and the lack of Canadian autonomy was focused on American defence policy.

ON NATIONALISM

Increasingly, Pauline came to believe that the Canadian Liberal Party was manipulated by American interests and that a movement towards continental integration was being fostered and accommodated by the Liberals. She was not alone in this view; across the country, groups of like-minded thinkers began to organize. At Carleton and other postsecondary educational institutions, departments of Canadian studies sprang up, whose mandate was to accentuate the ways in which Canadians are different from Americans:

Our own politics and society have received rather casual treatment in our schools and as a result the Canadian identity has appeared vague and uncertain to our own people. The heavy influences from abroad discourage the expression of personal feelings of attachment for the land and inhibit reflective comment on our own collective experience as a nation. But now this defensive attitude towards our culture must be reversed – not by building cultural walls to isolate this country from outside, but by awakening Canadians to their own heritage.[1]

A number of Canadian academics had identified the problems, though the solutions advanced were not always the same. As a short-term resolution to the nation-building issue, Pauline and other members of the CIC favoured the creation and expansion of Canadian studies departments both at the high school and postsecondary levels. For others, however, a more long-term change was advocated. George Grant, for example, believed that the best prescription to ward off this economic and cultural integration was an embrace of conservatism. This was the central theme of his book *Lament for a Nation*. Pauline and a number of other economic nationalists, who were strongly influenced by the new political economy, believed that the cure lay elsewhere. In her view, the ideological antidote to the spectre of economic integration was social democracy. Pauline's attitude towards nationalism permeated all other aspects of her political philosophy. The nationalism she espoused and passionately cared about could not survive with the liberalism that was being pursued by Lester Pearson and his successor, Pierre Trudeau. Yes, it is true that Pauline and Trudeau did have a clash of personalities and, yes, it is also true that Pauline was politically ambitious. However, neither of these factors formed her principal motivation for leaving the Liberals. It was more that, over a period of time, she began to have reservations about Canada's ability to survive in a political climate that was decidedly pro-American.

WOMEN AND SOCIAL EQUALITY

To what degree did feminism guide Pauline's political philosophy? She was convinced that the policies of the Liberal Party of Canada would not result in anything but formal and legal equality for women. After all, it had taken a virtual earthquake of public opinion to convince the Liberal Party to include section 28 in the Charter. Few in the party were concerned about the dearth of women seeking election for the Liberals, and issues that were of particular interest to women were rarely elevated to positions of prominence on the party's policy agenda. Simply stated, Pauline did not believe that feminism would be possible in the paradigm of liberalism espoused by the Canadian Liberal Party. She felt that the liberal creed of "equality of opportunity" and the use of the state to eliminate barriers that worked against this opportunity were destined to fall short. In 1970 the *Report of the Royal Commission on the Status of Women in Canada* identified multiple areas where Canadian women had been denied access to the corridors of power. Although it had been a useful process to document these areas, Pauline saw very little movement to address some of the more problematic issues. For example, women were still largely marginal players in the world of party politics, and until she assumed the mantle of president of Simon Fraser University in 1974, women continued to be denied access to the top rung of the ivory tower.

Early in Pauline's academic career, it was clear that she was an advocate of social justice for all Canadians. In 1957 she wrote a short piece in *Canadian Forum* on the Padlock Case. The Padlock Law, which had been passed by the Province of Quebec, had had the effect of restricting the religious freedoms and freedom of assembly of Jehovah Witnesses in Quebec. The law was challenged by a number of groups, and on 8 March 1957 the Judicial Committee of the Privy

Council, in an eight-to-one decision, ruled that the Padlock Law was beyond the power of the province to enact. In other words, the statute was ruled *ultra vires* (unconstitutional). In her article, Pauline wrote that the decision "brings to an end one of the most notorious invasions of freedom ever to disfigure the Canadian statute book."[2]

Around this time, Pauline also wrote an article that was critical of Diefenbaker's Canadian Bill of Rights. Her view was that the British North America Act, 1867, should be amended to include recognition of fundamental rights. The Bill of Rights, she argued, was flawed: "It would be far better to have no bill at all, or to have simply a resolution of the two Houses, than to have a bill which serves only to raise false hopes and false fears."[3] In her early writing, Pauline was the champion of justice for all Canadians – she did not focus on one particular group – but later in her political career she became more outspoken about equality as it affected women. In part, her increasing activism can be explained by the emergence of sexual equality as one of the issues of the day. However, as a woman who was in a position of political prominence, it was incumbent on her to give voice to the concerns of women in the House of Commons.

Certainly, as a young woman growing up in St Catharines, Pauline had endured her share of stereotypical snubs and of the sexism that permeated Canadian life. Yet these experiences did not awaken Pauline to the injustices that were experienced by most women. After all, she had been able to pursue a graduate education at two pre-eminent universities. And while it is true that she believed her work and scholarship had not always been taken seriously, she had been able to survive, complete her work, and eventually gain an entry-level teaching position at Carleton University. Life had not been all that bad or unjust, she told herself. Moreover, she had had the advantage of being raised in a home environment where her voice had been heard.

In 1948 Pauline was awoken from her belief that life was fair when she was dismissed from her job as an instructor at Queen's. Other experiences crystallized her awareness that Canadian women were far from being truly equal citizens in social, economic, and, most importantly, political terms. Although she won the nomination in Northumberland, it was largely achieved without the help of the Liberal electoral machine. Despite doing a good job for her constituents, she was not re-elected two short years later. Although she played by the rules and made a contribution to the extraparliamentary wing of the party by serving as its vice-president, she was demeaned by its new leader, Pierre Trudeau. By the end of the 1960s,

Pauline had become dispirited not only with the direction in which Canadian liberalism was going but also with the "chilliness" she believed was evident in the party establishment. If there was not a sense and commitment to equality within the party machinery itself, how could it be expected that this party would promote change in the real world?

Although Pauline had not been concerned with equality for women in particular during the early years of her political evolution, she had not ignored the subject. Fully five years before the release of the *Report of the Royal Commission on the Status of Women in Canada*, she had written a short paper entitled "The Working Woman," which illustrated very clearly the wage gap between men and women, based on 1961 census data. She wrote: "Most revealing of all, perhaps, is the fact that only 2.6 per cent of our working women have annual incomes higher than $5,000. This compares, incidentally, with the 22.2 per cent of men who are in this category. Clearly women are not very numerous at the top!"[4]

In December 1968, Pauline wrote a column for *Maclean's* entitled "Where were the MEN when Canada set out to find what makes life tough for women?" In this article she cited some examples of injustices towards women that had been presented to the Royal Commission on the Status of Women. These included remuneration levels for women faculty: "Even in our universities the average female faculty member earns $1,200 less than the average male with the same credentials, experience and rank."[5] She also pointed the finger at patriarchy as the underlying cause for the oppression of women:

It is the men, in the last analysis, who will decide the "fate" of women. Because they dominate the legislatures and bureaucracies of the nation, it is they who will decide whether equal-pay laws should be enforced, day-care centres set up, the dissemination of birth-control legislation information legalized, manpower retraining for women extended, and many other matters. And because they dominate the executive suites of industry, labour, the media and so on, it is these attitudes and practices and those of government, too, that will have to change before there can be much improvement in, say, the promotion of women to key jobs.[6]

Clearly, PJ's feminist consciousness had been piqued long before the activities of the Royal Commission on the Status of Women, though the evidence of discrimination documented by the commission undoubtedly served as a major catalyst in PJ's feminist awakening. It also helped her contextualize some of the things she had experienced – namely, her dismissal from Queen's and her election losses in 1962 and 1965. Although Pauline had felt isolated when those experiences occurred, she now realized that other women had suffered similar experiences. It was not a weakness in her own abilities that had cost her the position at Queen's and her seat in the House. It was outright gender discrimination. This realization came too late to restore Pauline's confidence in her writing ability and level of scholarship, but it was comforting to realize that others had suffered the same experience.

Despite the irrefutable conclusions reached by the researchers who prepared the *Report of the Royal Commission on the Status of Women in Canada*, improvements were not forthcoming in the 1970s. During this time, Pauline began to develop strong relationships which raised her consciousness and drew her attention to many issues of concern to women. In 1980 and 1981, women's groups lobbying for sexual equality guarantees in the constitutional discussions were disregarded by the powerbrokers in Ottawa. This was the final blow for Pauline. She spent the last twelve years of her life committed to the feminist cause – though this was still not her dominant focus. Her passion continued to be centred on social equality for all disadvantaged groups.

PEACE AND DISARMAMENT

Pauline's interest in peace and disarmament can be traced back to her years at Queen's. From the time she joined the Liberal Party in 1960, she had been strongly opposed to the Canadian government's adoption of nuclear weapons, and she never supported Lester Pearson's acquiescence to allowing limited nuclear weapons. The long-established "no nuclear" policy of the Co-Operative Commonwealth Federation and its successor, the New Democratic Party, was a strong attraction for Pauline. After she had made the switch to the NDP in 1971, Pauline never vacillated. She was strongly opposed to Canada's support of American defence policy and spoke out on this issue many times. For Pauline, Canada's external affairs policies had to be disentangled from American positions. Otherwise, our sovereignty as an independent nation would be in peril. Coercion by American interests simply had to be resisted.

As has also been documented, Pauline was a strong opponent of a series of American defence policies, including the testing of the cruise missile and Star Wars. It was not easy to take this position during the first Reagan administration, for Reagan's defence policy was supported by both the American public and multinational corporations. Pauline's philosophy on Canada's foreign policy was guided by two main principles – her profound belief that mutual deterrence was not an appropriate strategy and the immorality of spending such vast resources on military hardware. In terms of the former, she was convinced that the principle of common security as advocated by the International Commission on Peace and Disarmament Issues, and later by the New Democratic Party itself, was the only solution to ensure international security. She also believed that the plight of the Third World needed to be addressed by increased development assistance by First World countries such as Canada.

PARLIAMENT

As an academic, Pauline had always had a compelling interest in the machinery of government, and of Parliament in particular. As most students of Canadian government know, Parliament includes the House of Commons and the Senate, but when Pauline used the term she seems to have been referring exclusively to the House of Commons. As a New Democrat, she shared her party's antipathy for the Senate. Interestingly, when in 1966 she wrote a piece for the *Journal of Canadian Studies* entitled "The Reform of Parliament," not once did the word "Senate" appear.

As early as 1957, Pauline had talked about the abuse of power by dominant cabinet ministers such as C.D. Howe. What attracted her to Lester Pearson and the Liberal Party in the early 1960s was the widespread sentiment, shared by a number of new Liberals, that Parliament should be reformed and members should be empowered as important players in Canada's legislative system. Stronger committees, relaxed party discipline, and more emphasis on private members' business were all advocated as ways of restoring legislative authority to the parliamentarians. In 1966, a year after her electoral defeat, Pauline wrote about the reforms that had been recommended in 1963 by the Special Committee on Procedure and Organization (of which she had been a member) to speed up the pace of the House. After the interminable Flag Debate of 1964,[7] even the most traditional members agreed that change was necessary.[8] Most of the reform proposals were about saving time, for instance, by shortening Question Period and abolishing dinner adjournments. Pauline stated that while saving parliamentary time was important, the quality of debate should be rated equally important; yet the government did not seem concerned: "No effort was made, for example, to initiate new MPs into the complexities of existing legislation and departmental organization. No executive assistants were provided MPs to enable them to spend a little less time on routine constituency matters and a little more time delving into, and preparing speeches on, proposed legislation."[9]

Although the number of committees was increased and they were reorganized along functional lines, Pauline believed that "they were not given the time or the facilities to do the very best job possible."[10] She was in favour of strengthening committees and providing more staff and research resources for them, though she was not hopeful that Parliament was likely to be reformed in any meaningful way. In that same 1966 article she wrote: "It is difficult to see how MPs can take full advantage of the opportunities before them, how the quality of parliamentary debate, parliamentary scrutiny, and parliamentary criticism can be substantially improved, either in the House or in committee, while so many of the most needed parliamentary (and party) reforms remain to be implemented."[11]

One reason why meaningful reforms to Parliament are rarely implemented arises from the nature of Canada's parliamentary system. Like Britain and most former members of the British Commonwealth, Canada adopted the Westminster style of parliamentary government, which is characterized by a strong executive and a relatively weak legislature. Nelson Polsby, the eminent American political scientist,[12] classified the British Parliament (and by implication, the Canadian Parliament) as an "arena" type of legislature. Arena legislatures are essentially those that debate and scrutinize policy but have little role in actual lawmaking. Most parliamentary reformers advocate a major change from the type of legislature that Canada has. In terms of Polsby's classification system, they are advocating a "transformative" legislature, one that has the capacity to transform policy into law. The U.S. Congress is commonly cited as this type of legislature. It is important, therefore, that parliamentary reform be seen in the proper context. The strengthening of parliamentary committees, the loosening of party discipline, and the empowerment of backbenchers are all aimed at changing the nature of the Canadian House of Commons. Pauline was an advocate of this reform movement and believed that the Commons should be placed in a position of eminence in Canada's political system.

Epilogue
More than a Trailblazer

> Inherently all structures in society are male dominated. The problem is: How are we going to change that, and bring new attitudes in the command posts of society? In academia, politics and business women still need trail blazers. And the trouble with trail blazers is that nothing much happens afterwards. Just counting on trail blazers isn't nearly good enough.
>
> Pauline Jewett

Over the past eighteen months, I have had the pleasure of researching the life and accomplishments of a great Canadian. The legacy she leaves to her friends and family, to the women of Canada, and to all Canadians is a rich one indeed. As a public figure, Pauline will be fondly remembered for the spirit and conviction she brought to her work as a parliamentarian, teacher, university president, and humanitarian. In these roles, she demonstrated the dynamism and power one person can exert towards achieving the goal of a more humane, democratic, and peaceful place. Pauline Jewett did not change the world, but she did try to do so.

One cannot help but be amazed at the perseverance Pauline exhibited during her public life. It began with the completion of her PH D dissertation. A great many of those embarking on this degree do not finish. In fact, books have been written about the myriad pitfalls that confront PH D candidates. The selection of a "weak" thesis committee, financial difficulties, an uncertain employment market, and the alienation and isolation that students experience have all been cited as reasons for withdrawing from a doctoral program. What often separates those who do complete from those who do not is a need for closure in finishing what they have set out to do. Pauline was teaching part-time in Kingston, miles away from the faculty at Harvard who were supervising her work. Despite these obstacles, she ultimately defended her research and was awarded the degree. As we now know, her completion of the degree did not open doors to the academic world. For five years she applied for academic positions, and for five years her applications were rejected. Undaunted, she eventually found an institution prepared to give her a chance, and she became a valued member of the faculty at Carleton University.

Self-confidence and a strong belief in her own abilities were Pauline's benchmarks. She did not wait to be recruited for a position. In seeking both the nomination in Northumberland and the presidency at Simon Fraser University, Pauline was her own advocate; she was self-recruited. There were times when her lack of patience and her spontaneous nature may have worked against her. For instance, she did not always interpret the political climate accurately, and this led to personal setbacks in pursuing both the nomination in Burnaby in 1978 and the presidency of the New Democratic Party in 1989. When a man has a strong sense of self and self-confidence, these qualities are portrayed as positive, but when a woman has these same attributes, the negative connotations are accentuated – power hungry, blindly ambitious, aggressive, and shrill. Some of Pauline's critics undoubtedly saw her in this way.

Another powerful facet of Pauline's character was her persistence. When she decided to launch a run for the nomination in Northumberland, she did so knowing that the party establishment did not support her. Since she had not followed the conventional pattern of constituency and party service, she may well have been perceived as an overconfident upstart. This leap-frogging over conventional norms must have been all the more shocking because it was a woman who was defying the so-called rules. Yet even though many Liberals in the riding had profound reservations about a woman contesting the election, Pauline had no intention of abandoning her plans of being a parliamentarian. Such opposition only made her work harder. Similarly, the sense of injustice and defeat at losing the election in 1962 could have caused many people to abandon their political aspirations, but Pauline returned to the hustings and eventually was successful.

Even more remarkable was Pauline's desire to serve the people in such a hostile workplace as the House of Commons. As has been documented by a number of women legislators, Parliament was not a receptive place to women in the 1960s. For the most part, they were excluded from the cabinet table, and service on important legislative committees eluded them. They were unwelcome at certain clubs where the business of the nation was conducted. Marginalization was the order of the day. Pauline's second defeat against the high-profile former Conservative cabinet minister, George Hees, would have been enough to cause most parliamentarians to abandon their political ambitions. This 1965 defeat interrupted her movement up the political ladder and was one of those "fragmenting" events that required Pauline to improvise. Fourteen years passed before she re-entered the corridors of Parliament. Yet the defeat led Pauline to explore areas of intellectual interest to her. While at the Institute of Canadian Studies, she began to flesh out her philosophy on Canadian nationalism and the role of the university in our society. These two interests became intertwined and led to her next important life experience, the president's position at Simon Fraser University.

Three other decisions speak to the courage and commitment that Pauline demonstrated throughout her life. When she decided to switch her party affiliation, she knew there would be political repercussions both from her former colleagues and from her new ones. She also recognized that voters would be sceptical. There is no question that switching parties brought with it a huge risk. However, in her heart and mind she could no longer support the brand of liberalism espoused by the Trudeau-led Liberal Party. Staying true to her principles was always more important to Pauline than political opportunism. Her unpopular stance on the Meech Lake Accord was another example of her determination to make the right decision, even though it was not always the politically desirable one.

A third example of Pauline's commitment was her mission to restore academic credibility to Simon Fraser University. Confident of her ability to orchestrate consensual decision making, she was convinced that she could find a resolution to the censure that had been imposed on the university by the Canadian Association of University Teachers. This quest for consensus proved more elusive than she had anticipated, and it became physically exhausting for her. The institutional resistance that Pauline was confronted with would have precipitated an early resignation from most university presidents, yet Pauline persisted and ultimately resolved the dispute. It was with this same courage and strength of character, which Pauline had shown throughout her life, that in her final days she confronted the greatest enemy of all – terminal cancer.

One of Pauline's greatest concerns was that trailblazers come and go, their hard work and achievements being meaningful only if the torch is picked up by those who follow. Since her retirement from the House of Commons in 1988, more women than ever before have been elected. As a result of the June 1997 federal election, there were sixty women holding seats in the House. There is still a "long row to hoe" before the House of Commons can claim to be truly representative, but there are now enough women to fill at least three tables in the parliamentary dining room! Many of the women who sit in Parliament today acknowledge that the efforts of such predecessors as Pauline, Judy LaMarsh, and Grace MacInnis were crucial in making this presence possible.

Pauline was the first woman named as president of a co-educational Canadian university. As of 1998, there were eight women presidents of Canadian universities.[1] It is now common practice to have at least one woman short-listed for presidential competitions. What this figure tells us, however, is that women are not simply being short-listed as a token gesture; they are winning competitions because they have proved to be effective administrators. Pauline Jewett must be credited with setting the precedent by confirming that the top job in the ivory tower could be effectively performed by a woman.

In 1987, in celebration of her sixty-fifth birthday, Pauline was interviewed by CBC radio. When asked what she felt was her greatest contribution to public life in Canada, she responded: "If I had to pick one thing I would say my work in the area of peace and disarmament. This is where I found both the work that I was able to do as an academic and the work I have been able to do as a member of Parliament has been – I was going to say rewarding – has been personally rewarding even though one doesn't always see evidence every day of its being taken up by every person and every country of the world. And the almost equal great moment for me has been in helping to promote all aspects of equality – minorities of all kinds and, above all, equality of women."[2]

If Pauline Jewett were alive today, I believe she would be gratified with the accomplishments of women as we enter the new millennium. She would caution women that the struggle is far from over and would be dismayed at the dismantling of the social welfare state and the way government restructuring and deficit fighting has marginalized many Canadian citizens. As a strong supporter of accessibility to our universities and colleges for bright and deserving young people, Pauline would be outraged at the way this accessibility has been compromised by reduced government funding and escalating tuition fees. If Pauline Jewett were alive today, she would still be a voice for the disadvantaged and would still be encouraging those who wish to make a contribution to public life. She would especially be helping those with the drive and commitment to seek office in the Canadian House of Commons.

Pauline Jewett believed in Parliament. She was not an idealist – she knew that Parliament had its faults and that majority governments made effective opposition difficult. However, she was not a cynic; she believed that Parliament was the most important forum for debating major public issues. Even as a member of the opposition, she believed that parliamentarians had an important role. When asked in 1988 what she would miss most about politics, she replied:

I loved all parts of it. I loved campaigning. I loved door-to-dooring. I loved talking with people. I loved being an MP. I liked doing things for constituents. I liked tackling problems. I liked all the constituency side of it. But equally I liked the parliamentary side of it. It's very difficult when people ask me what I like most about it. But it's just not that part of it – the great public part of parliamentary life. It's the committee work. When I think back on being able to get my teeth into a really important committee report. Of all the things I love about politics – being an MP, representing a constituency, trying to think of a clever question in Question Period – I guess that's the part that has the most lasting effect upon me.[3]

From her early years, it was evident that Pauline had a mission, yet this mission was never more important than her friendships and her family life. These relationships sustained her through the setbacks she encountered as she went about her task of making Canada a better society, and it was these relationships that gave her not only her joy in life but the balance that is so vital for public figures who are making decisions that affect the lives of us all.

Notes

1 Denzin, *Interpretive Biography,* 70.
2 Ibid., 81.
3 Freccero, "Autobiography and Narrative," 16–29.
4 Cameron and Dickin, *Great Dames*, 15.
5 Edel, "Biography and the Science of Man," 9.

CHAPTER ONE

1 The second wave of the Canadian women's movement is generally considered to have begun in the early 1960s with the establishment in 1960 of the Voice of Women.
2 Pauline's brother Fred is the family historian who provided me with this genealogical information in an interview on 18 October 1996 at his home in Toronto.
3 This school still exists and has been renamed Trafalgar Castle School.
4 Frederick Chandler Jewett, Pauline's older brother, was known by family members as Chan while growing up in St Catharines. However, during his service in the Second in World War, he dropped Chandler in favour of Frederick.
5 Ridley College became co-educational in the late 1980s.
6 McKenzie, "Political Autobiography and Biography."
7 Goot and Reid, "Women and Voting Studies, 5–45.
8 Andersen, *To Change the World*, 15.
9 There was considerable concern among British leaders that they might lose the war if Germany began hostilities. Given this possibility, it was

important to establish a base elsewhere where British leaders could be airlifted in the event of a German invasion. In 1937 British officials began to plan the development of a base in Newfoundland. The economy of Newfoundland had collapsed during the Dirty Thirties, and in 1934 it had reverted to direct British rule under the Commission of Government, which remained in effect until 1949.

10 Coburn Jewett's contribution to the war effort was recognized by the British government when he was awarded the CBE in 1946.

11 Kushneriuk, "An Oral History of Pauline Jewett," 4.

12 Ibid.

13 Fred Jewett, interview by author, Toronto, 18 October 1996.

14 Kushneriuk, "An Oral History of Pauline Jewett," 5.

15 Gartner, "Shoot the Moon," 26.

16 Doris Anderson, letter to author, 30 December 1996.

17 Most Canadian women had the franchise federally by 1920, but Chinese and East Asian women were not allowed to vote until 1947, and native women on reservations were not allowed to vote until 1960.

18 Although a number of "persons cases" came before the courts, the best known is the one brought forward by five women from Alberta (one of whom was Nellie McClung), who sought the right for women to be appointed to the Senate. The federal government argued that the framers of the Constitution Act, 1867, had not intended women to be included as "persons" under section 24. The Supreme Court of Canada agreed with the federal position. However, until 1949, the highest court of appeal was the Judicial Committee of the Privy Council, and it overturned the decision of the Supreme Court in 1929. Senator Cairine Wilson, the first woman ever appointed to the Canadian Senate, was summoned to the upper house in 1930.

19 Beginning in 1954, Helen Koch, a psychologist at the University of Chicago, published ten articles on birth order. Many other studies have examined birth order, including that undertaken by Talcott Parsons and Robert F. Bales entitled *Family, Socialization, and Interaction Process*, published in 1955.

20 Sulloway, *Born to Rebel*, 85.

21 Ibid., 86.

22 Kushneriuk, "An Oral History of Pauline Jewett," 5.

23 Sulloway, *Born to Rebel*, 97.

24 Ibid., 98.

25 Andersen, *To Change the World*, 17.

26 See Eysenck, *The Psychology of Politics*.

27 Sulloway, *Born to Rebel*, 287.

28 Ibid.

29 Gartner, "Shoot the Moon," 27.

30 Andersen, *To Change the World*, 17.

31 "Normal school" is a term that used to refer to teachers' colleges.

CHAPTER TWO

1 Heap and Prentice, eds., *Gender and Education in Ontario*.

2 Neatby, "Preparing for the Working World"; Hitchman, "A Case Study of Status Differential," 138.

3 Ibid.

4 Neatby, "Preparing for the Working World," 332.

5 Ibid.

6 Prentice et al., *Canadian Women*, 326.

7 Harris, *A History of Higher Education in Canada*, 456.

8 Hamilton, *Queen's*, 37.

9 Ibid., 39.

10 Andersen, *To Change the World*, 20.

11 Harris, *A History of Higher Education in Canada*, 362.

12 Hooey, "The Marty Scholarship," xiii.

13 Aletta Marty was an outstanding graduate of Queen's. She graduated with an MA in 1894 and was awarded the University Medal in modern languages. In 1919, after a long history of teaching languages, she was named inspector of public schools in Toronto – the first woman to hold such a position in Ontario. She was the first Canadian woman awarded an honourary degree of Doctor of Laws, which she received in 1919. Beginning in 1937, a fellowship in her name (the Marty Scholarship) has been awarded to a woman holding an MA from Queen's for academic research.

14 Hooey, "The Marty Scholarship," xiv.

15 Queen's University, *Calendar of the Faculty of Arts*, 33.

16 Ibid.

17 Corry, *My Life and Work*, 70.

18 Ibid., 73.

19 Ibid., 73–4.

20 Ibid., 99–100.

21 Andersen, *To Change the World*, 27.

22 CTV, *Political Memoirs*, April 1992.

23 CBC radio, "Music in My Life," 11 December 1987.

24 Andersen, *To Change the World*, 27.

25 Kushneriuk, "An Oral History of Pauline Jewett," 6.

26 Hooey, "The Marty Scholarship," xix.

27 Hemlow, "A Marty Scholar's Adventures," 57.

28 Gibson, *Queen's University,* 163.

29 Andersen, *To Change the World,* 27.

30 Ibid.

31 See note 13 above.

32 Carver, "What Are We Doing Here?" 25.

33 Pauline's colleague in political science and eleven of the other women left to get married and did not complete their degrees (Kushneriuk, "An Oral History of Pauline Jewett," 7).

34 Andersen, *To Change the World,* 31.

35 Kushneriuk, "An Oral History of Pauline Jewett," 7.

36 Ibid., 10.

37 CBC radio, "Music in My Life," 11 December 1987.

38 Ibid.

39 Kushneriuk, "An Oral History of Pauline Jewett," 9.

40 Lyn Grey, interview by author, Victoria, 25 August 1997.

41 Lyn Grey, letter to author, 30 June 1996.

42 Andersen, *To Change the World,* 33.

43 Kushneriuk, "An Oral History of Pauline Jewett," 9.

44 Corry, *My Life and Work,* 101, 102.

45 Doris Anderson, letter to author, 30 December 1996.

46 Vickers and Adam, *But Can You Type?* 107.

47 Ibid, 142.

48 George Grant recalled meeting Corry and another professor from Queen's, Professor Macintosh, who belittled Grant for "giving up radical politics for the consolation of religion." In George Grant's view, Corry, Mackintosh, and others had influenced an entire generation of students who went into government and were "transforming Canada in ways he abhorred" (Christian, George Grant, 111).

49 Prentice et al., *Canadian Women,* 306.

CHAPTER THREE

1 Kushneriuk, "An Oral History of Pauline Jewett," 10.

2 Marion Dewar, interview by author, Toronto, 18 June 1996.

3 Kushneriuk, "An Oral History of Pauline Jewett," 11.

4 Christian, *George Grant,* 43.

5 Kushneriuk, "An Oral History of Pauline Jewett," 11.

6 Pauline was notorious for calling the men in her life by their first names only. None of her friends whom I interviewed could recall the last name of this suitor.

7 Kushneriuk, "An Oral History of Pauline Jewett," 11.

8 Carleton College, *Sixth Annual Calendar,* 4.

9 Ibid., 5.

10 Ibid.

11 Ibid.

12 Gzowski, "The New Women in Politics," 64.

13 Kushneriuk, "An Oral History of Pauline Jewett," 12.

14 Norm Fenn, interview by author, Renfrew, 18 September 1996.

15 The name of the lake is Constant Lake, but the Carleton people who cottaged there drew up the incorporation papers with the name Constan Associates. This error was never corrected, which explains the inconsistency.

16 Doris Anderson, letter to author, 30 December 1996.

17 Fred Jewett, interview by author, Toronto, 18 October 1996.

18 Many prominent people visited the lake. For example, Sylvia and Bernard Ostry were regular guests of the Porters.

19 In the April 1957 issue of *Canadian Forum*, she wrote a two-page commentary entitled "The Padlock Case" (7–8), and in the September 1957 issue she wrote an article entitled "Clarence Decatur Howe" (126–7). In March 1958 she wrote a column for the *Canadian Commentator* entitled "The Major Issues are Blurred" (3).

20 Lyn Grey, letter to author, 30 June 1996.

21 Jewett, "Clarence Decatur Howe," 127.

CHAPTER FOUR

1 In March 1956, C.D. Howe, the minister of trade and commerce, introduced a resolution to incorporate the Northern Ontario Pipe Line Corporation. The Ontario legislature approved a $35 million contribution to subsidize the construction of a nonprofitable section in northern Ontario, and Parliament was asked to estabish a crown corporation and provide $80 million in federal financing. The PCs led by George Drew and the CCF led by M.J. Coldwell were opposed to the plan and argued that Canadian taxpayers were being coerced into supporting a pipeline project that was largely dominated by American corporate interests. They proposed that the pipeline be built by an all-Canadian company. The debate became ugly, and eventually the Liberals used the closure rule to get the measure through Parliament so that construction could begin that summer. Given the dynamics of this debate and the questions relating to Canada's sovereighty, it is small wonder that Pauline felt uneasy with the Liberal government's position.

2 Stursberg, *Lester Pearson*, 39.

3 Ibid., 41.

4 McCall-Newman, *Grits*, 36.

5 Kent, *A Public Purpose*, 77.

6 Ibid.

7 Sharp, *Which Reminds Me*, 88.

8 Ibid., 89.

9 Ibid.

10 Ibid., 63.

11 Ibid., 64.

12 Cell 13 was the name given to a powerful group of Liberal activists that included Gordon Dryden, Keith Davey, Dan Lang, Paul Hellyer, Dick Stanbury, David Anderson, Royce Frith, Philip Givens, Joseph Potts, James Potter, James Service, Boyd Upper, James Scott, Gordon Edick, and Judy LaMarsh. Sometimes this group numbered more and sometimes less than thirteen. The cell was largely seen as the group that spearheaded the leadership victory for Lester Pearson after St Laurent stepped down as leader.

13 McCall-Newman, *Grits*, 36–7.

14 Kent, *A Public Purpose*, 79.

15 Ibid., 64.

16 McCall-Newman, *Grits*, 40.

17 Ibid., 40.

18 Kent, *A Public Purpose*, 90.

19 Ibid.

20 Ibid., 93.

21 Ibid.

22 Weber, *Politics as a Vocation*, 8.

23 Ibid.

24 Ibid., 41.

25 Ibid.

26 See Power, "Career Politicians"; Ward, *The Canadian House of Commons*; Kornberg, *Canadian Legislative Behaviour*; Kornberg and Mishler, *Influence in Parliament*; Harder, "Career Patterns"; and Docherty, *Mr Smith Goes to Ottawa*.

27 Franks, *The Parliament of Canada*, 72.

28 James Q. Wilson posits that there are two ideal types of American legislators – amateurs and professionals. The reward for the amateur is the self-satisfaction that comes with participation. For the professional, the reward lies in the extrinsic satisfaction of participation – power, status, or the fun of the game (*The Amateur Democrat*, 4–10).

29 Robert K. Merton, an American political theorist, claims that legislators have either "local" orientations (i.e., having lived in the community for many years, their interests are primarily local and community) or "cosmopolitan" orientations (involving minimal ties to a locality, but

a strong attachment to the "great society" of national and international problems, ideas, movements, fashions, and culture).

30 Jewett, "Run for Parliament," 8.
31 Kushneriuk, "An Oral History of Pauline Jewett," 13.
32 Aiken, *The Backbencher*, 16.
33 Kushneriuk, "An Oral History of Pauline Jewett," 13.
34 Kushneriuk, "An Oral History of Pauline Jewett," 14.
35 LaMarsh, *Memoirs of a Bird in a Gilded Cage*, 283.
36 Royal Commission on the Status of Women, *Report*, 339.
37 Ibid., 345.
38 Ibid., 349.
39 LaMarsh, *Memoirs of a Bird in a Gilded Cage*, 5.
40 At the time this interview took place, the newly configured CCF had not yet been officially renamed the New Democratic Party.
41 Gzowski, "The New Women in Politics," 52.
42 The tenor of Gzowski's article was a refreshing change from most media coverage of women politicians at the time. The usual approach concentrated on women's "biological" difference and described women politicians as "first women" and "token" in the nontraditional domain of politics. This approach led male reporters to query female politicians on a small number of women's issues, including social welfare, education, and health, rather than the "hard" issues of economics and foreign affairs. Even though many "first women" such as LaMarsh and Pauline had comparable educational and occupational backgrounds to their male counterparts, their visible biological difference became the primary point of reference. See Robinson and Saint-Jean, "The Portrayal of Women Politicians in the Media," 180–2.
43 Gzowski, "The New Women in Politics," 52.
44 Wyman, "Pauline Jewett: An Interview," 21.
45 Ibid., 21.
46 Gzowski, "The New Women in Politics," 52.
47 Ibid.
48 Jewett, "The Working Woman," 219.
49 Ibid., 218.
50 *Report of the Chief Electoral Officer: General Election 1962*, 994.
51 Wyman, "Pauline Jewett: An Interview," 21.
52 Ibid.
53 Andersen, *To Change the World*, 39.
54 This is a phenomenon that refers to the tendency of the federal Progressive Conservative Party not to support its leader. Political scientist George Perlin has written a book entitled *The Tory Syndrome* on the topic.

55 *Report of the Chief Electoral Officer: General Election 1963*, 996.

56 Docherty, *Mr Smith Goes to Ottawa*, 84.

57 Jewett, "What Every New MP Should Know," 11.

58 Ibid.

59 Aiken, *The Backbencher*, 180.

60 McCall-Newman, *Grits*, 44.

61 Porter, *The Vertical Mosaic*, 405.

62 Franks, *The Parliament of Canada*, and Sutherland, "The Consequences of Electoral Volatility," 306.

63 Kent, *A Public Purpose*, 209.

64 Ibid., 232.

65 Andersen, *To Change the World*, 43.

66 Canada, House of Commons, *Debates*, 17 May 1963, 22.

67 Ibid.

68 Ibid., 24.

69 Ibid., 24–5.

70 Kent, *A Public Purpose*, 231.

71 CBC television, *Across Canada* (the observer), interview by Lloyd Robertson, 3 June 1965.

72 Ibid.

73 Stursberg, *Lester Pearson*, 383.

74 Kushneriuk, "An Oral History of Pauline Jewett," 15.

75 *Ottawa Citizen*, 21 May 1964.

76 LaMarsh, *Memoirs of a Bird in a Gilded Cage*, 9.

77 McLaughlin, *A Woman's Place*, 27–8.

78 LaMarsh, *Memoirs of a Bird in a Gilded Cage*, 289.

79 McCall-Newman, *Grits*, 48.

80 Ibid.

81 Campbell, "Jewett versus Hees," A29.

82 Ibid.

83 Ibid.

84 *Report of the Chief Electoral Officer, General Election 1965*.

85 Fisher, "The Understated Charm of Pauline Jewett," C12.

86 Kent, *A Public Purpose*, 414.

87 "Major Job of Cabinet Building Ahead for Trudeau," *Globe and Mail*, 8 April 1968, A10.

88 Jewett, "Run for Parliament," 8.

89 Andersen, *To Change the World*, 54.

90 Kushneriuk, "An Oral History of Pauline Jewett," 20.

CHAPTER FIVE

1 Carleton University, *Twenty-Eighth Calendar, 1969–70*.

2 Pat Armstrong, interview by author, Toronto, 21 July 1997.

3 Kome, *Women of Influence*, 85.

4 Ibid., 87.

5 See Firestone, *The Dialectic of Sex*, and Millett, *Sexual Politics* for these radical critiques.

6 Jewett, "Run for Paliament."

7 I interviewed several Liberal women in 1992 who referred to Trudeau's "quota" for women as cabinet ministers. This quota, they said, was well known on the Hill.

8 Jewett, "How Can the Greatest Number of Canadians," 14.

9 Stainsby, "Jewett Says She's Had Terrific Go at Politics," c9.

10 CTV, *Political Memoirs*, April 1992.

11 Rotstein and Lax, *Getting It Back*, 313–14.

12 Ibid., 314–15.

13 Ibid., 196.

14 Committee for an Independent Canada, *Brief Submitted to the Standing Committee on Finance, Trade and Economic Affairs of the House of Commons concerning Bill C-132*, 17.

15 Ibid., 18.

CHAPTER SIX

1 Mills, "Festival at Simon Fraser," 232–3.

2 This debate was portrayed in a CBC documentary shown on *Dateline Special* entitled "Two Schools of Thought," which was aired on 3 April 1977.

3 Yandle, "The End of PSA at Simon Fraser University," 16.

4 Canadian Association of University Teachers (CAUT), "Report on the Simon Fraser Dispute," 42.

5 Smith, "Faculty Power and Simon Fraser," 122.

6 Ibid.

7 Yandle, "The End of the PSA at Simon Fraser University," 16.

8 CAUT, "Report on the Simon Fraser Dispute," 42.

9 Ibid., 46–7.

10 Yandle, "The End of the PSA at Simon Fraser University," 16.

11 Ibid.

12 CAUT "Report on the Simon Fraser Dispute," 48.

13 Ibid.

14 Yandle, "The End of the PSA at Simon Fraser University," 17.

15 One of the suspended instructors died before the dispute was settled.

16 Yandle, "The End of the PSA ar Simon Fraser University," 19.

17 McKeown, "The Determined Miss Pauline Jewett," 7.

18 Sawatsky, "Jewett Gets Job as SFU President," 1–2.

19 Cocking, "The Knives Are Out for Pauline Jewett," 17–18.

20 Jill Vickers, interview by author, Ottawa, 18 September 1996.

21 Andersen, *To Change the World*, 59.

22 McKeown, "The Determined Miss Pauline Jewett," 8.

23 Cocking, "The Knives Are Out for Pauline Jewett," 18.

24 Mills, "Festival at Simon Fraser," 228.

25 "$1 Million Job for Jewett," *Ottawa Journal*, 13 March 1974.

26 Cocking, "The Knives Are Out for Pauline Jewett," 19.

27 Ibid.

28 Sawatsky, "Jewett Gets Job as SFU president," 2.

29 "Not for a Million Dollars," *Time Canada*, 1 April 1974, 9.

30 McKeown, "The Determined Miss Pauline Jewett," 7.

31 Levitch, "From Instant University to Academic Disaster," 21.

32 Cocking, "The Knives Are Out for Pauline Jewett," 20.

33 Campbell, *Time and Chance*, 38.

34 CBC television, "Two Schools of Thought," 1978.

35 Jewett, "Who's Being Hired to Teach in Our Universities?" 10.

36 Cocking, "The Knives Are Out for Pauline Jewett," 17.

37 Ibid., 19.

38 CBC television, "Two Schools of Thought," 1978.

39 *Chatelaine*, December 1977, 106.

40 *Time Canada*, 7 July 1975, 10.

41 Ibid.

42 Ibid.

43 Cocking, "The Knives Are Out for Pauline Jewett," 18.

44 Ibid.

45 University of British Columbia, *Calendar of the Fifty-Seventh Session*, 76.

46 This story was told me by Dr Ruth Syme, Muriel Uprichard's minister in Toronto in the 1980s, in a conversation in February 1998. Dr Syme is currently a minister in Deep River, Ontario. Dr Uprichard passed away in December 1997.

CHAPTER SEVEN

1 This was an affectionate term used by Pauline to describe her constituents in Northumberland. After she was elected in New Westminster–Coquitlam, she referred to a number of constituents as her fishermen.

2 The late Frank Underhill, a prominent Canadian political scientist, postulated that Canadian voters have a predisposition to support a different party at the provincial level from the one in power in Ottawa. When the Social Credit Party was in power in British Columbia (which was the case during Pauline's entire tenure as an MP for the province, (1979–

88), British Columbians tended to support the NDP at the federal level. Underhill termed this predisposition the "theory of counterbalance."

3 Margaret Mitchell, interview by author, Vancouver, 26 August 1997.
4 Ibid.
5 Margaret was defeated in the 1993 general election.
6 Margaret Mitchell, interview by author, Vancouver, 26 August 1997.
7 Kome, *Women of Influence*, 107.
8 Ibid.
9 Margaret Mitchell, interview by author, Vancouver, 26 August 1997. Audrey McLaughlin also refers to Pauline's indirect recruitment in her memoir *A Woman's Place*, 8.
10 Margaret Mitchell, interview by author, Vancouver, 26 August 1997.
11 Ibid.
12 The three other women elected in 1963 were Jean Casselman (PC, Grenville-Dundas), Judy LaMarsh (Liberal, Niagara Falls), and Margaret Konantz (Liberal, Winnipeg South).
13 McLaughlin, *A Woman's Place*, 26.
14 McCall-Newman, *Grits*, 378–9.
15 Docherty, *Mr Smith Goes to Ottawa*, 98.
16 CBC television, *The Journal*, 28 October 1983.
17 Canada, House of Commons, *Debates*, 10 September 1987, 8825.
18 Ibid.
19 Hedlin, "Miss Jewett's Scheme Is a Pure Disgrace," 9.
20 Gibson, "History Shows Jewett Realistic on South Africa," 11.
21 CBC television, *The Journal*, 10 February 1983.
22 Jewett, "Toward an Independent Foreign Policy," 9–10.
23 Ibid., 10.
24 CBC television, *The Journal*, 10 February 1983.
25 Jewett, "Should Canada Test the Cruise?" 89, 91.
26 CBC television, *The Journal*, 10 February 1983.
27 Riley, "Boys' Games Played in Secret," 28.
28 The senators on the committee were Jean-Maurice Simard (joint Chairman), Richard Doyle, Jacques Flynn, Philippe D. Gigantès, Jerahmiel S. Grafstein, and Peter Stollery.
29 Canada, Parliament, Special Joint Committee of the Senate and of the House of Commons, *Canada's International Relations*, 1.
30 Jewett, "NORAD," 13.
31 Ibid., 12.
32 Independent Commission on Disarmament and Security Issues, *Common Security*, xiii.
33 Ibid., 176.
34 New Democratic Party, *Canada's Stake in Common Security*, 2.

35 Ibid.

36 Ibid.

37 Anderson, *Rebel Daughter*, 233.

38 Ibid., 234.

39 Ibid., 235.

40 Ibid., 239.

41 Ibid., 241.

42 CBC television, *The National*, 14 February 1981.

43 Kome, *Women of Influence*, 129.

44 Anderson, *Rebel Daughter*, 244. Originally, it had been thought that the conference would attract only 500 delegates, but well over twice that number attended.

45 Ibid., 244.

46 Kome, *The Taking of Twenty-Eight*. Section 28 was the clause added late in the constitutional discussions which states: "Notwithstanding anything in this Charter, the rights and freedoms referred to in it are guaranteed equally to male and female persons."

47 Canada, House of Commons, *Debates*, 6 October 1986, 6661–2.

48 The five senators were Arthur Tremblay (joint chairman), Philippe D. Gigantès, Nathan Nurgitz, Raymond J. Perrault and Yvette Rousseau.

49 Canada, Parliament, Special Joint Committee on the 1987 Constitutional Accord, *Report*, 5:82.

50 The final accord was approved by the first ministers after an all-night negotiating session held in the Langevin Block on Parliament Hill.

51 Canada, Parliament, Special Joint Committee on the 1987 Constitutional Accord, *Report*, 16:25.

52 Ibid.

53 Ibid.

54 Margaret Mitchell, interview by author, Vancouver, 26 August 1997.

55 Canada, Parliament, Special Joint Committee on the 1987 Constitutional Accord, *Report*, 10:55.

56 Ibid., 2:26–7.

57 Ibid.

58 Margaret Mitchell, interview by author, Vancouver, 26 August 1997.

59 Ibid.

60 Brown, *Being Brown*, 137.

61 Copps, *Nobody's Baby*, 65.

62 Campbell, *Time and Chance*, 232.

63 Mishler, "Nominating Attractive Candidates for Parliament," 581–99. See also Fenno, *Home Style*.

64 Dawn Black, interview by author, Vancouver, 26 August 1997.

65 Ibid.

66 "Pulling the vote" is a phrase used by campaigners and canvassers that refers to a practice whereby workers make sure that those voters who have been identified by canvassers as party supporters are encouraged to go and vote. In some cases, campaign workers drive people to the polls, provide babysitting, and so on.

67 Dawn Black, interview by author, Vancouver, 26 August 1997.

68 Ibid.

69 Ibid.

70 Ibid.

71 Doris Anderson, letter to author, 30 December 1996.

72 Ibid.

73 Ibid.

74 Margaret Mitchell, interview by author, Vancouver, 26 August 1997.

75 "Ex-MP Pauline Jewett runs for NDP presidency." Montreal *Gazette*, 20 November 1989, A7.

CHAPTER EIGHT

1 Robinson and Saint-Jean, "The Portrayal of Women Politicians in the Media," 180–4.

2 Ibid., 181.

3 McKeown, "The Determined Miss Pauline Jewett," 7–9.

4 CTV, *Political Memoirs*, April 1992.

5 Clement, "John Porter and Sociology in Canada," 583.

6 Ibid., 584.

7 Vallee, "Obituary: John Porter," 14.

8 Clement, "John Porter and Sociology in Canada," 584.

9 Forcese, "The Macro-sociology of John Porter," 651.

10 Clement, "John Porter and Sociology in Canada," 585.

11 Hofley, "John Porter," 596–7.

12 Ibid., 596.

13 Forcese, "The Macro-sociology of John Porter," 651.

14 Ibid., 654.

15 Ibid., 653.

16 Anne Porter, interview by author, Toronto, 25 September 25, 1997.

17 Clement, "John Porter and Sociology in Canada," 585.

18 Norm Fenn, interview by author, Renfrew, 18 September 1996.

19 Anderson, *Rebel Daughter*, 218.

20 Doris Anderson, interview by author, Toronto, 8 December 1996.

21 Anderson, "Jewett Set Example Few Dare to Follow," A17.

22 Nichols (with Jane O'Hara), *Mark My Words*, 129.

23 Ibid., 171.

24 Ibid., 10.

25 Ibid., 19.

26 Ibid., 172.

27 Ibid., 1.

28 Lyn Grey, interview by author, Victoria, 25 August 1997.

29 McLaughlin, *A Woman's Place*, 48.

30 "Ex-MP Pauline Jewett Runs for NDP presidency," Montreal *Gazette*, 20 November 1989, A7.

31 Stainsby, "Jewett Says She's Had Terrific Go at Politics," C9.

32 Davis-Barron, "Friends in Need," A2.

33 Archer, "Women," 21. Archer states that the "queen bee syndrome" indicates that women who have made it in a man's world occupy privileged positions themselves and are often not willing to share them with others.

34 McMartin, "Life Lived Full of Fun, Purpose," A3.

35 Elizabeth Moore, interview by author, Ottawa, 1 June 1998.

CHAPTER NINE

1 McMartin, "Life Lived Full of Fun, Purpose," A3.

2 Marion Dewar, interview by author, Toronto, September 1996.

3 Lyn Grey, interview by author, Victoria, 25 August 1997.

4 Davis-Baron, "Portrait of a Fighter," A1-A2.

5 Taber, "An Honourable Woman," A4.

6 There were other significant contributions made to this scholarship fund, including $25,000 gifts each from Nova Corp (Alberta) and the Maurice Price Foundation. Pauline's will left her Registered Retirement Savings Plan moneys, in the amount of $550,000, to Carleton University for the express purpose of creating a foundation that would administer a scholarship plan. It was her intention that high school guidance counsellors would identify promising but financially needy students to high school liaison officials at Carleton University. She believed that this early identification was an important element of her vision, as these students would be able to finish their grade 13 year without the worry of wondering how they could afford to pay for their university education. This notion of identification was an important element of Pauline's scholarship plan. It was also her wish that the financial assistance would be considerable and would continue for the duration of the student's undergraduate education. Unfortunately, she was not able to orchestrate and organize this plan before her death, and her vision for this scholarship as originally intended has never materialized. Nevertheless, in the 1997–98 academic year, forty-five bursaries, in the

amount of $500 each, were awarded from the Pauline Jewett Scholarship Fund.

CHAPTER TEN

1 Page, "Canadian Studies," 175–6.
2 Jewett, "The Padlock Case," 7.
3 Jewett, "Mr Diefenbaker's Proposed Bill of Rights," 201.
4 Jewett, "The Working Woman," 217.
5 Jewett, "Where Were the MEN," 15.
6 Ibid., 11.
7 The Flag Debate lasted thirty-three days.
8 Jewett, "The Reform of Parliament," 11.
9 Ibid., 13–14.
10 Ibid., 14.
11 Ibid., 16.
12 Polsby, "Legislatures."

EPILOGUE

1 These women are Janyne Hodder (Bishop's), Martha Piper (UBC), Jacquelyn Thayer Scott (Cape Breton), Sheila Brown (Mount Saint Vincent), Elizabeth Parr-Johnston (New Brunswick), Elizabeth R. Epperly (Prince Edward Island), Marsha Hanen (Winnipeg), and Lorna Marsden (York).
2 CBC radio, *Sunday Morning*, 11 December 1987.
3 CBC radio, *The Early Edition*, 18 March 1988.

Bibliography

Aiken, Gordon. *The Backbencher*. Toronto: McClelland and Stewart, 1974.

Ambert, Anne-Marie, ed. *Sex Structure*. 2nd edn. Toronto: Longman, 1976.

Andersen, Doris. *To Change the World*. Toronto: Irwin, 1987.

Anderson, Doris. "Jewett Set Example Few Dare to Follow.". *Toronto Star*, 27 July 1992.

– *Rebel Daughter*. Toronto: Key Porter, 1996.

Archer, Maureen. "Women: A Minority Group in the Academic Professions." *Branching Out*, March/April 1974.

Bashevkin, Sylvia. *Toeing the Lines: Women and Party Politics in English Canada*. 2nd edn. Toronto: Oxford University Press, 1993.

Brown, Rosemary. *Being Brown*. Toronto: Random House, 1979.

Cameron, Elspeth, and Janice Dickin, eds. *Great Dames*. Toronto: University of Toronto Press, 1997.

Campbell, Kim. *Time and Chance*. Toronto: Doubleday, 1996.

Campbell, Norman. "Jewett versus Hees: The Battle Commences. *Ottawa Citizen*, 25 September 1965.

Canada. House of Commons. *Debates*, 1963, 1986, 1987.

Canada. Parliament. Special Joint Committee of the Senate and of the House of Commons on Canada's International Relations. *Canada's International Relations*. Ottawa: Supply and Services Canada, 1986.

– Special Joint Committee of the Senate and the House of Commons on the 1987 Constitutional Accord. *Report*. Ottawa: Queen's Printer, 1987.

Canadian Association of University Teachers. "Arbitration at SFU: The Popkin Case." *Bulletin*, Winter 1971.

– "Report on Simon Fraser University, 3." *Bulletin*, Winter 1972.

– "Report on the Simon Fraser Dispute." *Bulletin*, Winter 1970.

– "Simon Fraser University." *Bulletin*, Autumn 1970.

- "Special Document: Simon Fraser University – Professor Prudence Wheeldon Dismissal Hearing Report." *Bulletin*, Autumn 1971.
Canadian Broadcasting Corporation. cbc radio. *The Early Edition*, 18 March 1988. Audiotape.
- "Music in My Life." *Arts National*, 11 December 1987. Audiotape.
- *Sunday Morning*, 11 December 1987. Audiotape.
- cbc television. *Across Canada*, 3 June 1965.
- *The Journal*, 20 December 1982, 10 February and 28 October 1983, 6 March 1984, 30 July 1987.
- *Midday*, 24 July and 23 August 1985.
- *The National*, 14 February and 13 July 1981, 15 July 1983, 23 August and 4 December 1985, 14 February and 26 June 1986, 13 September 1987 (*Sunday Report*), 16 April 1988 (*Saturday Report*), 14 July and 23 November 1988, 6 July 1992.
- "Two Schools of Thought." *Dateline Special*, 3 April 1977.
Carleton College. *Annual Calendar*, 1942–43, 1947–48, 1950–51, 1954–55, 1955–56.
Carleton University, *Twenty-Eighth Calendar*, 1969–70.
Carver, Anne Harley Sedgewick, "What Are We Doing Here?" In *Still Running*, ed. Joy Parr. Kingston: Queen's University Alumnae Association, 1987.
Christian, William. *George Grant: A Biography.* Toronto: University of Toronto Press, 1993.
Cinman, Israel. "Boycott Suspended: Censure Remains." caut *Bulletin*, December 1974.
- "caut Board Suspends Simon Fraser, University of Ottawa and Mount Allison Censures." caut *Bulletin*, April 1977.
Clement, Wallace. "John Porter and Sociology in Canada." *Canadian Review of Sociology and Anthropology* (Special Issue in Memory of John Porter 1921–79), December 1981.
Cocking, Clive. "The Knives Are Out for Pauline Jewett." *Saturday Night*, November 1975.
Committee for an Independent Canada. *Brief Submitted to the Standing Committee on Finance, Trade, and Economic Affairs of the House of Commons concerning Bill C-132*. Ottawa: 21 June 1973.
Committee on the Status of Women. *Status of Women in Provincially-Assisted Ontario Universities and Related Institutions 1985–86 to 1994–95*. Toronto: Council of Ontario Universities, 1996.
Copps, Sheila. *Nobody's Baby: A Survival Guide to Politics*. Toronto: Denear, 1986.
Corry, J.A. *My Life and Work: A Happy Relationship*. Kingston: Queen's University Press, 1981.

CTV. *Political Memoirs*, April 1992. Videotape.

Davis-Baron, Sherri. "Friends in Need: Support Helps Jewett Battle Cancer." *Ottawa Citizen*, 15 January 1992.

– "Portrait of a Fighter." *Vancouver Sun*, 17 January 1992.

Denzin, Norman K. *Interpretive Biography*. Newbury Park: Sage Publications, 1988.

Docherty, David. *Mr Smith Goes to Ottawa*. Vancouver: UBC Press, 1997.

Dunn, Christopher, ed. *Provinces*. Peterborough: Broadview Press, 1992.

Dyck, Rand. *Provincial Politics in Canada*. 3rd edn. Scarborough: Prentice-Hall, 1996.

Edel, Leon. "Biography and the Science of Man." In *New Directions in Biography*, ed. Anthony M. Friedson. Honolulu: University of Hawaii Press, 1981.

Eysenck, Hans J. *The Psychology of Politics*. London: Routledge and Kegan Paul, 1954.

Fenno, Richard F. *Home Style: House Members and Their Districts*. Boston: Little, Brown, 1978.

Firestone, Shulamith. *The Dialectic of Sex: The Case for Feminist Revolution*. New York: Bantam, 1970.

Fisher, Douglas. "The Understated Charm of Pauline Jewett." *Toronto Sun*, 12 July 1992.

Forcese, Dennis P. "The Macro-sociology of John Porter." *Canadian Review of Sociology and Anthropology* (Special Issue in Memory of John Porter 1921–79), December 1981.

Franks, C.E.S. *The Parliament of Canada*. Toronto: University of Toronto Press, 1987.

Freccero, John. "Autobiography and Narrative." In *Reconstructing Individualism: Autonomy, Individuality, in Western Thought*, ed. Thomas C. Heller, Morton Sosna, and David A. Wellbery. Stanford: Stanford University Press, 1986.

Gartner, Zsuzsi. "Shoot the Moon: Clio and Urania, Thelma and Louise. *Western Living*, November 1992.

Gibson, Frederick W. *Queen's University, 1917–1961*. Vol. 2. Kingston and Montreal: McGill-Queen's University Press, 1983.

Gibson, Gordon. "History Shows Jewett Is Realistic on South Africa." *Financial Post*, 21 September 1987.

Goot, Murray, and Elizabeth REID, "Women and Voting Studies: Mindless Matrons or Sexist Scientism?" *Sage Professional Papers*. 1975.

Gordon, Walter L. *A Political Memoir*. Toronto: McClelland and Stewart, 1977.

Gray, Charlotte. "Women MPS: A New Breed." *Chatelaine*, October 1979, 178–9.

Group of 78. *Canada and Common Security: The Assertion of Sanity*. Ottawa, 1987.

Gzowski, Peter. "The New Women in Politics." *Maclean's*, 21 April 1962, 30–1, 52, 54.

Hamilton, Herbert J. *Queen's*. Kingston: Alumni Association of Queen's University, 1977.

Harder, Peter V., "Career Patterns and Political Parties at the National and Sub-National Levels in the United States and Canada." In *The Canadian House of Commons Observed*, ed. Jean-Paul Gaboury and James Ross Hurley. Ottawa: University of Ottawa Press, 1979.

Harris, Robin S. *A History of Higher Education in Canada, 1663–1960*. Toronto: University of Toronto Press, 1976.

Heap, Ruby, and Alison Prentice, eds. *Gender and Education in Ontario*. Toronto: Canadian Scholars' Press, 1991.

Hedlin, Ralph. "Miss Jewett's Scheme Is a Pure Disgrace." *Western Report*, 28 September 1987.

Hemlow, Joyce. "A Marty Scholar's Adventures." In *Still Running*, ed. Joy Parr. Kingston: Queen's University Alumnae Association, 1987.

Hitchman, Gladys Symons. "A Case Study of Status Differential: Women in Academics." In *Sex Structure*, 2nd edn., ed. Anne-Marie Ambert. Toronto: Longman, 1976.

Hofley, John R. "John Porter: His Analysis of Class and His Contribution to Canadian Sociology." *Canadian Review of Sociology and Anthropology* (Special Issue in Memory of John Porter 1921–79), December 1981.

Hooey, Margaret. "The Marty Scholarship: An Informal History." In *Still Running*, ed. Joy Parr. Kingston: Queen's University Alumnae Association, 1987.

Independent Commission on Disarmament and Security Issues. *Common Security: A Blueprint for Survival*. New York: Simon and Schuster, 1982.

Jewett, Pauline. "Clarence Decatur Howe." *Canadian Forum*, September 1957.

– Honourary degree address, Carleton University, 12 June 1987.

– "How can the greatest number of Canadians participate in day-to-day politics and influence MPs?" *Maclean's*, November 1968.

– "Let Ottawa money play a larger role in education." *Maclean's*, 8 February 1964.

– "The Major Issues Are Blurred." *Canadian Commentator*, March 1958.

– "Mr Diefenbaker's Proposed Bill of Rights." *Canadian Forum*, December 1958.

– "NORAD, the Trojan Horse Bringing Star Wars." *Canadian Dimension*, April 1986.

– "Ottawa starts a department to fight poverty in our hard-up regions. Let's hope it doesn't have to fight existing federal agencies – and the provinces, too." *Maclean's*, February 1969.

– "The Padlock Case." *Canadian Forum*, April 1957.

- "The provinces are hushing it up, but Ottawa still pays for higher education. Here's why Ottawa should take it all over. And how ..." *Maclean's*, January 1969.
- "The Reform of Parliament." *Journal of Canadian Studies*, November 1966.
- "Run for Parliament and you invite exhaustion, frustration. An ex-MP tells why people do it." *Maclean's*, August 1968.
- "Should Canada Test the Cruise? In My view, No." *Readers Digest* (Canada), May 1984.
- *A Structure of the Canadian Nurses' Association*. Montreal: Canadian Nurses' Association, 1952.
- "Toward an Independent Foreign Policy." *International Perspectives*, November/December 1985.
- "Trudeau's vision of government: Why he needs the people "plugged in" to make it work. *Maclean's*, September 1968.
- "Voting in the 1960 Federal By-elections at Peterborough and Niagara Falls: Who Voted New Party and Why?" *Canadian Journal of Economics and Political Science*. 28, no. 1 (February 1962).
- "What every new MP should know – from a writer who learned the hard way: as an MP." *Maclean's*, October 1968.
- "Where were the MEN when Canada set out to find out what makes life tough for its women?" *Maclean's*, December 1968.
- "Who's being hired to teach in our universities? Foreigners, mostly. We used to be short of qualified Canadians. Now we're turning out many more of them; but we don't give them jobs." *Maclean's*, March 1969.
- "The Working Woman." *Continuous Learning*, September/October 1965.
- "You're the prime minister. You want constitutional reform – but the public and many politicians apparently couldn't care less. How can you stir their interest? Here are some things you could do, Mr Trudeau ..." *Maclean's*, May 1969.
Kent, Tom. *A Public Purpose*. Kingston and Montreal: McGill-Queen's University Press, 1988.
Kome, Penney. *The Taking of Twenty-Eight: Women Challenge the Constitution*. Toronto: Women's Press, 1983.
- *Women of Influence*. Toronto: Doubleday Canada, 1985.
Kornberg, Allan. *Canadian Legislative Behaviour: A Study of the Twenty-Fifth Parliament*. New York: Rinehart and Winston, 1967.
Kornberg, Allan, and William Mishler. *Influence in Parliament*. Durham, N.C.: Duke University Press, 1976.
Krangle, Karen. "Jewett Breaks Her Silence over Future at SFU." *Vancouver Sun*, 15 October 1977.
- "Jewett Considers Political Bid after Cutting Short SFU Term." *Vancouver Sun*, 16 August 1978.

- "Jewett Tells SFU Governors She Won't Seek Second Term." *Vancouver Sun*, 2 November 1977.
Kushneriuk, Pauline (Coupar). "An Oral History of Pauline Jewett." Unpublished manuscript. Private collection, 1983.
Lamarsh, Judy. *Memoirs of a Bird in a Gilded Cage*. Toronto: McClelland and Stewart, 1968.
Levitch, H.G. "From Instant University to Academic Disaster." *Saturday Night*, March 1971.
McCall-Newman, Christina. *Grits: An Intimate Portrayal of the Liberal Party.* Toronto: Macmillan, 1982.
McKenzie, Judith. "Parliamentary Careers in Canada, 1958–1993." PH D thesis, University of Toronto, 1994.
- "Political Autobiography and Biography: Towards a New Approach to the Study of Women in Politics." Paper presented at the annual meeting of the Canadian Political Science Association, Memorial University, St John's, Newfoundland, 1997.
McKeown, Robert. "The Determined Miss Pauline Jewett." *Weekend Magazine*, 12 October 1974.
McLaughlin, Audrey, with Rich Archbold. *A Woman's Place*. Toronto: MacFarlane Walter Ross, 1992.
McMartin, Pete. "Life Lived Full of Fun, purpose." *Vancouver Sun*, 7 July 1992.
Masleck, Carolyn. "CAUT Council Rejects Simon Fraser Agreement." *Bulletin*, February 1976.
Millett, Kate. *Sexual Politics*. New York, Avon Books, 1971.
Mills, John. "Festival at Simon Fraser." *Queen's Quarterly*, 82, no. 2, Summer 1975.
Mishler, William. "Nominating Attractive Candidates for Parliament." *Legislative Studies Quarterly*, November 1978.
Neatby, Nicole. "Preparing for the Working World: Women at Queen's during the 1920s." In *Gender and Education in Ontario*, ed. Ruby Heap and Alison Prentice. Toronto: Canadian Scholars Press, 1991.
New Democratic Party of Canada. *Canada's Stake in Common Security.* August 1993.
Nichols, Marjorie (with Jane O'Hara). *Mark My Words: The Memoirs of a Very Political Reporter*. Vancouver: Douglas & McIntyre, 1992.
Page, P. "Canadian Studies: The Current Dilemma." In *Getting It Back*, ed. Abraham Rotstein and Gary Lax. Toronto: Clarke, Irwin, 1974.
Parr, Joy, ed. *Still Running*. Kingston: Queen's University Alumnae Association, 1987.
Polsby, Nelson W. "Legislatures." In *Governmental Institutions and Processes: Handbook of Political Science*. Vol. 5, ed. Fred I. Greenstein and Nelson W. Polsby. Reading, Mass. Addison-Wesley, 1975.

Porter, John. *The Vertical Mosaic*. Toronto: University of Toronto Press, 1967.

Porter, Marion. "John Porter and Education: Technical Functionalist or Conflict Theorist." *Canadian Review of Sociology and Anthropology* (Special Issue in Memory of John Porter, 1921–79), December 1981.

Power, C.G. "Career Politicians: The Changing Role of the MP." *Queen's Quarterly*, Winter 1956–57.

Prentice, Alison, et al. *Canadian Women: A History*. Toronto: Harcourt Brace Jovanovich, 1988.

Queen's University. *Calendar of the Faculty of Arts*. Kingston: Jackson Press, 1939, 1940, 1945, 1947, 1948.

Report of the Chief Electoral Officer: General Election. Ottawa: Queen's Printer, 1962, 1963, 1965, 1979, 1980, 1984, 1988.

Riley, Susan. "Boys' Games Played in Secret." *Maclean's*, 7 July 1980.

Robinson, Gertrude, and Armande Saint-Jean, "The Portrayal of Women Politicians in the Media." In *Gender and Politics in Contemporary Canada*, ed. Francois-Pierre Gingras. Toronto: Oxford University Press, 1995.

Rotstein, Abraham, and Gary Lax, eds. *Getting It Back: A Program for Canadian Independence*. Toronto: Clarke, Irwin, 1974.

Royal Commission on the Status of Women. *Report of the Royal Commission on the Status of Women in Canada*. Ottawa: Information Canada, 1970.

Sawatsky, John. "Jewett Gets Job as SFU President." *Vancouver Sun*, 20 March 1974.

– "$1 Million SFU Contract Jewett Price for Presidency." *Vancouver Sun*, 12 March 1974.

Sharp, Mitchell. *Which Reminds Me ... A Memoir*. Toronto: University of Toronto Press, 1994.

Skeet, Jillian. "A Report on the NDP Security Policy." *Peace Magazine*, June/July 1988.

Smith, J. Percy. "Faculty Power and Simon Fraser. *Canadian Forum*, September 1968.

Stainsby, Mia. "Jewett Says She's Had Terrific Go at Politics." *Vancouver Sun*, 4 February 1989.

Stanley, Don. "A Look at What Makes Pauline Run." *Vancouver Sun*, 22 October 1977.

Stoffman, Daniel. "Pauline Jewett: NDP's New Jewel." *Toronto Star*, 30 July 1979.

Stursberg, Peter. *Lester Pearson and the Dream of Unity*. Toronto: Doubleday, 1978.

Sulloway, Frank J. *Born to Rebel*. Toronto: Random House, 1996.

Sutherland, Sharon. "The Consequences of Electoral Volatility: Inexperienced Ministers 1949–1990." In *Representation, Integration, and Political Parties in Canada*, ed. H. Bakvis Toronto: Dundurn Press, 1991.

Taber, Jane. "An Honourable Woman, Oath or No Oath." *Ottawa Citizen*, 15 September 1992.

University of British Columbia. *Calendar*, Vancouver: UBC Press, 1971, 1972.

Vallee, Frank. "Obituary: John Porter." *Society*, 15 September 1992.

Vickers, Jill McCalla, and June Adam. *But Can You Type? Canadian Universities and the Status of Women*. Toronto: Clarke, Irwin, 1977.

Ward, Norman. *The Canadian House of Commons: Representation*. Toronto: University of Toronto Press, 1950.

Weber, Max. *Politics as a Vocation*. Philadelphia: Fortress Press, 1965.

Wilson, James Q. *The Amateur Democrat*. Chicago: University of Chicago Press, 1965.

Wyman, Georgina. "Pauline Jewett: An Interview." *Branching Out*, September/October 1974.

Yandle, Sharon. "The End of PSA at Simon Fraser University." *Canadian Dimension*, February/March 1970.

– "Ex-MP Pauline Jewett Runs for NDP Presidency." Montreal *Gazette*, 20 November 1989.

– "Jewett Faces Her Toughest Battle." Montreal *Gazette*, January 1992.

– "Jewett Given Nod as NDP Candidate." *Vancouver Sun*, 11 September 1978.

– "Law Student Defeats SFU Head Jewett for NDP Nomination in Burnaby Riding." *Vancouver Sun*, 3 October 1977.

– "Mixed Reaction Greets Jewett's Nomination Bid." *Vancouver Sun*, 27 September 1977.

– "Not for a Million Dollars." *Time Canada*, 1 April 1974.

– "No Women Allowed." *Time Canada*, 7 July 1975.

– "SFU Governors Fully Back Jewett." *Vancouver Sun*, 7 January 1978.

Index

abortion, 125–6
academics: discrimination against women, 34; importance of publication to, 37; recruitment of Canadian faculty, 102
Adam, June, 34
Advisory Council on the Status of Women, 123–4; resignation of Doris Anderson, 125
Aiken, Gordon, 57
ambition and career expectations, 53, 55–6; amateurs and professional, 182n28; apprenticeship, 65; cosmopolitan orientation, 55, 182n29; progressive ambition, 65. See also Docherty, David C.; Franks, C.E.S.; Weber, Max
Anderson, Doris, 12, 124, 129, 137, 148–50, 159–61
apartheid, 114–17
Armstrong, Pat, 80
Axworthy, Lloyd, 123–4

backbenchers and caucus solidarity, 64. See also House of Commons

Ban Righ Board, 21
Ban Righ Hall, 21
barons of SFU, 97; support of Brian Wilson, 97
Barrett, Dave, 139
Beattie, Munro, 41, 43. See also Constan Associates
Betty Ford Center, 133, 153, 158
Black, Dawn, 109–10, 134, 138, 155
boycott, 100–1. See also Simon Fraser University
British Columbia Women's Rights Committee, 112, 129
Broadbent, Ed, 110–12, 128, 132, 138

cabinet: appointment to, 56, 64–5, 76; tokenism in, 65. See also women in politics
Cameron, Elspeth, xiv
Campbell, Kim, 101
Canadian Association of University Teachers (CAUT): academic boycott, 100–1; imposition of censure on Simon

Fraser University, 94–7, 99–100
Canadian Charter of Rights and Freedoms, 125; s. 15, 124–5, 129; s. 16, 128; s. 28, 125, 127–9, 188n46
Canadian Nurses' Association, 38. See also Uprichard, Muriel
Canadian Society for the Abolition of the Death Penalty, 69–70
Carleton College, 41
Carleton University, 35; chancellorship of, 140. See also Institute of Canadian Studies
cell 13, 51, 182n12
chilly climate for women legislators, 70–1, 173–4. See also women in politics
Cocke, Dennis, 107–8, 161
Cocke, Yvonne, 107–8
Commander of the British Empire (CBE), 178
Committee for an Independent Canada, 88–9
committees, in House of Commons:

political careers, 84. *See
also* Weber, Max;
Franks, C.E.S.;
Docherty, David C.
Political Science, Sociol-
ogy, and Anthropology
Department (PSA) at
Simon Fraser Univer-
sity, 93–7, 99
Polsby, Nelson, 171
Porter, John, 45–6, 65,
144–7; *The Vertical
Mosaic*, 46, 65, 145. *See
also* Constan Associates
Porter, Marion, 45. *See
also* Constan Associates
Prentice, Alison, 19, 20,
35
Privy Council, 160

Queen's University:
alumnae association,
20; army reserve unit,
24; Department of
Political and Economic
Science, 29; enrolment
of women, 19; regula-
tions against sororities,
21. *See also* Corry, J.A.;
Douglas, Alice Vibert;
Royce, Jean

Radcliffe College, 26, 89
Rideau Club, 71
Rioux, Marcel, 80–1
Robinson, Svend, 107–8,
133
Royal Commission on the
Status of Women, 82,
166, 168–9; on nomina-
tions, 59–60
Royce, Jean, 24–5, 32, 144

St Laurent, Louis, 49
Sharp, Mitchell, 51, 73, 75
Shortt, Dr Elizabeth, 20

sibling rivalry, 13, 178n19.
See also Sulloway, Frank
J.
Simeon, Richard, 127–9
Simon Fraser University
(SFU), 91; barons of, 97,
103; imposition of boy-
cott on, 96; imposition
of censure on, 94–8,
100–1; PSA seven, 99,
101; strike, 96
Simpson, Morley, 5
Simpson, Nathan Alonzo,
5, 11
Skelton, O.D., 40
Special Joint Committee
of the Senate and
House of Commons on
Canada's International
Relations, 120–3
Special Joint Committee
on the Meech Lake
Accord, 126–31; Doris
Anderson's position,
150; impact of the dis-
tinct society clause on
s. 28, 128; Liberal
Party's position, 129;
National Action Com-
mittee's reaction to,
128–9; NDP addendum
to final report, 129–30.
See also Meech Lake
Accord
Spector, Norman, 128
Strand, Kenneth, 94, 96–7,
133
Sulloway, Frank J., 15–16

theory of counterbalance,
110
Trudeau, Pierre, 74–6, 123

United Empire Loyalists,
4
United States: invasion of
Grenada, 114; Equal

Rights Amendment,
123
university presidencies: at
Simon Fraser Univer-
sity, 91, 97–100; at
University of Prince
Edward Island, 90; at
York University, 90–1
Uprichard, Muriel, 38–9,
105–6
Urquhart, M.C., 29

veterans' preference pol-
icy, 35
Vickers, Jill, 34, 97, 161

Wallin, Pamela, 152
War Measures Act, 86
Wartime Prices and Trade
Board, 35. *See also* C.D.
Howe
Weber, Max, 53–4. *See also*
political careers
Welland Canal expansion
project, 7
Wellesley College, 27
Whitehead, K.B., 24
women in politics:
appointment to cabinet,
65; media stereotypes
of women politicians,
141, 183n42; recruit-
ment of women
candidates, 59; repre-
sentation of women in
House of Commons,
57, 112; women in the
Liberal Party, 113. *See
also* chilly climate; Liberal Party of Canada;
loneliness factor; New
Democratic Party

Yerxa, Elijah, 4
Yerxa, Harriet Elizabeth
(Jewett), 4